Real
Swansea

For my brother Martyn and my sister Carey

Real
Swansea

Nigel Jenkins

Series Editor: Peter Finch

seren

Seren is the book imprint of
Poetry Wales Press Ltd
Nolton Street, Bridgend, Wales
www.seren-books.com

© Nigel Jenkins 2008
Series Introduction © Peter Finch 2008

ISBN 978-1-85411-484-6

A CIP record for this title is available from
the British Library

The publisher works with the financial assistance
of the Welsh Books Council

Printed by Bell & Bain, Glasgow
Maps by: Anna Ratcliffe
Frpnt Cover Image David Williams/Photolibrary Wales

Also in the Real Wales series
Editor: Peter Finch:

Real Aberystwyth – Niall Griffiths
Real Cardiff – Peter Finch
Real Cardiff Two – Peter Finch
Real Newport – Anne Drysdale
Real Wrexham – Grahame Davies

Coming Soon:
Real Liverpool – Niall Griffiths
Real Merthyr – Mario Basini

CONTENTS

2 km

Morriston•

River Tawe

Lower
Swansea
Valley

Morris Castle •

•Gowerton

•Penlan

Landore•

•Fforestfach

Bonymaen•

Kilvey Hill

•Dunvant

Cockett•

•Townhill

•St Thomas

10
High Street
11 The Kingsway
Oxford Street
King Edward Road

Quay Parade
SA1

Crymlyn•

Sketty•

Uplands•

1
9
Wind St
13
4
8
3 7
12
Maritime
Oystermouth Quarter
Road

2
6

Brynmill•

5

The Promenade

Clyne Valley

Fish Weirs

N

Swansea
Bay

1. Castle Square
2. Dylan Thomas Centre
3. Leisure Centre
4. Morgan's Hotel
5. Patti Pavilion
6. Queen's Hotel
7. Swansea Jack
8. Swansea Prison
9. The 'No Sign'
10. The Windsor Lodge Hotel
11. The Mansion House
12. The Tower of the Ecliptic
13. World's End

Mumbles

Southend•

Pier

Langland
Bay

Prouder cities rise through the haze of time,
Yet, unenvious, all men have found is here.

from Vernon Watkins' 'Ode to Swansea'

PREFACE

When I first arrived in Swansea it was a return to the industrial heart of the nineteenth century. This was in 1958 and no one had yet thought about clearing up the wreckage. No one could afford to. Austerity, bomb sites, supply failures, shortages. Rock and roll had only just begun to brighten up the night skies. The place was bashed, bust and breaking apart, the parts I saw, steaming in on the Western Region, along the Neath and then the Tawe. Down the valley through Plasmarl, Landore, and Hafod. I was crossing a landscape I'd only ever experienced before in the novels of Edgar Rice Burroughs and H.G. Wells. A red, broken-brick fantasy of furnace, yard, smokestack, and collapsing workers' housing mixed with slop and slag on a cinder-black ground. Could this be hell? It could, but hell deserted. Hell with no one around. This was the Lower Swansea Valley after the tinplate and copper and spelter had been abandoned. Swansea Vale, Villiers, Landore Sulphate, Middle Bank, Upper Bank, Llansamlet, Mannesman Tube Works, White Rock, Hafod Phosphate, Hafod Isha Nickel and Cobalt, Morfa. "The most extensive contiguous area of industrial dereliction to be found anywhere in the United Kingdom," said a contemporary report.

I knew nothing about what I could see beyond the sheer and obvious hell of it. I learned later that this was heavy industry, smoke-filled, fire breathing, lung wrecking heavy manufacture at the point of no return. This was the bed on which Swansea had been built. By the middle of the twentieth century it had been run onto the rocks by underinvestment, world depression, foreign competition and the depletion of native ores.

My train from Cardiff took me into Swansea High Street station. High Street is a dead end. The train from London to Carmarthen leaves the way it came. Trains come in, stop, then reverse back out. Dust. Echo. Victorian cast iron. Platform tickets. Uniformed porters with trolleys. Guards with flags. None of that with the downmarket First Great Western Swanline Arriva diesel transport of today.

Off the train and into the city. Wind Street takes the baton from High Street running south from the station to the water. This former banking and business district has today totally given way to pleasure. Piss-up bladdered belch hammered shot-shooting sprawling on your long legs or in your shirt. Lloyd's Bar, Walkabout, Yates, SoBar, Varsity, Bar,Co, Adelphi, The Bank Statement. I take a look down

Salubrious Passage, once home of poetry readings and second-hand book shops. Deserted. A hand-written sign on a store door says 'open afternoons only' but the space beyond it is empty. Another bar soon, more space for vertical drinking.

At the lower end there's a subway which runs to Somerset Place, home of the Dylan Thomas Centre built into the refurbished Old Guildhall. The Centre, known as Tŷ Llên (House of Literature), was opened in 1995 when for twelve months Swansea was created U.K. City of Literature. A home for bards, novelists, and literary raconteurs. Tŷ Llên is clearly a hard name to pronounce. Hardly anyone calls it that now. Inside are the doors to Dylan Thomas' writing hut lifted from a skip at Laugharne. These are the originals. At Laugharne the refurbished hut on the cliff side has yet another set, also original. These are twenty-first-century equivalents of the bones of saints, fragments of the true cross, the chisel which Moses used. On e-bay recently someone was selling a pair of Dylan Thomas' trousers. Do not destroy, recycle. The subway is scrawled with DT quotations, posters replaying Fern Hill for the hundredth time. "Oh as I was young and easy in the mercy of his means.... "The poem rolls on wall and floor, printed, painted, carved in benches, on plaques and in stones right the way across the southern part of western Wales. Dylan in our hearts and in our souls. In our beer and our cafes. On our plates and our tea towels. Our shortbreads and our jams. They visit here in their hundreds to touch the places where that short, stubby man once walked. Where he talked. Where he dreamed.

Swansea is built at a rivermouth with its town rising up the escarpment of Mount Pleasant, like Edinburgh but without the grandeur. 6000 people in 1801. Sveinn Sae'r. Sweynesse. Sweinesei. Sweyn's Ey. Swanzey. Scandinavian. Germanic. Little to do with Swans. Nothing to do with the sea. No Romans. Only a dubious connection with Welsh saints. "The haunt of gull and plover". The industrial revolution made the place, the smelting, the mining, the tinplace works, the ferrous metals and the port through which everything travelled. For a hundred and fifty years Swansea boomed. Then the Depression hit and hard. And during World War Two so did Hitler. The town centre was flattened in a series of vast raids and rolling firestorms.

Swansea Bay is a great arc of sand running from the docks right round to the world's most eruditely named village, The Mumbles. A train, one of the earliest of passenger rail links, once ran the whole length of this great curving. It's now gone. Ripped up. Replaced by bikeways, covered in tarmac, Mr Softee Vans parked along it, kids with skateboards, baseball caps and cans. The tram ran along a sort of bund, with a wall on the seaward side. Peversely from the present road you can't see the water at all, a Swansea bay of endless sky. Full of size and light.

Swansea became a city in 1969 when Charles, as part of his princely investiture, made it one. Swansea Jacks had long reckoned that the place should also be the Welsh capital, lost, fought hard to become the home of the National Assembly, didn't succeed, got instead the Maritime Museum hacked apart in Cardiff and rebuilt here as a high-tech all singing and dancing make the computer displays work just by waving your arms family-friendly second prize.

Swansea believes in itself, circles around itself, honours itself as a great city and the real psychological authority behind everything Wales does. There's an air of this in the streets and the bars and the places where Swansea boys doing Swansea things gather. In their suits and their shoes. It's slick but it isn't the West End. Swansea power. You can feel its sea-blown grip weaken as you cross the Tawe going east or the Loughor to the west. Swansea, the town on a hill, stretched back behind you like an urban myth. And as you head away on the clogged M4 you wonder was the city there or did you imagine it. The lovely rubbery Dylan town, old, faded, but with new gleaming glass and concrete right along its front. Swansea where everyone is still talking and nobody hustling. Bars, cafes, new generation SA1 waterfront cool and yet hundreds of brown-stained ancient pubs.

Peter Finch, 'Real' Series Editor.

INTRODUCTION

Borders

What begins for you
where the waves break
– sea or land, land or sky –

depends on where
you're coming from, depends
on where you're going to

and whether you
have legs or fins, lungs or gills.

Although more than 80 kilometres west of the Wales/England border, Swansea – Abertawe in Welsh – owes much to the fruitful interaction within its magnetic field of a range of frontiers. There are the natural ones: land and sea; hill and coastal plain; Pennant sandstone and Coal Measures, Millstone Grit and limestone. And there are those derived largely from the human presence: east Wales meets west Wales; rural and urban (there are cows grazing on Kilvey Hill, within a mile of the city centre); Welsh language and English language (and Arabic, Bengali, Cantonese, Polish, Somali, Urdu – among Swansea's scores of languages); blinkered opulence and stultifying poverty; the unparalleled Beauty of the Gower coast cwtshed up to the ugly Beast of post-industrial banality.

Between such nodes the currents continue to leap, generating still the kind of energy that transformed what, a thousand years ago, was "but a stretch of sand, the haunt of sea-gull and plover" into the metallurgical capital of the world and, during the nineteenth century, the undeclared metropolis of Wales. "Of all the cities and towns of Wales," the historian Glanmor Williams has written, "Swansea has a history unsurpassed in length, importance, variety, and interest". Forget the tiresome dead-hand of Swansea being 'the graveyard of ambition', which Dylan Thomas is supposed to have coined (he didn't), and take your Swansea bearings instead from a message inscribed in the paving outside High Street station, 'Ambition is critical'. Facing travellers, crucially, as they enter the city rather than as

they leave it, this 'micro-poem' by David Hughes was a riposte, in Thatcherite times, both to quietist acquiescence and to the thoughtless, selfish kind of ambition that characterised the greedy 1980s. Far from being a dozy backwater, the scale of Swansea's ambition, past and present, can be measured in an extraordinary range of achievements, from the development of the open-hearth furnace (which revolutionised steel-making in the later nineteenth century) to the poetry of Dylan Thomas, from William Grove's invention of the fuel cell to the music of John Cale (Wales's one world-class innovator in both rock and art music), from the world's first passenger railway (1807) to the art of Ceri Richards – to name but a random handful.

In the past, as a sea-trading and manufacturing town, Swansea was Cardiff and Merthyr Tydfil rolled into one. Today, as Swansea comes to terms with one of its periodic identity crises, it's finding a post-industrial role for itself as a centre for service industries, education, leisure and tourism[1]. Britain's wettest town, the city of broken umbrellas, may not know exactly where it's going (and its rash heedlessness of its past is a disabling weakness), but it's going there anyway – with the determined gusto of a bunch of stylish revellers on Wind Street. The city's twenty-first-century ambitions are declared at its eastern gateway by the vaunting postmodernism of the SA1 development around the redundant Prince of Wales dock (but don't spoil the party by mentioning climate change and rising sea levels), and its status as the nation's second city has been enhanced recently by its adoption of two national institutions, the Wales National Pool and the National Waterfront Museum.

When and how Swansea began is difficult to pinpoint. The Romans appear to have forded the Tawe near today's High Street station, but the only signs of Roman or Romano-British settlement are the *tesserae* of a pavement at Oystermouth. The not unreasonable proposition of a pre-Viking settlement on the sandy banks of the Tawe (poor as its farming would have been) greatly exercised Colonel W. Ll. Morgan in the early twentieth century. Morgan argued that Swansea was originally a Celtic settlement known as Senghenydd (Sein + Henyd(d)), after one of Wales's two saints Cenydd; it may therefore also have been known as Llangenydd (or Llangeneu or Llanngemei or Lan Gemie: the church of Cenydd, Morgan maintained, stood where the Normans later built their castle). Although a fascinating, convoluted argument, it's pursued, according to the historian Gerald Gabb, with "unapologetic pigheadedness" and is "far beyond the bounds of common sense".

Then there's the "swirling mass of dubious data" concerning Swansea's supposed Viking origins – enshrined, for instance, in the iconography of the Guildhall (1934), with its Viking prows jutting out above the clock faces on its 48.8-m tower. The popular notion that the town was founded when some Viking notable by the name of Sweyn (or Sveinn) established a settlement on an 'ey' (island) in the mouth of the Tawe – Sweyn's ey – is a myth, but a myth with just enough substance to support the possibility of its containing an element of truth. There's no denying that the name 'Swensi', in one form or another, was being used for the area from about 1140 (although it would take until the 1730s for it to become 'Swansea'). Gerald Gabb speculates that the Vikings' chosen 'ey' may not have been some shifty mudbank in the estuary but somewhere more typical of the secure, raised sites the Scandinavians normally favoured, namely the tidal island of Mumbles Head. Gower may have the most Norse finds of any part of Wales, but they number only five. The most persuasive evidence (so far) of Swansea's Viking beginnings is how local people pronounce the place name: not with a soft second 's', as would many an English or American visitor, but with a buzzing, 'z'-sounding 's': the 'ey' may no longer be with us, but memory of its possessor seems to be inscribed in the way we harden that second 's'.

The name has nothing to do with sea-borne swans – although swans can indeed be seen gliding on the sea when the tide's in and the water's calm, and Cyril the Swan parades the pitch at the beginning of every home match played by the zealously supported Swans, whose swan logo is omnipresent. However, it's the name of the rugby team, the Ospreys, that evokes Swansea's genuinely heraldic bird: an osprey with a fish is featured on the earliest seal of the borough (c.1158-84), and a stylised, rather phoenix-like image of an osprey looms large today in the city's official insignia.

Whether or not there was a settlement at the *aber* (mouth) of the Tawe when the land-grabbing Normans conquered Gower c.1100, they seem to have been content to adopt 'Swensi', or some variant thereof, as the name of the caput, with its castle and walled town, which they established here. They had a stab at 'Abertawe' too, but it tumbled awkwardly from their mouths as Hakkydeweye (today's Pentregethin Road, the old Swansea to Carmarthen road, was once called Hakkydeweye; as Swansea's oldest-known street name, there's surely a case for its restoration).

With the dispossessed native Welsh deeply resentful of the Anglo-Norman occupation, and inclined to launch sometimes devastating attacks on the alien stronghold, early Swansea, for the best part of three hundred years, was a frontier town in a defensive, military sense. In the more peaceful conditions that followed Owain Glyndŵr's challenge to English rule in the early fifteenth century, Swansea settled down as a market town, serving the agricultural industry of its hinterland, and as a port. Several other industries grew in importance: ship-building, tanning, weaving and, above all, coalmining. By the 1630s, when Swansea was exporting 12,000 tonnes a year, in Britain it was third only to Newcastle and Sunderland as a coal port.

The choice of an osprey – a riverine rather than a maritime bird – as Swansea's emblem was fitting, for it was the Tawe, a navigable river flowing through coal-bearing land, which was the key to Swansea's eventual prosperity. Because it took 18 tonnes of coal and 4 tonnes of ore to produce 1 tonne of copper, it was cheaper to ship the ore to the coal – even from as far away as Chile – than to take the coal to the ore. No other industrial centre with metallurgical pretensions had Swansea's in-built natural advantage. By 1810, when Swansea was producing 60% of the world's copper, the town could truly claim the title of Copperopolis. And by the late nineteenth century, Swansea could claim a comparable dominance in tinplate production. As copper production declined in the 1880s, the output of zinc (or spelter) burgeoned: by 1914, Swansea was producing 75% of Britain's zinc.

The development of what is the oldest industrial town in Wales was dependent on both a highly skilled workforce and the determination of its industrialists and entrepreneurs to be at the very forefront of scientific and technological change. The town's 'coming of age' in the 1780-1855 period, as Louise Miskell argues in her aptly titled *Intelligent Town*, owed much to the comparatively gradual nature of its development. Industry was not the traumatic novelty that it was in areas such as the Rhondda and Merthyr Tydfil, with their patterns of

boom and bust, demographic surges and ethnic conflict, bitter industrial strife and truck-shop exploitations. With a variety of industrial
undertakings and small manufactories, together with relatively
mature commercial, craft, retail and service sectors, and the ability to
maintain, well into an increasingly sulphurous nineteenth century, its
dual reputation as 'the Brighton of Wales', Swansea had the economic
diversity, the experience and the time to adapt to change. Evolving
rather than mushrooming, Swansea absorbed industry, rather than
being absorbed by it.

The democratisation of local government, the paving and lighting
of the central streets, the growth of banking, educational and health-
care facilities, the founding of libraries and the advent of important
publications such as *Seren Gomer* and *The Cambrian* were essential
factors in Swansea's emergence, by the early nineteenth century, as the
capital of Wales in all but name. Eventually, thanks largely to the
corporation's interminable wrangling over the construction of a floating dock, Cardiff stole a march on its dithering neighbour, and
Swansea's primacy as a coal-shipping port was lost. But science,
antiquarianism and the arts burgeoned. The Swansea Scientific
Society, founded in 1835, was re-launched in 1838 as the Royal
Institution of South Wales and housed from 1841 onwards in Wales's
first purpose-built museum (today's Swansea Museum). Among the
RISW's members were some of the most gifted scientists and technological pioneers of their time. Like *The Cambrian* newspaper, the
RISW conceived of itself as an institution with a national remit. It
placed the intellectual and cultural life at the centre of Swansea's
urban identity, Louise Miskell observes, "making this probably the
clearest feature distinguishing Swansea from other Welsh towns in the
eyes of both its own inhabitants and outside observers."

The stage was set for a remarkable artistic starburst in the twentieth century. Dylan Thomas, of course, was its most luminous shaft.
But there were other 'Kardomah Boys' who achieved international
renown, among them Vernon Watkins, tipped for the role of Poet
Laureate shortly before he died in 1967, Daniel Jones, Wales's first
symphonist, and the painter Alfred Janes. The roll-call of nationally,
if not internationally, significant Swansea-born or Swansea-resident
artists since those days is a long one: the English-language poets Harri
Webb and John Ormond (also a film-maker), the Welsh-language
poets Pennar Davies, Alan Llwyd and Emyr Lewis, the stained-glass
artists Amber Hiscott, David Pearl and Catrin Jones, the painters Ceri
Richards and Glenys Cour, the novelists Kingsley Amis, Paul Ferris,

Alun Richards, Iris Gower and Stevie Davies – to name only a tiny handful of the more prominent. And Swansea is a bountifully musical city – from Bonnie Tyler and Spencer Davis, at the rock end of the spectrum, to the West Glamorgan Youth Orchestra which, at its best, is indistinguishable from an orchestra of seasoned professionals.

Swansea's darkest hour, by contrast, was during the Second World War. Between June 1940 and February 1943, the town suffered 44 air raids, the worst of which was the Three-Nights Blitz of 19-21 February 1941, in which 239 people lost their lives. The German bombers, aiming to cripple Swansea as an oil and coal port, failed to destroy the docks, and they missed many fine buildings nearby – an area today which still has the architectural charm of pre-war Swansea. But, intending also to undermine civilian morale, they inflicted major damage on several suburbs and they wiped out the town centre. The poet Waldo Williams, 75 kilometres away in north Pembrokeshire, later recalled in 'Y Tangnefeddwyr' (The Peacemakers) how he could see "Uwch yr eira, wybren ros, / Lle mae Abertawe'n fflam ..." (Above the snow, a rose-red sky / Where Swansea is aflame).

Builders redeveloping the city centre sometimes unearth near ground level a layer of dark red ash, a poignant memento of that three-nights' conflagration. For much of the 1950s and 1960s, the town I knew as a child was a bomb-site, in which a replacement, functional, grossly unimaginative Swansea gradually rose from the ashes of those narrow, canyon-like streets, with their proud, decorative façades – a lost Swansea for which my parents' generation have such an aching *hiraeth*.

If the architectural banality of the city centre is an ever-present reminder of the devastation of the blitz, it can't be said that the war did lasting damage to the Swansea spirit, which is as spry and resourceful as ever, having managed with relative ease the post-war transition from a heavy-industries economy to a services-based economy. The city, says Mike Parker in the latest *Rough Guide to Wales*, is "breezy and resurgent". It's also confidently Welsh. In the devolution referendum of 1997, Swansea – unlike the equivocal capital – voted in favour of the National Assembly for Wales, and then campaigned vigorously (although unsuccessfully) for the Assembly to be based in Swansea.

Swansea became a city in 1969. It's taken many a downtown Swansea Jack a while to catch up with Swansea's elevation ("Yea I knowzits u city / burile olliz call it town", says a character in one of

David Hughes's dialect poems). But if Swansea can shrug off what remains of its provincialism, stop looking edgily over its shoulder towards Cardiff, and trust in its numerous assets and indigenous strengths, it may yet arrive, in more than just name, at that desirable condition of urbanity. It may have its faults, but there's no better place than Swansea for the fulfilling of all manner of ambitions.

Brogarwch[2]

Swansea man weds Swansea bride
in Swansea:
Abertawe honeymoon

This book's allotment of some 65,000 words is nowhere near sufficient to the task of adequately representing such an intriguing city. I am all too aware that many communities and institutions that are of the essence of Swansea – from Morriston to the Guildhall, from Penlan to the Glynn Vivian Art Gallery, from Waunarlwydd to Tŷ Tawe, that powerhouse of the Welsh language in Christina Street – are barely touched on here, if they are mentioned at all. There simply hasn't been the space in one volume to encompass Swansea in all its richness and variety. I hope, though, that if this book sells well enough to justify a follow-up volume, I will soon find myself at work on *Real Swansea 2*.

notes

1. Tourism, attracting some 4 million visitors a year to Swansea, is said to be worth over £255m to the local economy.
2. Love of one's native patch or 'bro'.

SOUTH

SWANSEA BAY

If you stand at Mumbles when the tide's in, with perhaps a rowing team slicing over the bay's glassy surface and a dozen mute swans tacking and preening on the almost imperceptible swell, you could think yourself on the edge of a lake in Switzerland, there being no sign in this apparently land-bound scene of any egress to the Severn Sea.

> tide in, skiers out
> — dollar signs carved
> from shore to shore

You have to move a kilometre or so towards town before the open-armed crescent of Swansea Bay declares itself wide to the oceans of the world.

The English poet Walter Savage Landor (1775-1864), recalling in later life the view at the end of the eighteenth century, famously declared, "The gulf of Salerno, I hear, is much finer than Naples; but give me Swansea for scenery and climate"; he found it "the most beautiful coast in the universe." The occasional palm tree may indeed lend the bay a Mediterranean ambience, but it can also have its darker moods, as when Siberian winds turn the sea's edge to a rubble of ice, or when, twice daily, the tide, falling by nearly ten metres, exposes a vast expanse of oleaginous mud (the Glamorgan–Gwent coast's tidal reach being second only to that of the Bay of Fundy in Canada, thanks to the classic funnel shape of the Severn Sea). I've heard it rumoured in Mumbles that students hoping to take a short cut to the university across the low-tide quagmire have never been seen again.

If the bay has delivered prosperity to Swansea, it has also at times threatened it with invasion. The keels of Viking marauders would have scrunched ashore here, as Sweyn (if he existed) eyed up the river mouth for the settlement of the 'ey' that is believed to have borne his name, and the alien ships of the Normans would not have been too many decades behind them. A feared French invasion during the Napoleonic Wars led to Mumbles Head being equipped with four eighteen-pounders; the lighthouse island was further fortified in the 1860s. During the Second World War, the bay was ringed with what was hoped would be an impenetrable barrage of eight-tonne concrete blocks. A pillbox from that time, up to its eye-holes in sand, can still be seen at the foot of the dunes between the university and Blackpill.

That German visitation never came, but the sea itself might prove a devastating invader before long. Climate-change experts have predicted that a rise in sea level of about one metre over the next 100 years will render low-lying cities such as Swansea uninhabitable well before the end of the present century. And they are not alone: on walls and garage doors all over

Swansea in 2006 there appeared a chalk line, with the caption 'sea level in 2059' (and other dates for other locations). Such dangers are foreseeable. Less predictable and more immediately cataclysmic would be a tsunami – a word not known to the Welsh when, in 1607, both shores of the Severn Sea were devastated by what an eye-witness described as "mighty hilles of water tumbling over one another … as if the greatest mountains in the world had overwhelmed the lowe villages … Sometimes it dazzled many of the spectators that they imagined it had bin some fogge or mist coming with great swiftness towards them." This would accord with descriptions of the Indian Ocean tsunami of Boxing Day, 2004, although it is only since 2002 that scientists have considered it likely that the great 'flood' of 1607 – which killed at least 2,000 people and drove almost six kilometres inland in Monmouthshire – was in fact a tsunami, triggered perhaps by a submarine landslide south of Ireland.

It was the greatest environmental disaster in British history. The damage in Cardiff was extensive. What happened in Swansea is little attested, although the tsunami – whose effects were felt as far north as Cardigan – must have had an impact. It certainly seems to have made its mark east of the river in the hamlet of St Thomas, where it swept away most of the ancient and historic chapel of St Thomas the Martyr[1].

Could there be another tsunami here? Yes, according to tsunami expert Professor Mike Disney of Cardiff University. "There is no need to panic," he has written, "but in low-lying cities … the risk is not negligible." A tsunami of 1607 dimensions could sweep away half a million souls in this more densely populated age. So if, one day, you hear that half of the island of La Palma has slipped at last into the

Atlantic or that a large meteorite has hit the ocean, and it looks as if Swansea Bay is about to pay the city the most intimate of visits, you are advised by Professor Disney not to jump into your car and take to the roads (which would quickly become traffic jams to drown in), but simply to take to the nearest high ground (or a multi-storey car-park). A stout sea wall is recommended as a longer-term precaution, but this Swansea has only here and there.

That the bay offers Swansea so yieldingly to penetration is explained by the relative softness of the underlying Coal Measures and the Millstone Grit shales.

> Branches of coal
> spread out beneath us,
>
> a language of the sun,
>   locked
>   by the ancient trees in their cells,
> and translated again
>   by the green sun
>   that goes whispering
>   through sinew and bone.

Running in parallel across the neck of peninsular Gower and out under the bay, these rocks were more easily eroded by ice and water than the comparatively resistant Pennant sandstone and limestone which flank them north and south, constituting the more elevated parts of Swansea. What is now Swansea Bay was dense with vegeta-tion from soon after the thaw began towards the end of the last ice age until nearly 9,000 years ago, when the sea broke in, covering the fertile river plain that stretched from here to Devon. The black and waterlogged remains of those ancient trees – stumpy trunks, branches, root systems – can be seen on the foreshore at Blackpill and near the Vivian stream outfall pipe in front of the university. Elsewhere on the beach, fisherman digging for bait often find their spades striking bits of Stone Age woodland. Boreholes out in the bay have reached peat as deep as 20m, evidence that in the late glacial period plants grew in Swansea Bay some 20m below the present sea-level.

Various local traditions suggest that the present bounds of Swansea Bay were established much more recently than the end of the last ice age. There's the folk memory of a bridle path used by the lords of Gower, connecting Penrice with Margam, which hugged the coast until it reached Mumbles Head, where it cut across what is now the bay toward the woods at Margam. It's thought to have been swept away by the 'flood' of 1607, as was Grove Island, with its farm (belonging to the Angel family), which was situated off Mumbles Head in the region of what is known to sailors to this day as the Green Grounds. In 1885, there was dragged up on the Green Grounds a slab of chiselled stone, with cement attached, which was believed to have come from the old farmhouse. There are, by now, no Angels left in Mumbles, but there are still locally-born people who remember the family's name and that spectral farm beneath the sea.

For over a century, until 1999's inauguration of the new sewage treatment plant, the Green Grounds might have been more accurately described as the Brown Grounds. Twice a day, on the flood tide, the raw sewage of the entire population of Swansea was pumped into the bay from an outfall off Mumbles Head – the third largest in Wales. I was on board the paddle-steamer *Waverley* when, rounding the head after an evening's cruise, we found ourselves afloat on a stinking brown swell of sewage blooming up from the pipe beneath us. For years, the used condoms on local beaches outnumbered the jellyfish, although things improved a little in the 1980s when Neil Kinnock opened a screening and mashing plant at Mumbles: you'd still be swimming in sewage at Langland and Caswell, but at least, now, there'd be less of a frisson of recognition. It was at about this time that notices warning people not to eat shellfish from the bay suddenly disappeared – presumably to avoid scaring off visitors. Although sewage continues to be pumped into the bay from Neath and Port Talbot, and there seems to be no way of cleansing the bay of industrial-era contaminants such as zinc and cadmium, there has been a radical improvement in water quality since Swansea stopped pumping its sewage into the sea. In a seafront restaurant, I recently enjoyed a plateful of the largest and most succulent mussels I have ever tasted, and asked where they were from. "Out there," said the waitress, gesturing towards the bay, where at that moment the red-hulled *Swansea Bay*, one of the visual delights of a high blue tide, was busily working the mussel beds.

In comparison with the industrial era, when there could be scores of ships riding at anchor as they waited to enter the port, and when public holidays saw thousands of workers and their families thronging the sands, Swansea Bay today is relatively deserted. Days can pass without a single freighter crossing to or from the twin piers of the port. Joggers, dog walkers, five- to twenty-aside footballers, kite flyers, windsurfers, the odd sunbather are common sights on the foreshore – but with hectares, usually, of empty beach between them.

The largest vessel regularly to cross the bay, until late 2006, was the Swansea–Cork *Superferry* (1972; rebuilt 1991), a heavily smoking, white leviathan of a tub that had more in common with a supermarket than a ship. In 2005, some 116,000 passengers used the ferry – a considerable decline from the 1995 figure of 163,000, resulting apparently from the growing low-cost airline market. At the height of the season, the ferry would round Mumbles Head at about 7 p.m., and a couple of hours later it would be belching back across the bay on its ten-hour journey to Ireland.

> smacking lushly ashore
> from the bay long becalmed –
> the vanished ferry's wake

Swansea–Cork sailings for 2007 were cancelled, the company claiming it had failed to secure a replacement vessel for the *Superferry*. They hoped to resume the service in 2008.

Most vessels of any size have to take a pilot on board when approaching or leaving the port. Swansea's early pilots, who were fiercely competitive (and bibulous) freelances, were often Gower men – such as the Aces. In 1803, it was ordered that "no person who Keeps a public House be appointed [as a pilot] in future". The pilots eventually amalgamated and by the end of the nineteenth century they were working from a steam cutter, the Beaufort – named after the dukes of *Beaufort*, seigneurial lords of Gower and major players in the life of the port. The *Beaufort* was succeeded by the *Roger Beck*, named after the last chairman of the old Swansea Harbour Trust, which in turn was succeeded, in 1959, by the *Seamark*, whose distinctive red and yellow paintwork made her an instantly recognisable feature of Swansea Bay for over forty years.

My grandfather[2] having been chairman of the pilotage authority

and my grandmother, consequently, having been invited to launch the *Seamark* at Appledore in Devon, I and other members of the family enjoyed several days aboard the *Seamark* during the 1960s, bustling around among the tankers and freighters, as we put pilots aboard the incoming ships and took them off the ships that were outward bound, towering above us, as we came alongside, like impossible steel cliffs. It was especially exciting at night, particularly if the wind was up: the closer we'd sidle to a tanker's hull, the wilder would the sea boil between the two vessels, as the pilot – in anorak and trilby, and bearing a briefcase – would balance himself on the *Seamark*'s gunwale and then, when the angle was right, hurl himself over the roiling divide toward a rope ladder dangling down from the tanker.

The more stressful aspects of the job were compensated for by long lulls between ships, when the *Seamark* would drift for hours in the bay; then, perhaps, it would be time for a nap, or a read, or some television in the upward-sloping lounge, with a tumbler of something restorative from the drinks cabinet. The pilots, in those pre-breathalyzer days, were generous hosts. When, on one of our visits, it was noticed that there were no lemons for the gin-and-tonics, it was no trouble at all to chug back into port to pick up a lemon or two from the red-brick, castellated Pilot House. At the end of her sea-going life, the *Seamark* was donated to the Cardiff sea cadets, and lies now in the Roath basin. Her successor (from 2001) is another *Beaufort*. A chunky, utilitarian craft, the *Beaufort* is capable of 18 knots – twice the speed of the *Seamark* – which means quick drop-offs and returns, and no more hanging about for hours in the middle of Swansea Bay, chatting about music and books while waiting for tardy hulks of the deep.

A regular and distinctive visitor to the bay – black hull, white superstructure, yellow, squared-off 'A' lifting gear at her prow – whose identity and purpose often puzzle the casual observer, is the Trinity House tender *Mermaid* (1987). Based at Swansea, her job is to ferry to and from Trinity House's west-coast base at Swansea every buoy on southern Britain's western seaboard when it's due for

its five-yearly refurbishment. The buoys – the bigger, older ones weighing six tonnes or more – are picked up and later repositioned with pinpoint, satellite-navigated accuracy. They are hoisted aboard along with the 50-metre chains that tether them to the 'sinkers' – huge bath-plug-like weights (of between 1 and 5 tonnes) – which rest immovably on the sea bed. The *Mermaid*'s crew of seventeen spend three weeks aboard, and then take three weeks off. Her sister ship, the 'yacht' *Patricia* (1982), based at Harwich and responsible for the buoys on the eastern seaboard, is an occasional visitor to Swansea. Slightly smaller but notably plusher, the *Patricia* is equipped with state rooms for the English royal family and accommodation for paying guests; her cruises to Ireland and around the Severn Sea are much in demand.

Regular summer-season visitors to the bay include the motor cruiser *Balmoral* (1949) and her older sister ship the *Waverley* (1947), which claims to be the last ocean-going paddle-steamer in the world, and is evocative of the White Funnel Fleet steamers, such as the *Glengower*, the *Cardiff Queen* and the *Westward Ho!*, which used to ply regularly between Swansea and Ilfracombe until the mid twentieth century. The *Balmoral* and the *Waverley* offer cruises along the Gower coast and trips to Ilfracombe and Lundy – rather too raucously boozy, on occasion, for some tastes. Then there are the regattas, the flotillas of tiger-moth dinghies, the pleasure craft of sail and motor, the jet-skis of macho egomaniacs desperately trying to prove something – and the windsurfers. In April, 2006, a Swansea windsurfer, Adam Cowles, hit the headlines after a quick scoot across the bay turned into an epic – and potentially lethal – adventure. He realised things were getting out of hand when the shoreline behind him vanished and he passed a huge cargo ship. "It was at that point I had a moment of inspiration," he told *The Evening Post*. "I just thought I would carry on and head towards Devon." Three hours later, he stumbled ashore 65 km from where he had started, at what some surprised locals informed him was Woody Bay, near Lynton.

> high tide after the storm,
> the bay bobbing with
> bits of forest

Swansea Bay, over the years, has seen some curious sights. The sands near the west pier were Swansea's first airport: in the early decades of the twentieth century, the post would be delivered to the town by a flimsy, two-seater aircraft, its approach requiring someone to clear a landing strip among the bathers – who'd later be offered, for a fee, a ride over the bay in this newfangled contraption. Until the end of the century, when most travelling shows stopped using animals, every circus that came to town would take its elephants for a wallow in the sea at Brynmill. More recently, *The World* (2001), that restlessly nomadic floating city for the super-rich, dropped anchor in the bay, to enable its denizens to stock up on essentials at Sainsbury's and Tesco. Homes aboard The *World*, which is on a continuous circumnavigation of the globe, cost nearly $2m dollars apiece, offers considered only from those with assets of $5m or more.

If plans to site a 30-turbine nest of 134-m high cash generators around the Scarweather Sands – the biggest offshore wind farm in Britain – proved highly controversial, there is considerable (and not, generally, unfavourable) public interest in an ambitious scheme to build in Swansea Bay the world's first tidal lagoon for generating electricity. Constructed of rock, slate, sand and gravel, it would look like a circular island at low tide and be invisible at high tide; covering around 5 sq km, it would generate, on both incoming and outgoing tides, enough electricity to provide power for 10,000 homes. But the plan has been undermined by a report from the Department of Trade and Industry which claims that the scheme is not economically viable. The lagoon's many supporters have vowed to continue the campaign for its construction, arguing that for the same price as the proposed (and ecologically damaging) Severn barrage at least 150 lagoons could be constructed. Generation costs from a lagoon, they say, would be around 2.5 pence and from the barrage 5.5 pence per kilowatt hour.

> hooter booms –
> and a slice of the city
> sails into the night

QUAY PARADE

The name of Quay Parade, the main southern gateway to Swansea, evokes the quay that was situated here, at the confluence of the Tawe and the Pill (or the town ditch or moat) – the Tawe then, of course, flowing alongside the Strand. The Pill was a tidal creek which ran roughly along the line of today's Quay Parade – necessitating a bridge at the town's South Gate (at the bottom of Wind Street). It was fed by two streams, one winding through the (then open) Burrows and another created by springs rising on Mount Pleasant. The latter hugged the town's medieval wall, flowing through the present St David's shopping centre and along what is now Rutland Street, towards the southern end of today's Princess Way. Here it joined the stream winding town-wards over the Burrows, from the direction of the National Waterfront Museum.

The only thing that flows along Quay Parade today is traffic. As a gateway to the city, Quay Parade conveys a mixed, inauspicious message, the vaunting ambition of the new Sail Bridge to your left undermined by the tin retail sheds of Parc Tawe and the passé glass pyramid (1990) of Plantasia (trying hard to be 'modern') to your right. They advertise a seam of philistinism embedded deep in Swansea's soul – a philistinism which, paradoxically, may have consti-tuted for its artists the irritant grit that has cultured many a pearl. As you speed across the Tawe on the New Cut Bridge, you might miss David Backhouse's graceful sculpture *Flying Figurehead* (1989) in the bushes at the edge of Sainsbury's car park, but there's no escaping the bridgehead's louring gun-on-a-plinth on the opposite side of the

road. This is intended not to take out unwelcome guests or fugitive natives but to mark the fiftieth anniversary of the cessation of hostilities in Europe and to commemorate the 387 people who died in air raids in Swansea. Few would quarrel with that intention, but many have questioned the lumpish literalism of deploying an actual anti-aircraft gun as a memorial, rather than a work of art (see, by way of contrast, bombed Rotterdam's formidable *Verwoeste Stad* (The Razed City; 1946) by Ossip Zadkine). Its unveiling in 1995 sounded the death knell for Swansea's brief period as a European leader in the field of public art.

The bridge, opened in 1965, is the fifth to span the Tawe at this point. It succeeded a combined road and rail bridge (1897) which swung open to allow the passage of ships. Travelling over the old bridge as a child in the 1950s and along the road's jostle of tarmac and rail was a thrilling experience, as you half expected your family's saloon to be pancaked any second by a thundering coal train.

Harbour Road, as Quay Parade was then known, was dominated horizontally by railways: not only the tracks embedded in the road, but, even more of a presence, the railway viaduct – supported by a row of arches and a metal bridge across the bottom of Wind Street – which ran parallel with the road until it crossed it just west of the Museum, taking coal trains to the South Dock. Two massive stone piers standing in the Tawe just south of the New Cut Bridge are the remains of a railway bridge over the Tawe, which fed trains onto the Harbour Road viaduct. The viaduct's arches – echoed by the arched frontages of the new Salubrious Place development – were home to various concerns, including, in the 1960s, the offices of two of Swansea's three large taxi firms, Streamline Taxis and Davey's Taxis (the third was Glamtax in York Street), with their Austin Cambridges, Ford Cortinas and Wolseleys.

The area was dominated vertically by that major Swansea landmark, Weaver's flour mill which looked like a broad, off-yellow, windowless skyscraper and stood towards the northern end of

Sainsbury's car park, on the edge of the half-tide basin of the North Dock (which forms the rest of the Sainsbury's site). Built between 1897 and 1898, to a design by the French firm of Hennebique, it was perhaps Europe's first ever reinforced-concrete building. This great slab of a building – which had a 91,000-litre reservoir on its roof – used imported wheat to produce 900 bags of brown bread flour an hour, for distribution to dozens of small bakers all over town. The growing popularity of white bread from abroad during the 1920s began the slow decline of Weaver's fortunes, and the mill closed in 1963. Various schemes were mooted that might have saved this architecturally important building, including converting it into a gallery of modern art, but its structure was deemed intractable, and it was demolished – with considerable difficulty – in 1984. All that remains is one of its reinforced columns preserved, with plaque, on the riverside walkway nearby.

Opposite Weaver's, near the grass verge in front of Toys R Us, stood one of Swansea's more colourful pubs, the Cuba, named after the copper ore trade with that island. Often known as The Gateway to Swansea, it was the last port of call for sailors returning to their ships – or the first when they came ashore, thirsty and ruttish after weeks at sea. Working girls would sit around the bar in their short skirts, with their prices – £3, £5 – written with chalk from the darts board on the soles of their shoes. Competition with girls from the Queen's in Gloucester Place would sometimes get physical, with the girls barging into each other's pubs for a scrap over the poaching of clients. The pub, demolished in the 1960s, had an old pot-bellied fire in the middle of the room. A long-standing Swansea councillor (who asked to remain nameless) told me he'd nearly got himself killed one drunken night when he decided to relieve himself on the iron casing of the fire, filling the bar instantly with clouds of urinous steam.

The Buck brothers' famous 1748 print of The East View of Swansea, in the County of Glamorgan names the north bank of the Pill – at the bottom of the Strand, where the Bank of Scotland and Swansea Civil Justice block now stands – as the Parade and it shows a neat row of about fifteen lime trees, which stood there until 1805. The Bucks also show, nearby, a curious stone-walled, earthen platform known as the Mount, which stood on a plot at the bottom of Wind Street, next door to the café-bar La Prensa, on which the Brasseria restaurant, in 2006, opened an alfresco terrace. It has puzzled generations of historians. W.H. Jones, in the 1920s, proposed this as the site of Swansea's very first, wooden-built castle, overlooking the supposed 'ey' in the aber of the Tawe, and possibly thrown up and fortified by the Danes. The Mount was removed in 1804, to make way for the Oystermouth (later, Mumbles) railway.

MORGAN'S HOTEL

Ever stayed in a five-star hotel? Me neither – not until a Friday in March 2007 when I got to stay, free of charge, at Swansea's only five-star hotel: Morgan's, in Adelaide Street, diagonally opposite the site of the long-vanished Mount. My compañera, the jazz singer Margot Morgan (no relation), had earlier performed in an NSPCC fund-raising evening at Morgan's – the first live-music event to be held in the hotel's bar – and, by way of thanks, the management offered Margot and mate a night at Morgan's, on the *maison*. (The place encourages alliteration – there are Ms for Morgan everywhere.)

I'd been to Morgan's once before, on a post-gig, Shiraz bender with Spencer Davis, but my recollections of the place – although we spent hours at the bar – were rather unfocused. Here, now, was an opportunity to experience la vie de luxe from the inside.

We could have walked the couple of kilometres from Margot's house in Brynmill quicker than we got there by car on traffic-jammed Oystermouth Road. But we thought we had better arrive at our five-star hotel in four-wheeled style.

We squeeze the rusting Ford Ka between a Jaguar and a BMW in the hotel car park (which, in the eighteenth century, was a slaughter-house on the southern bank of the Pill) and stand for a moment to admire a building which, when it opened in 1903, was said by *The Cambrian* to have "remodelled the whole appearance of this part of Swansea".

Built as offices for the Swansea Harbour Trust, and speaking eloquently of the town's global significance as a centre of trade and

industry, it was designed by Edwin Seward (1853-1924) of Cardiff – whose other notable buildings include Cardiff's Free Library (1882) and the Coal Exchange (1885). It's an exuberantly confident essay in Arts and Crafts Baroque, counterpointing red Catty-brook brick with bands of Portland stone, and revelling in a richness of detail, from its domed tower mantled with statuary, to art nouveau light

fittings and external railings. It eventually became the offices of Associated British Ports and served briefly as the offices of the UK Year of Literature (1995) before its conversion to a hotel, in 2002, by Martin and Louisa Morgan.

They've succeeded triumphantly in conveying a sense of the unashamedly modern while making the most of the historic features of this Grade II★ listed building. The commodious bar, the first area you enter from the street, with its "hot chocolate and cool cream leather chairs and sofas", strikes the right, welcoming note from the outset. You might be, like me, a paid-up member of the riff-raff, but there's no suggestion you shouldn't be here, no one at the door in a uniform to tell you that your face and scruffy denims don't fit.

The reception desk is at the foot of the main staircase, which is crowned by one of the glories of the building, a cupola pierced by eight stained-glass roundels characterising the trade winds as human types, from hoary old north to sensuously fecund south.

We are shown to the Zeta suite. The holy Catherine and her husband have not, we're told, stayed in this particular room, although they were regular guests at Morgan's before the completion of their Ponderosa at Mumbles. It is, nevertheless, a boudoir fit for a movie queen: suede curtains, a ceiling so high that our exploding champagne cork fails to reach it, an emperor-size bed with – at its head – a glass shelf for our drinks and a huge mirror that must have seen all manner of action, and a king-size, wooden-floored bathroom with 'daring double showers'. The décor, in contrast to all this potential for excitement, is cream-and-brown understatement and beige restraint. There's just one painting – by Nick Holly, of scarf-waving football fans leaving the Vetch.

A bottle or two of champagne later, we head for the dining room, which was originally the Harbour Trust's sumptuous boardroom. It's still a magnificent room, with its varnished wooden floor, its barrel-vaulted ceiling, two *trompe-l'œil* door frames (in the corridor outside are, conversely, real frames surrounding *trompe-l'œil* doors), and –

above a brace of glass-panelled doors – an intriguing crescent-shaped mural depicting sailing ships laid up in the Tawe, with the castle itself seeming to flare up out of the timber-work of a ship in the process of being built.

Apart from a low-volume, twenty-strong hen party, most of the other diners – cutlery and crockery studiously a-clatter – are couples in their thirties. Enter, later, one of Wales's finest (Marxist) playwrights, Gareth Miles, and his wife Gina, who are spending a night at Morgan's in celebration of their fortieth wedding anniversary. The presence of the impeccably left-wing Gareth in this seat of five-star indulgence relieves me forthwith of any lingering socialist qualms about our luxury escapade. From the first bite of oven-fresh bread, via scallops, pheasant paté, guinea fowl and lamb, to the last mouthful of macaroon cheesecake, the meal is an honorary fat-cat's delight. And we still manage to find room, at ten o'clock the next morning, for the full Welsh breakfast.

Magnificent, munificent – and Swansea-made – Morgan's.

THE LEISURE CENTRE

Ugly but much loved, the Leisure Centre reopened in March 2008 after a £32m refurbishment designed, in part, to overhaul its notoriously dowdy image.

'The Lehjer', as it has been fondly known, stands roughly where the old Victoria railway station used to be, with its extensive coal marshalling yard spreading a dozen parallel sets of railway lines over what is now the car park opposite Tesco. Until its closure in the 1964, Victoria station was the point of departure, on the LMS[3] line, for Shrewsbury, Liverpool, Manchester and points further north.

When the Leisure Centre opened in 1977, people said it was built back to front, offering nothing to Oystermouth Road but the appearance of a stultifying brown shoebox. By 2003, it had fallen into such disrepair that it was suddenly closed and threatened with demolition. But, following a change of municipal heart, a programme of wholescale refurbishment was decided on. Its interior was scooped out and completely remodelled, and its drab exterior was given a make-over. New attractions include indoor surfing, a four-storey play zone and a rooftop gym with sweeping views over the bay. It's supposed to be good for another 25 years.

Despite the Leisure Centre's universally derided exterior, its sports and fitness facilities and its swimming pool – with wave machine, shutes and thrilling slides – proved so popular that its overnight closure may have been the deciding factor in Labour being voted out of local authority power, in 2004, for the first time in over twenty years. It was used by 800,000 people a year and – astonishingly – it routinely beat St Fagans, the National Museum and the great Norman castles of the north to top place in the official ranking of national tourist attractions (which must surely have had more than a little to do with Swansea's high rainfall and the lack of wet-weather options for visitors).

Almost everyone can remember good times at the ugly old Lehjer – from romping with the kids in its Jolly Roger foam-rubber funland, to seeing Chuck Berry, live on stage in the gym, well into his sixties and still delivering the famous duck-walk.

Its reopening, under the management of a not-for-profit company, was heralded by a new logo and name, The LC2, which the council paid a private PR firm over £11,000 to dream up. They await anxiously to see if the people of Swansea take to the new name. Perhaps, in time, they'll come round, and drop 'The Lehjer' in favour of a visit to Elsie's.

OYSTERMOUTH ROAD

A city by the sea that seems to care not a seagull's fart about being by the sea, that's Swansea. Nowhere illustrates this indifference better than Oystermouth Road, that 1.5-km stretch of the Swansea–Mumbles road (the A4067) which begins roughly at the Leisure Centre and ends roughly at Victoria Park, where it continues as the Mumbles Road. It's topped and tailed by two ghosts of bridges: the railway bridge that used to cross the road just west of the Museum, of which no trace remains, and the Slip bridge for pedestrians, which was removed in 2004, in a squall of controversy, leaving its two stone abutments bereft of a role.

Oystermouth Road, with its constant barrage of traffic, keeps people away from the beach as efficiently as would a moat full of piranhas. And if you manage to cross safely to the beach, where then might you find any refreshment, apart from the ice-cream van by the Slip – if it's there? An ambitious plan advanced in recent years was to drop the road into a tunnel (allowing the traffic to re-emerge in the region of Sainsbury's), thereby cementing an intimate relationship between the city and its seafront. But, as ever in Swansea, it's traffic that rules and the scheme was rebuffed.

The Swansea to Oyster-mouth connection goes back a long way. After the main Roman road from Nidum (Neath) to Leucarum (Llwchwr) crossed the Tawe – at a ford situated to the east of the high ground on which High Street station now stands – a track veered south-west,

cutting across the Burrows, in the direction of a certain seaside village renowned for its oysters. Some Romans, indeed, settled in Oystermouth, as evidenced by the tesserae of a Roman pavement discovered at the parish church in the nineteenth century. This track may in time have become the road across the Burrows that was laid down in the early nineteenth century, roughly along the route of the present road.

One of the few pleasures for the eye in today's Oystermouth Road, as you approach from the east, is the National Waterfront Museum. Its airy, uplifting aesthetic is in marked contrast to much of what follows.

It was in a shed in Rutland Street (opposite Victoria station, now the Leisure Centre) that the famous Mumbles trains were parked overnight. Every morning, the traffic in Oystermouth Road would be held up for the tramcar-like train to cross the road on a track – embedded in the tarmac – which arced westward and carried the red, two-car units, powered by overhead electricity cables, alongside the main road towards Mumbles. For most of the length of Oystermouth Road the tracks of the Mumbles train and of the LMS line ran side by side.

Tesco occupies the site of what was Oystermouth Road's most prominent landmark, the gas works. From 1924, when the manufacture of gas transferred to a new works at Morriston, the site became a distribution centre, with its four gasholders rising over the town and sinking back again as the gas levels fluctuated. Operations ceased here in the later twentieth century, when the depot lay abandoned for some years and was considered briefly as the site for a piazza. Then

Tesco barged in, and out went the idle dream of a civic amenity.

Two mostly unloved buildings glower at each other across the middle section of Oystermouth Road: the dark sandstone prison (1861) and the sprawling, off-white County Hall, often referred to as the Taj Mahal (in recognition of what it is not). Built as West Glamorgan County Hall on a magnificent seafront site in the early 1980s, the subtext of its design, like that of the prison, is that it's representative of power – municipal power in this case, suggested by the processional ramp of purple brick leading up to its imposing entrance, above which the council chamber looms. These portals look down on you; make you feel – the British way – more a subject than a citizen. But it's been a happy place for some: registry office marriages are solemnised here as are gay partnerships; Swansea, in 2002, was the first place in Wales to offer same-sex commitment ceremonies.

In 2006, plans were announced to spend £13m transforming County Hall into a civic centre fit for the twenty-first century. The (not very central) Central Library in Alexandra Road would be moved to the (not very central) County Hall, and this new civic centre would include a family history centre and archive, seafront café, public exhibition area and a council services contact centre (centre upon centre upon centre). It was opened in March 2008.

After the stiff formality of the prison and County Hall, Oystermouth Road goes wildly higgledy-piggledy with the pubs, B&Bs, small hotels and dodgy dives that fill up most of the rest of its length: Sea Beach, Sandpiper Guest House, Arches Hotel and Tea Rooms, Ye Famous Abertawe Alehouse Hen Dafarn, Tudor Court

Hotel, Camelot, Lotus Restaurant, Beachcomber, Trafalgar, The Glengarrif Hotel, Leonardo's .... The chaos of their names reflects the visual anarchy of their frontages. Some of these (originally attractive) buildings have been sympathetically restored, inside and out, but many have been refurbished as thoughtlessly and cheaply as possible, contributing to the row's unfortunate rough-and-ready image. In comparison with the Marriott across the way (£119 per night), these places are cheap (£20 per night, for instance, at the Tudor Court). In the heyday of Swansea's theatres, scores of actors and actresses used to board here, as, today, do reps and travellers of all kinds, clandestine lovers and parties from the Valleys down in Swansea for a lively weekend.

The last in this row of hostelries (or the first if you're coming from Mumbles) is the Bay View Hotel. It was built in 1859 at what was then an isolated spot, notorious for robberies, known as 'the finger post at St Helen's'. The Bellevue Recreation Ground, as it was called, was intended as an early kind of leisure centre, comprising a hotel, sanatorium, bowling green, billiard room, skating rink, pleasure gardens and a high-level promenade where customers could take refreshments and enjoy the sea views. Too far from town to make economic sense, the struggling enterprise was described as "the biggest white elephant to be built in the name of the licensing trade", and soon earned itself the nickname of Jack's Folly. When the Swansea Baths and Laundry was opened opposite in 1884 (on what is now a car park for Guildhall employees), it abandoned its health and fitness pretensions and became the Bay View pub.

From the Bay View's front door you gaze on blank sky where, until 2004, the sturdy black struts of the Slip bridge commandeered the view. The bridge was opened on a wet and windy October day in 1915, as flags fluttered and the great and the good cowered in the archways of its stone supports. For the best part of a hundred years, it provided a safe crossing over both the road and (until the 1960s) the two railways that passed in parallel beneath it. The Slip was Swansea sands' entertainments mecca, with swings, round-abouts, helter-skelter, Punch and Judy show, ice-cream booths under striped canvas awnings, and a lean-to stall selling tea, coffee and cocoa.

Holidaymakers would have poured in their thousands over the Slip bridge, descending directly onto the hot sands. They couldn't do so today. For its cross-span is to be found 700 metres away, on the

foreshore footpath opposite the Recreation Ground, bridging nothing. In 2004, the reputedly deteriorating span was moved 'for safety reasons' (and nothing, surely, to do with clearing a lucrative view of Mumbles for the occupants of the new Morgan Court flats). It was then settled on chocks on the Recreation Ground while the council indulged in a £35,000 consultation exercise intended to find out whether the people of Swansea wanted the bridge fully restored – at a cost of £700,000 – or scrapped. The results of the exercise were inconclusive, claimed the council – which then proceeded with a refurbishing and re-siting plan, which no one had voted for at all and which cost local taxpayers £120,000. Council leader Chris Holley later admitted the authority had dropped a clanger. The re-sited Slip bridge has been known ever since as Holley's Folly.

But let's end our tour of Oystermouth Road on a positive note. A few metres from the bridge's northern abutment is a (defunct) fountain erected by public subscription and dedicated to the memory of the local engineer and philanthropist Henry Evans Charles MRCS, who died in 1907. The inscription informs us simply that 'He went about doing good'. Who could hope for a more wholesome epitaph?

WORLD'S END

The nondescript Albert Row, opposite the Oystermouth Road car park, is little more than a conduit for vehicles leaving the Quadrant and Tesco's deliveries bay. The long-demolished streets around here constituted a wretchedly poor quarter of Swansea known aptly as World's End. Forgotten by all, the area nevertheless deserves to be remembered for an intriguing literary association.

It was in a hovel at the junction of Thomas Street and Edward Street, named incongruously Major Roteley's Cottage, that the pioneer of the novel in Wales, Thomas Jeffrey Llewelyn Prichard

(1790-1862), met his grim demise. Builth-born, he ended up in Swansea after an itinerant and frequently poverty-stricken existence as strolling player, bookseller, publisher, accountant and – determinedly – professional writer: his biographer Sam Adams describes him as "the first conscious … Anglo-Welsh writer".

Prichard's one popular success as a writer, *The Adventures and Vagaries of Twm Shon Catti* (1828), based on the legendary exploits of the 'Welsh Robin Hood', Thomas Jones (c.1530-1609) of Tregaron, is often referred to as the first Welsh novel. He published it himself and sold it, as he sold his other books, by tramping all over Wales and hawking it from door to door. But wide-scale pirating of the book, and the comparative failure of his other titles, deprived him of much in the way of financial reward for his literary labours, and his prospects as an actor were dashed when he lost his nose in a fencing accident. The wax nose he wore as a substitute, held in place by his spectacles, made him a figure of vicious fun to the urchins of World's End, who would hurl stones at his house, followed by foul-mouthed abuse when he came to his door to complain.

Detached from his family and with few friends, his last days in his single room in Swansea were fraught with ill health and destitution. One winter's night, the 71-year-old father of the Welsh novel fell drunkenly into his fire; the shock and his injuries killed him. His grave can be seen in Danygraig cemetery.

THE PROMENADE

The 9.5-km walk from Swansea's West Pier to the pier at Mumbles, most of which can be cycled, begins in the sand dunes that gave name to the Burrows of pre-industrial Swansea. Reaching, on average, 275 metres inland from the high water mark, and stretching originally 2 km from the Tawe to Brynmill, the Burrows formed an extensive tract of marram grass, sand couch, sea-holly, sand-sedge and other dune plants. Only a small fraction survives – a segment shaped like an isosceles triangle, about 700 metres long, between the river and the beginning of the paved promenade.

Criss-crossed by sandy paths and pocked with hollows, the dunes provide shelter from the wind – and prying eyes – for impromptu barbecues, day-long drinking sessions and clandestine encounters, some involving syringes. The twining of two lovers in one of these hollows reminds me of Walter Savage Landor's historic encounter hereabouts, in 1796, with the 17-year-old beauty Rose Aylmer. The 21-year-old poet fell instantly in love with her, but their trysts on Swansea's "lonely strand", which seem to have haunted him to the end of his days, lasted only eighteen months before she was whisked away to Calcutta by her aunt. There, in 1800, at the age of twenty, she died – possibly from cholera, possibly from dysentery caused "by indulging too much with that mischievous and dangerous fruit, the pineapple."

When I visited Calcutta in 1992, I managed to find her grave in South Park Street Cemetery, a high-Anglican necropolis for the captains of Empire. Inscribed at the base of her tomb are the best-known lines of Landor's entire oeuvre and the most famous of all imperial epitaphs:

> Ah, what avails the sceptred race!
> Ah, what the form divine!
> What every virtue, every grace!
> Rose Aylmer, all were thine.
>
> Rose Aylmer, whom these wakeful eyes
> May weep, but never see,
> A night of memories and sighs
> I consecrate to thee.

He composed them, apparently, "when I was cleaning my teeth before going to bed".

Where the dunes end, the promenade proper begins, running along the top of the new sea defences on which stand, also, the pale green, Regency-inflected town houses of Marine Walk, with their magnificent views across the entire sweep of Swansea Bay.

> mobile in right hand,
> she trades sweet nothings
> as her left scoops poop

The strong tower motif along Marine Walk is inaugurated by the *Tower of the Ecliptic* astronomical observatory (1991), and followed up by artworks such as Rob Conybear's octagonal *Lighthouse Tower* (1987) winking playfully at its serious big brother across the bay at Mumbles Head; Robin Campbell's *Copper Flame* (1989), which is a tribute both to the transformation of ore to metal, and, in Martin

Williams's ceramic panels, to wind forces one to eight; and, on the other side of the Seagate – the main access to the beach – the *Zeta Mnemonical* (1989), also by Robin Campbell. The *Zeta Mnemonical*, packed with intriguing detail, celebrates the four winds and the Swansea Cape Horners, the *Zeta* having been a barque-rigged steamer launched in 1865 for Swansea's copper ore fleet (the most-beautiful-Welshwoman- in-Hollywood is named, via her grandmother, after the *Zeta*).

These artworks have not been maintained, and the ravages of time, the elements and vandalism are increasingly evident. Some, such as Ian Hamilton Finlay's boarded up *Tower of the Nets* (1987), opposite the *Tower of the Ecliptic*, were never completed; others, like Robin Campbell's *Boatshed Doors* (1990), are left to flake and fade, until they are sad, indecipherable ghosts. Several sandstone plaques along Marine Walk, many of them relating to the science of light, have been weather-blasted beyond restitution. The beautiful exhortation on one of them, "Bless the vast planetary abstraction of the ocean", is by now entirely unreadable.

At the Heath Robinson-ish *Lighthouse Tower*, the seaward side of the promenade drops down to a lower level so that you are walking parallel with the beach about half way down the sea-defence wall. Inscribed in the concrete along this stretch are the names of some notable Swansea Cape Horners: *The Jonas of Swansey, Blithe de Swaynseye, Ianthe, Chelhydra, Capricorn, Pacific, Antarctic, Topaz, Cypher, Flora, Darwin, Orient, Ocean Rover, Glamorgan, Galatea, Mohican, Zeta, Epsilon, Delta, Gamma, Beta, Alpha*. The Cape Horners, ships of almost mythic renown, would sail out with cargoes of coal or patent fuel (briquettes made of coal dust and tar pitch) and return from Chile laden with even heavier copper ore.

A voyage round Cape Horn to Chile and back – west under sail, east under steam – could last six to nine months and could take a heavy toll on both crew and ship. Between 1873 and 1899, over 200 Swansea ships were wrecked or lost without trace. Many sailors survived the hazards of passage only to succumb to disease. Yellow fever was among the most feared, so many sailors dying of it that Santiago in Chile was nicknamed 'Swansea cemetery'. Swansea is the only town in Britain known to have suffered an outbreak of this acutely infectious disease: in 1865, when the barque *Hecla* returned from Cuba several of the crew had died from it; a further seventeen townspeople would also die.

The foreshore in front of the Marriott Hotel and County Hall used to be the realm of the bathing machine. Useful only when the tide was in, the bathing machine – horse-drawn to the water's edge – was basically a hut on four large wheels, with steps at the front down which the disrobed bather would slither into the water. Many swam naked, and mixed bathing was not permitted. There was a set of machines for women and another for men, separated from each other by half an acre of beach patrolled by a policeman with a large cane, to ensure that the men kept out of the women's area.

Some of these machines operated in association with a now long vanished but once notable Swansea institution, the Bathing House. Built towards the end of the eighteenth century and occupying roughly the site of the western wing of County Hall, it stood for many years on the Burrows in complete isolation. It was run for a time, unprofitably, by the Worcester-born poet and novelist Julia Ann Hatton (1764-1838), known as Ann of Swansea, who was the sister of the famous tragedienne Sarah Siddons. Sarah seems to have more or less bribed Ann – after a series of scandals – to live at least 150 miles away from London, in return for a sum of £20 a year. So, the lame (in more than one sense) 'poetess' pitched up in Swansea, where she lived for most of the rest of her life. Her verse aspires effortlessly to the ambitions set for it by the title she chose for one of her collections, *Poetic Trifles* (1811). But she was popular in her day and warmly appreciated by Swansea people. Settling eventually in Park Street, she suffered ill health, poverty, neglect and loneliness in old age. Buried in the churchyard of what is now St Matthew's in High Street, Ann of Swansea took with her, as Jim Davies has observed, "what little remained of Swansea's ambitions to be a genteel seaside resort."

At the western end of the County Hall car park, a favourite if frequently besanded night-stop for lorries, the promenade joins the route of the old LMS Swansea–Shrewsbury line which, running roughly parallel with Oystermouth Road, will take us as far as Blackpill. Sandwiched between the LMS line, on its raised bund, and the road was the Mumbles railway. Accompanying us from here all the way to Mumbles is another thoroughfare that's largely invisible, the Mumbles–Swansea sewage main. For much of the route, it's directly underfoot, but from here to Brynmill it's buried under the sand on the south side of the sea wall.

The dunes of the old Burrows may have disappeared almost entirely under concrete, stone, brick and tarmac, but their sandy ghosts have struggled ever since to recover lost ground. The frequent sanding of the promenade and the seafront road by the prevailing south-westerlies has long been an expensive headache for the authorities. The council has decided to tackle the problem not by fighting the dune ghosts but by encouraging them. On the beach in front of the Patti Pavilion is the largest of two or three dune-building projects. A length of black nylon mesh fencing is being used to trap wind-blown sand, gradually accumulating around the fencing – with the aid of sand-fixing marram grass – a new dune habitat. The aim is to encourage the dunes to form seawards, away from the promenade, which eventually will push the high-tide line back. It's early days yet, but the signs are that the ghosts are happier than they used to be and may soon rematerialize as fully-fledged dunes.

A small car park occupies the site of Swansea Bay station, whose purplish brick walling is still sturdily in place. Here the promenade path is divided – for about 500 metres – by a long grassy island which is host to a series of monuments.

The first, made of a tonne and a half of Penzance granite, commemorates one of Swansea's most famous sons, the life-saving, black Labrador retriever Swansea Jack.

> first rain in weeks,
> slugs risking freedom
> on the busy path

A few metres west of Swansea Jack's resting place is a monument – originally sited in Victoria Park – to local men who fell in the South

African wars. The moustachioed and rifled warrior who stands in
alabaster glory atop the pinkish plinth was modelled, in 1904, not on
a veteran of the Boer War but on Sergeant-Major Andrew Bird of
Sketty, a swagger-sticked disciplinarian who taught French and PT to
thousands of boys, including Dylan Thomas and Wynford Vaughan
Thomas, at Swansea Grammar School. Oiseau – as, of course, he was
known – would never admit to having been the model.

You can count the names of the 43 who fell in South Africa.
Almost beyond counting (and beyond the imagination's reckoning of
grief) are the hundreds and hundreds of names inscribed inside the
cenotaph enclosure which dominates this length of promenade and
which commemorates the dead of the First World War, the Second
World War and more recent conflicts.

At the western end of this islet of municipal mourning is a recent
and distinctly unofficial expression of the most raw and ragged of
popular griefs: the cellophane bouquets, potted plants, Swans flags,
poems, photographs and messages of love for Ben Bellamy, a gifted
and popular Olchfa School A-level student, who was murdered on
the beach near here one early Sunday morning in September 2005.
The seventeen-year-old had been walking back to his Sketty home
from 'Cinders' nightspot at Mumbles pier when he was set upon by
three feral youths who had initially seemed to befriend him. They
beat him unconscious, robbed him, stripped him and dumped him in
the sea. His body was found by a jogger a few hours later. The killing
was met with anger and dismay by people all over Swansea.
Eventually, two of Ben's attackers were found guilty of murder and
one of manslaughter (the manslaughter charge was subsequently
quashed; he was convicted simply of robbery).

On the promenade at this point, we come to the first of three
clumpingly ugly 'stone waves' (the others are at Blackpill and West
Cross) which were erected in 2006 – at around £16,000 a time – to
do little more than display two posters apiece. Thirty minutes of
physical activity five times a week, advises one of the posters. This
popular stretch for joggers, walkers and cyclists is also the starting
and finishing point of the Swansea Bay 10k race, which usually
attracts over 4,000 runners.

Sex is also supposed to be good exercise. According to some,
there's a lot of it going on in the dunes either side of the car park at
the bottom of Sketty Lane. With Penllergaer Woods and the car park
at Caswell, this is supposed to be the 'dogging' capital of Swansea.
I can't say that in my years of cycling past here at least twice a day,

I have noticed much in the way of open-air orgies. Just shifty, unprepossessing loners – always men, never women – mooching around behind the red glow of a fag, their sad gazes begging for a little companionable friction.

> cycling home, not
> aware until a cyclist
> sweats by towards town
>
> that the wind
> has been behind me

From the car park at the bottom of Sketty Lane to Blackpill was the final seafront kilometre for the old LMS line, which used then to sweep north and head up Clyne Valley. The trains, as they banked before crossing the bridge over Mumbles Road, were – for kids splashing below in the Blackpill lido – an incredible vision of steam, smoke and clanking metal. The promenade descends steeply here to bridge the Clyne stream and find a new, lower level which is almost that of the beach. Having arrived at Blackpill largely on the route taken by the old LMS line, we travel the rest of the distance to Mumbles pier (1898) along the water's-edge route taken by the Mumbles railway. It was not until 1900 that the railway took the sea-shore route. Prior to this, the Blackpill to Oystermouth section continued along the then narrow and leafy Mumbles road. Much of the sea-shore route was laid on slag from the former Cwmfelin steel-works. A couple of oblique slipways down to the beach are constructed of large, irregular, slag slabs.

If the authorities hope eventually to solve Swansea seafront's sand-drifting problem, another 'natural' problem – actually resulting from human agency many years ago – is proving less tractable: the relentless prolif-eration, between Blackpill and West Cross, of that mud-binding invader cord grass (*Spartina anglica*), which was well established here by the late 1960s. It was introduced in many places in the nineteenth century to protect foreshores or to 'reclaim' mudflats for grazing, but, with its extensively creeping rootstock, it has often established itself where it's not wanted. Unless its spread can be controlled here the circular patches it has established in recent decades may coalesce eventually into a continuous sward, turning the mud-rich foreshore into something approaching a salt marsh.

This would be a view unlikely to appeal to Bonnie Tyler, whose palatial establishment, Fernhill, overlooks this stretch of the promenade. The Skewen-born singer (born Gaynor Hopkins), world famous for hits such as 'Lost in France', 'Total Eclipse of the Heart' and 'Holding Out for a Hero' has lived in Mumbles – with her husband, former Welsh judo champion and businessman Robbie Sullivan – since the 1970s. They lived initially in a modest detached house in Norton Road, but moved in the 1980s to her present abode which, with its night-time floodlighting (red at Christmas), is more in keeping with rock queen expectations.

> above the pines
> Bonny Tyler's palace
> outshines the moon

With a house in Portugal and busy touring, she hasn't had time lately to spend more than about a month a year in Mumbles. But when she's back she makes herself unpretentiously at home, and you may well find yourself bagging vegetables alongside her in the Choice is Yours fruit and veg shop or rubbing shoulders with her in Pepper's wine bar. She makes a point of returning to Mumbles for Christmas, and throws a party at Fernhill every Christmas morning.

Nestling in the grass just before the West Cross Inn is an oval plaque (English only) dedicated to the memory of one of the most colourful members of Swansea's renowned Dillwyn family, Amy (1845–1935). An independent-minded, cigar-smoking (from the age of eleven) eccentric, Amy Dillwyn managed the family's spelter works at Llansamlet after her father's death, campaigned for women's rights, wrote literary criticism and produced several novels, among them the well-regarded *The Rebecca Rioter* (1880), which is set chiefly in Swansea. She grew up at Parc Wern (later Parc Beck) and Hendrefoilan, but she spent her last years in the twin-gabled Tŷ Glyn (now much extended as the Mumbles Nursing Home) a few metres away from this seafront plaque, on the other side of Mumbles Road

– where, at the entrance, there is a companion plaque.

Just beyond the West Cross Inn, is a row of large seafront houses divided by broad expanses of grass. There were similar houses on these vacant plots until the 1980s, but the council spent hundreds of thousands of pounds buying them up, as they came on the market, and knocking them down – their policy being to open up the view of the bay  along this stretch of Mumbles Road. It seemed perverse that round about the same time they began to entertain – as they are still entertaining – a developer's ambition to deposit a large chunk of Torremolinos bang on the seafront at the Dunns, which would not only obscure the view from Mumbles Road but seriously frustrate the crescentic sweep of the promenade. There was a time in the 1980s, indeed, when the developer was proposing building out into the bay. One or two of the marker posts he used to describe his desired bulge can still be seen sticking out of the mud. Also to be seen, in the lee of the sea wall, is the seaweed-covered stump of an ancient tree.

If you're interested in gabions (who isn't?) you'll find one on the foreshore – as long as the tide isn't in – before you reach the Dunns. About 140 m down the beach at Norton is a low wall of quarry stones held together in a wire mesh – a pilot gabion. It was put there in 1978 to see if it would encourage a build-up of sand; then a series of breakwaters bigger than ordinary groynes would be built between Blackpill and Oystermouth, to create a new, 3-km stretch of sandy beach. The experiment doesn't seem to have worked.

The extension of the railway in the 1890s, from the Dunns to what would become the pierhead, called for the reclamation of a substantial, crescent-shaped section of the foreshore between the Dunns and Southend, involving the construction of an embankment (1893) along which the railway (and now the promenade) would run. It's on this reclaimed land that there stand today Boots the chemist, CJ's restaurant, Safeway, the Tivoli and associated shops, the tennis courts, the bowling green, the houses of Cornwall Place, Devon Place and Promenade Terrace, the crazy golf course and the children's play park. The area was formerly a natural harbour, known as Horsepool, where the oyster skiffs used to lie up. The skeletal remains of a dozen of them protrude through the mud here. Just left of the slip in front of the Antelope is a twin crescent of stumps, about half a metre high, which is all that remains of a jetty constructed by the railway company to replace the harbour.

> the ocean shredded
> by jet-ski boymen …
> the biding waves waving

The tang of espresso, as you pass Verdi's by the slipway at Knab Rock, is difficult to resist. Another dark liquid lurks nearby which it's as well you don't get a whiff of. Few of those who use the extensive car park at Knab Rock realise that beneath their feet are four vast sewage tanks, each big enough to drive a double-decker bus into, and each with a capacity of two million gallons. It's not often that they are full. Part of Swansea's new sewerage system, they are there for emergencies – such as when particularly heavy rain threatens to overwhelm the sewage treatment plant at Fabian Way. Such emergencies are rare, but there have been several occasions on which these tanks have proved a vital safety valve for an overloaded system. They are only a few metres away from the great storage tanks that were built under Mumbles Hill when the town's main drainage scheme was completed in the 1930s. Behind large wooden doors in the cliff face, Swansea's sewage was stored in a chamber hollowed out from the limestone; when the tide was right, it was released through an outfall off Mumbles Head.

The promenade, from Promenade Terrace to Knab Rock, has been a lying-up place for boats since the railway embankment was built. These days, the bigger craft tend to be stored at the Promenade Terrace end, and the lighter, more frivolous vessels – with names to match – at the Knab Rock end: Itchy Pussy, Tipsy, Giggle Goo, Bass King, Sticky Bits, Little Feat, Why Worry?

> gull hooked, trailing
> from its beak a yard of line –
> o for a gun

The last building of note on the final furlong of our walk, on the approach road to the pier, is the original Mumbles lifeboat station

(1883), situated opposite its slipway. The slip is used these days for launching the inshore lifeboat from its new base opposite, while the old lifeboat station provides the Mumbles rowing club with a store-room for their long, sleek craft.

The promenade ends where the Mumbles train used to meet the buffers, just short of the pier café. Note the railway's old traction posts now serving as lampposts.

THE TOWER OF THE ECLIPTIC

Standing proud of the eastern end of the promenade, on its own deep-piled plinth, is the Tower of the Ecliptic astronomical observatory (1991), designed by the artist and architect Robin Campbell who, as the council's then special projects officer, was responsible for commissioning the unprecedented amount of art that gives the Maritime Quarter so much of its historical and ludic intrigue.

Here he got to do his own thing – a hymn to light, the 'ecliptic' being the imaginary line along which each planet travels. The tower was originally to have been hexagonal, rather than four-sided, and six storeys high, but the engineers took fright and insisted on both a scaling down and the provision of a separate access tower. The equipping of the observatory was left to Swansea Astronomical Society, which has been running for nearly fifty years and is Wales's oldest. Their Dr Fred Jenkins (1918-95), a Sketty-born GP and restlessly resourceful model-maker and inventor, used to while away his on-call time with lens grinding, and became sufficiently expert both to construct the tower's 510-mm telescope – Wales's biggest – and to grind its lenses.

Although the telescope, in the observatory's rotating dome, can point in any direction, in practice it's only ever pointed out to sea – because of severe light pollution emanating from Swansea. A solar telescope attached to it enables you to look safely at sunspots and the surface of the sun boiling and exploding.

Organising the artwork was left to Robin. Keen to involve artists at the design stage rather than follow the usual architectural (mal)practice of "slapping lipstick on the gorilla" as an afterthought, he called a meeting of practitioners to discuss the possibilities over a pint. Present at the Golden Hind (now the Tug and Turbot) that evening were, among others, the sculptor Rob Conybear, the artist Uta Molling, the stained-glass artist David Pearl, Robin and myself. We made little headway with our ruminations until one of us noticed a round table, so we abandoned our rectangular board, took up new positions in a democratic circle – and the ideas started to flow.

Within days, I received from the council an official – and somewhat alarming – order for "six short texts on the cosmos" ('texts', Robin explained, rather than 'poems', because if 'they' realised they were commissioning poems, they'd cancel the order forthwith). My cosmological knowledge was woefully inadequate, so I loaded myself up with books, made an office out of a ceramicist's[4] workshop in the artists' studios above the Dylan Thomas Theatre, and set to self-educational work, casting my imagination far out towards the immensity of quasars and deep into the internal vastnesses of the atom. Life-altering stuff. But could I make poems out of this vital matter? Research eventually had to give way to creativity, and I chose to adapt for my 'cosmic gnomes' a three-liner known as the *englyn penfyr*, one of the oldest of the Welsh bardic forms. It seemed an appropriate model for a commission touching on both cosmological and human affairs – for the early Welsh nature gnomes, which combine the classification of natural phenomena with aphoristic wisdoms, represent perhaps the beginnings of science. My friend the poet Menna Elfyn translated the verses into Welsh, and the slate plaques were carved by the calligraphic artist Ieuan Rees of Rhydaman.

Not all of the observatory's artwork is as readily visible as its beclouded heads-on-sticks or Rob Conybear's lissome female – a weather vane representing the Goddess of the Ecliptic – that tops the access tower (it's taken from a nude cast of the artist Uta Molling). Hidden from sight, apart from when the building is open to the public, is – at Uta's toe tips – the observatory's glory, the access tower's glass roof. Designed and made by David Pearl, this light-sensitive diachroic glasswork fills the spiral-staircase tower with a rainbow-like refulgence that changes subtly as the light outside changes. You enter the tower beneath a plaque inscribed with signs of the zodiac – somewhat to the discomfort of the astronomers, for whom astrology is a long-discredited pseudo-science.

AND

'Kath' perhaps and 'Crow' maybe - two
names in the sand at half-past midnight
when I step down from the city
to take a leak upon the strand.

A rushed and perchance exuberant script
on a slate washed clean
by the vanished tide,
two longish extra lines unreadable,

but precise too: 29 Jan, 9.35 p.m.

Though many a tide has turned
in much less than three hours,
I wish all lovers well
and dedicate the pleasure
of this piss to them,
Kath perhaps and Crow maybe,

where the sea meets the city,
the orange lights an incoming dark.

FISH WEIRS

Almost as difficult to locate as the lost farm of the Angels, I'd heard,
are the post-medieval – or even medieval – fish weirs on the
foreshore. Richard Porch, in *Swansea: History You Can See*, describes
them as "the most easily overlooked historic features in this book and
perhaps the most elusive." I'd seen a bird's-eye plan of them, like
clusters of primitive or modernist chevrons, and then from the top of
Kilvey I caught promising sight of one or two unnaturally straight
lines emerging from the water as the tide retreated.

Encouraged by this, I head out one warm afternoon in wellies and
shorts, feeling like some oddity from *Little Britain*. There are, apparently, a couple of these structures about a kilometre off Oystermouth,
but I'm concentrating on the two largest groups, one to the south of
Brynmill and the other in front of County Hall. It's 3.00 p.m, which
should give me enough time, either side of low water at 3.30, to spot

a fish weir or two. What I'm looking for are two shallow walls, up to 200m long, converging at an angle of between 60 and 90 degrees to form a seaward-facing V-shaped funnel. With a net or basket positioned at the V's apex, these stone pools would become traps for fish as the tide receded. Documents from the sixteenth century onwards suggest that Swansea's fish weirs – which included those in Fabian's Bay where the eastside docks were later constructed – were valuable assets; they often came with property and would be rented out to fishermen on an annual basis. In the 1880s, says Richard Porch, the fish being taken included cod, conger, bass, mullet, whiting, sole, plaice, brill, turbot, salmon – although pollution, dredging and over-fishing were already combining to reduce the variety and quantity of catches. Another, less durable kind of Swansea Bay fish weir, consisting of stakes and nets (or wattle, earlier) raised about two metres high, was in use at Mumbles as late as the mid twentieth century.

Although the going is firm initially, I'm soon up to my calves in a broad sump of grey slime which tops a greater thickness of black mud. Remembering those tall tales (surely?) about the lost students, I begin to wish I'd brought my mobile phone with me. The beach offers surer footing as I gain an extensive tract of the blue alluvial clay – topped with a thin layer of sand – that is characteristic of the estuarine deposit which, inter-bedded with peat, covers much of Swansea Bay. And here – there's no doubting that rough V shape – is my first fish weir … and there another and there yet another. They are not so much walls as arrangements of rubble surmounted in every case by a thick superstructure of coagulated sand – the work, it would seem, of some sort of sea worm. It is perhaps only this amplification by nature of these man-made structures that makes them visible at all after so long in such an exposed situation. I trudge eastward then and find fairly easily the second large group of weirs in front of County Hall. The arms of several of the Vs are slightly curved; others are fragmented and sketchy; but some of the weirs, like some in the Brynmill group, still manage to retain a good depth of water, higher than the top of my boots – and fish.

The modern approach to foreshore fishing involves the use of a long net – about 70 metres long and 2 wide – which is pegged to the beach along one length and fitted with floats along the other, so that it's raised to a vertical plane by the incoming tide. I'm examining the meagre haul of one of these nets – a bass and, arching in spasms as they drown in air, three small dogfish – when I notice a man with two pendulous plastic bags hastening towards me, evidently a fisherman doing the rounds of his nets, concerned no doubt that an interloper is about the snaffle his catch. But we soon get talking. Medieval fish weirs? Never heard of them, he says – although we're standing less than 200 metres from one.

This latest in the line of foreshore fishermen tells me he comes down from the Sandfields at every low tide to gather what the sea has left him. The takings, he laments, have been poor for years, and there's been no improvement even after they stopped pumping raw sewage into the bay. "I blame the greed of the fishing fleet," he says, bagging the bass and leaving the dogfish to their slow deaths.

Later, at the university's school of biological science, I ask John Lancaster about those wormy encrustations on the fish weirs. He tells me they are an agglomeration of tubes formed by the marine bristle worm *Sabellaria alveolata*, better known as the honeycomb worm. It's common in this area wherever there is sheltered, muddy sand and something hard – such as the stone of a fish weir – on which its larvae can settle. The worms mix mucus and sand to form a cement-like material with which they construct the tubes in which they live and from which, when immersed, they extend tentacles to filter their food. They intertwine with other tubes, and future larvae can settle on the existing tubes; over time, they can develop into a reef of considerable size and substance. Brittle as these structures are if you step on them, it's likely that without the industry of the honeycomb worm there'd be no trace by now of Swansea's ancient fish weirs.

THE PATTI PAVILION

> I like to eat bananas ...
> Cos they got no bones.
> I like marijuana ...
> Cos it gets me stoned.

Well, I don't like marijuana much (it makes me feel paranoid) but I can't stop this catchy Man band jingle springing to mind when I pass the Patti Pavilion at the junction of Gors(e) Lane with the Mumbles Road. It was Man that brought worldwide renown to the Patti with their fêted album *Man at the Patti*, recorded live in 1972, at the first of their many Patti Christmas parties.

Of the celebrated rock venues of the 'sixties and 'seventies – the Embassy (later Barons), the Tower Ballroom on Townhill, the Tivoli in Mumbles, the Top Rank on The Kingsway, the Ritz, Skewen, the Ritz, Llanelli – only the Patti, the best loved of them all, has survived. It's as good a place as any to take stock of Swansea's musical life. Like a Welsh San Francisco, Swansea has generated more than its share of rock and pop's front-liners: not only the enduringly popular Man band (far bigger in France and Germany than they are at home), but Spencer Davis, Bonnie Tyler, Mary Hopkin, Badfinger, the Dire Straits and Meatloaf drummer Terry Williams, Karl Jenkins of Soft Machine – and John Cale, Wales's one world-class rock innovator and probably the greatest Welsh musician, across all genres, of modern times. Then there are the up-and-coming headliners such as The Storys and Viva Machine.

The story of Swansea's hundreds of bands and solo performers is complex and fascinating. All I can do in a paragraph or two is to list fairly randomly some who spring to mind. The Jets were about the first. They amalgamated with Deke Leonard's Llanelli band The Corncrackers to form Dream, renowned for their pacey cover versions and their psychedelic light shows; Lynn Mittel, better known these days as Owen Money, was their singer. Two significant bands of the same era were The Eyes of Blue and The Bystanders, with their close-harmony vocals and exuberant instrumental jamming (who can forget their version of 'Light My Fire'?). Dream and the Bystanders amalgamated to form Man in 1968. With Deke Leonard on guitar and vocals, the band has modified personnel constantly; prominent members have included Martin Ace, Clive John, Micky Jones, John Pugwash Weathers – and lately the sons of various Men: Josh Ace (who has his own band, Ringolevio) and Micky Jones's son George.

There have been numerous spin-offs, cross-overs and splinter groups – Gary and Taff (Gary Pickford-Hopkins and Ray 'Taff' Williams), The Barrow Boys, Poco Loco, The Breeze, Deke Leonard's Iceberg, and so on and on) – and all sorts of dipping in and out of each others' combos – and houses: if the Dire Straits drummer drops in on a guitarist pal and there are no drums available for an impromptu jam, he'll make do with tapping out the beat on a leather chair.

Musicians from 'the sticks' tend to gravitate to London and other far-flung 'centres', but for most of Swansea's successful musicians the centre has remained Swansea. Sure, there have been deaths, divorces, poisonous business deals, dope- and booze-rot and the escape hatch of religion. The fate of Badfinger is one of the most tragic in the history of rock. Signed to the Beatles' Apple label in

1969 – having changed their name, at Paul McCartney's suggestion, from the Iveys[5] to Badfinger – the Townhill lads had a string of hits, with Harry Nilsson's rendition of their lachrymose 'Without You' (penned by guitarist Pete Ham and bassist Tom Evans) topping the charts worldwide. But they were bedevilled by financial mismanagement, and by 1983 both Ham and Evans had killed themselves (drummer Mike Gibbins died, of natural causes, in 2005). But most Swansea rockers have survived both the dangerously high times and the sloughs of unfashionability – not least through having at least one foot planted firmly on home ground.

Jacks n drugs n rock n roll would not have been what Madame Adelina Patti (1843-1919) had in mind when she donated the winter garden of her home at Craig-y-Nos Castle to the people of Swansea in 1918 (because of the war, it wasn't erected in Victoria Park until 1920). As the most celebrated singer in the world, she could command the equivalent in today's money of £60,000 per gig. Born in Madrid to Italian parents and raised in New York, Patti eventually made Europe her base and bought Craig-y-Nos, in the Upper Swansea Valley, in 1878. She would process like royalty through the streets of Swansea, and thousands would turn out to cheer her coach and horses.

The pavilion was built in about 1881. With its corrugated-iron roof like an overturned boat, its cast-iron frame and sidewalls of glass, it's been used on its present site for meetings and as a tea-room, for beer festivals, cabarets, school jamborees, an examination hall for the university and a sorting office for Christmas mail. But it's most famous for its rock nights. By rock stadium standards, it's a tiny venue, but some of the greatest acts in the world have played the Patti. Arthur Lee and a rejuvenated Love gave an astonishing performance there not long before he died in 2006.

The Patti, for years, has been showing its age, in spite of the 72-hour facelift it was given by Anneka Rice in 1994 for her television makeover programme. In 2005, the grand dame of Swansea venues closed, for an ambitious £1.7m refurbishment to turn it into a 900-seat auditorium with café bar and restaurant – and Man played her out for the season at a gala Christmas bash.

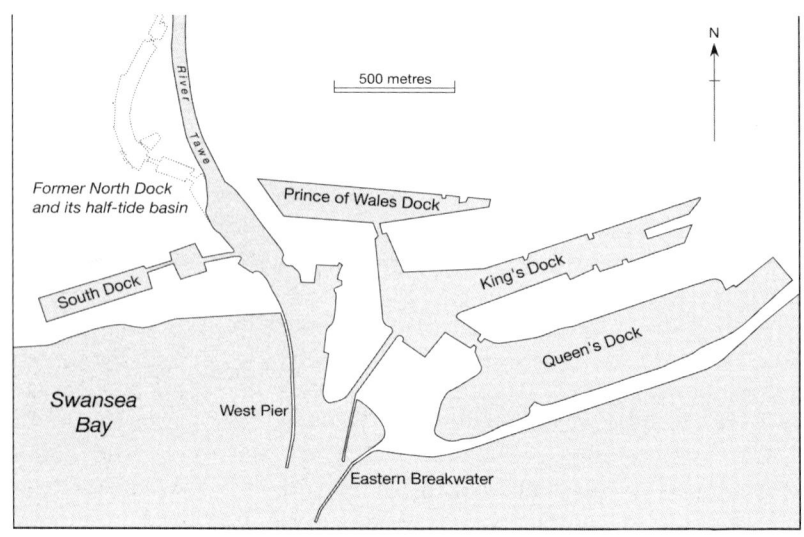

DOCKS, WESTSIDE

"Swansea, in point of spirit, fashion, and politeness," declared *The Gloucester Journal* in 1786, "has now become the Brighton of Wales". Equipping itself with all the trappings of a refined and stylish place of resort – pleasure gardens, bathing machines, circulating libraries, theatres, public assembly rooms and, by 1804, a newspaper – Swansea might indeed, at that juncture, have taken the seaside route to genteel (if relatively modest) prosperity. But coalmining and the smelting of lead, zinc and copper were already gathering implacable momentum in the Lower Swansea Valley, and Swansea was well on its way to becoming 'Copperopolis', the copper-smelting capital of the world, with steel and tinplate destined to supplant copper as major forces in the local economy. What was called for now was a proper dock, in which cargoes could be loaded and unloaded regardless of the tide.

The commercial port's high visibility at the city's eastern gateway tends to nurture the assumption that the eastside is where Swansea's docks began. Hindsight suggests that they should have begun there, but – with the exception of a small-scale (and tidally compromised) 'shipping place' with quay walls at Port Tennant (c. 1824) – they didn't. The river itself, navigable at high tide for nearly five kilometres upstream, is where the first quaysides were built, some of which are still robustly present.

The expense, inconvenience and risks that accrued from vessels having to lie on river mud when the tide was out led to demands from traders and industrialists for a 'floating' harbour. But, before the 1790s, Swansea's conservative burgesses, preoccupied with accruing personal wealth, consistently refused to counte-nance such demands, which would have meant them spending money on projects which could have benefited the town as a whole. The Duke of Beaufort's all-powerful steward, Gabriel Powell, was implacably opposed to Swansea going 'industrial' rather than 'seaside'. It was not until Powell's death in 1788 that the chief obsta-cle to harbour improvements was removed, although progress was painfully slow. Work on deepening a channel through the notoriously obstructive nine-foot 'bar' of sand and gravel across the river and on the construction of piers at the river mouth – with stone quarried on Kilvey Hill – was not completed until 1810. It would be another forty-two years before Swansea acquired its first 'wet' or 'floating' dock – decades behind its competitors, Bristol (1809), Llanelli (1828), Cardiff (1839) and Newport (1844).

This was achieved between 1840 and 1852 by excavating a new channel for the Tawe – the New Cut – and using a stretch of the river's original course at the Strand, locked at both ends, to make Swansea's first permanently water-filled dock, the Town Float or North Dock as it was later known. The 4.14-ha dock, in the lee of the castle, exported coal from its western side and patent fuel from its eastern, where there were grain warehouses and copper-ore yards. The North Dock, which in its heyday could be crossed by walking from ship to ship, closed in 1928, unable to accommodate the increasingly bulky vessels frequenting the port. It's the site today of the Parc Tawe retail and leisure sheds. Its 1-ha half-tide basin, to the south of what is now Quay Parade and occupying the Sainsbury's site, was retained until the early 1960s for ships serving Weaver's Flour Mills. Following Weaver's closure in 1963, the half-tide basin –

which was the 'valve' through which ships entered the North Dock from the Tawe (or left it) – was filled in; as wasteland in the 1970s, it was often home to groups of travellers and their caravans. At the eastern end of Sainsbury's, behind the café extension, you can see exactly where the basin connected with the Tawe: two sets of four cast-iron mooring bollards and curved features on the ground mark either side of the basin's entrance. Most of the old bollards dotted around the Maritime Quarter and along the banks of the Tawe are dated and inscribed 'S.H.T.' (which has inspired many a chalk-equipped wizard of spelling to supply the missing vowel). The initials stand for Swansea Harbour Trust (motto: 'By Industry We Flourish'), which was the body that managed the port from 1791 until 1923, when the Great Western Railway Company took over. The dating of the bollards – one of the Sainsbury's group is inscribed 1858 – tells us exactly when they were put in place, and speaks eloquently of their historical context.

The decades it took to negotiate and finally construct the Town Float so frustrated the coppermaster John Henry Vivian that he formed a company to build a masonry dock on that elongated triangle of seafront Swansea once known as the Burrows, which stretched from what is now the Dylan Thomas Centre beside the Tawe to westerly Brynmill. The eastern portion of the Burrows had been the modish heartland of polite, early nineteenth-century society; many were aghast at the prospect of their sumptuous pleasure gardens becoming a vast hole in the ground and of steam engines thundering along the elegant Georgian terraces. But there was no arguing with 'progress'. "One must not think of the beautiful," exhorted Clark Russell in 1882, "but of the useful, with a capital U. Nobody talks of sea views or mountains here, but of how many ships were cleared last week, and what the export and import returns were ...".

Nearly eighty thousand people turned out in 1852 to see the first sod raised by the marquess of Worcester; but it was not until 1859, after a series of disputes, strikes, financial problems and a take-over by the Harbour Trust, that the 5.3-ha South Dock opened. Coal was shipped from the north side of the dock and at the western end there were timber yards. Fish were landed at the south side of the 1.6-ha half-tide basin, where there was a wholesale fish market. There still is a fish wholesaler's here; most of today's fishing fleet of some two or three dozen vessels moors nearby, in the (barraged) river, at Pilot House Wharf – conveniently outside the fish restaurant.

The opening of the South Dock was hailed by *The Cambrian* as "incomparably more important to us, as an industrial and commercial community, than any event that ever transpired in our midst". But it was clear by the 1870s that the two westside docks were unable to keep pace with Swansea's burgeoning coal, copper, iron and steel trade. The eastside's time had come.

THE MARITIME QUARTER

Eighteenth-century Swansea having chosen the industrial route, to vastly greater wealth (for some) than might have strewed the seaside path, the Brighton option – the attractions of coastal Gower notwithstanding – remained the road not taken. By the mid twentieth century, Swansea's 250-year industrial bacchanal had given way to a seemingly incurable hangover, in the form of the most derelict and polluted landscape – in the Lower Swansea Valley – of any in Britain.

The road not taken looked like the road beyond repair. But as Swansea muddled through yet another of its periodic identity crises, the worst of that post-industrial squalor was gradually cleared away (along with a lamentable quantity of Swansea's historic industrial architecture), and the seaside path beckoned once more as a possible route for the future.

The old Burrows – evoked by Burrows Road in the Sandfields and East Burrows Road which runs parallel with the river – was for centuries an uninhabited area of grass-covered dunes, with marshy grazing land along its northern margin; this, in the later eighteenth century, was enclosed as fields. The word 'Burrows' takes us back to the time of the Norman incursions, when the invaders introduced the cony (or rabbit) to Britain (there was no indigenous word for rabbit in either Welsh or English), often setting aside areas of dune for rabbit warrens. Most dune systems in the Swansea and Gower area are still called burrows. The sole building on the Burrows, as late as 1748, was an inn which survived until 1947 as the Beaufort Arms. It served the ferry which, until 1850, was the only means of crossing the lower Tawe, and was situated on what is now Sainsbury's service yard, off the street that is still known as Ferryside.

Swansea's long tradition of public open spaces dates back to 1789 when the corporation opened pleasure gardens on the Burrows. Although the onward march of industry was by now unstoppable, the Brighton dream persisted, and Swansea's new fashionable quarter was laid out on the Burrows between about 1790 and 1830, largely to the

designs of Georgian Swansea's principal architect William Jernegan (1751-1836). Some of the finest of these streets – Prospect Place, Somerset Place, Gloucester Place – have survived both the bombs of the second world war and the neglect of the industrial and post-industrial periods. The most delightful of them is a sequence of eight tall red-brick houses, with their canopied and balconied windows, on the northern side of Cambrian Place. John Newman describes them as "Highly eccentric and rather lovable." Also in Cambrian Place is another Jernegan creation, the Assembly Rooms, which were intended to provide polite society with a new focal point for concerts, balls, public meetings and breakfasts, billiards, card games and reading. Work started on this building in 1811, but the money ran out and it was not until 1821, after the corporation took possession, that the building was completed. The project seems to have bankrupted Jernegan, but he soon worked his way back to relative prosperity. The gravestone of this seminal Swansea maker – whose local works include Mumbles lighthouse, Marino (later incorporated into Singleton Abbey), Kilvrough Manor, Stouthall, Sketty Hall, St Matthew's church in High Street and Brynymor House in Eaton Crescent – is set in the pathway on the north side of St Mary's church.

Even before their completion, the Assembly Rooms were too small for Swansea's growing population, and by about the 1850s – when the South Dock was carved out of the park-like core of the Burrows, and railway lines were laid down the middle of elegant streets – commerce and industry had overwhelmed the area, and 'people of quality' had decamped to the Uplands and Glanmor. The Assembly Rooms were used for the 'ticketings' (price setting) of the Swansea copper trade and served briefly as public baths before becoming offices – of Cory Brothers, for about a century, and then of the National Coal Board. After an anxious period of dereliction in the 1970s and 1980s, the distinctive façade was saved and the remainder of the building was reconstructed as flats.

In the aftermath of industry's "melancholy, long, withdrawing roar", dereliction characterised almost the whole area. Of the few who lived here, several did so unofficially. There was Phil the Div, for instance, who lived within the (now demolished) ice factory opposite the Pump House in a caravan he'd brought down from the Swansea Valley. With his seven Alsatians, he was a formidable sight roaming the pubs of Swansea. This ramshackle part of town attracted those who  couldn't or wouldn't adapt to more mainstream conventions elsewhere, but there was no room for them when the Brighton option began its resurgence.

"All yachts and yuppies – ach y fi! Where's my box of England's Glory?" ran the received Welsh wisdom on marinas and all who sailed in them when these new yacht havens began to appear around the coast in the 1980s, Swansea's being the first to be completed. It could have been a disaster, certainly. Swansea is blighted by some of the ugliest buildings that utilitarian 'architecture' has been able to devise.

When the council bought up the redundant South Dock in 1969, the architectural precedents were not good. As the dried out sump – berthing place once for banana boats from the Caribbean – gradually filled up with rubbish, they wondered what to do with it. A dual carriageway? A sunken garden? An estate of council houses? Executive luxury bungalows? Then somebody noticed, winking at them just over the southern retaining wall, the sea – which they promptly let back in to the dock. They began to address not a problem but an opportunity. By 1980, the council, who had been purchasing run-down workshops and scrap-yards plot by plot, were owners of the whole development area. They had considerable powers, therefore, to determine the nature and style of that development.

Swansea, in spite of notorious own goals, sometimes gets lucky. Few could have realised it at the time, but when the local authority's planning department took on the Scottish artist and architect Robin Campbell as special projects officer in the mid 1970s, they were hiring the services of a visionary. It's thanks largely to him that Swansea's unhappy architectural precedents were not replicated in the South Dock scheme – although the imaginative scope of his initial design brief suffered a considerable watering-down in the execution. Enough of that original spark remains, however, to distinguish the South Dock scheme as uniquely responsive to the spirits of time and place.

As work on the South Dock scheme proceeded, not everyone was convinced. The poet David Hughes caught a vox-pop scepticism in his splendid local dialect poem 'Swonzee Boy See?'

> Ayve done some fancy work rounair, avenay?
> Sorl been tarted up like
> Roun byer Lehjer un South Dock.
> Ew doan see flats ly cat up Blineymice.
> Meenmy brother ewster dive inner dock
> – few trydit now ewed crackew ed onner yot.

The marina no doubt has its oiling of toffs. If you're Taff, 23 and unemployed, the good ship Euphoria, Feelfree, Smooth Torquer, Lazy Dreamer, High Society, Beautiful Freak is unlikely to be yours. One of the most curious of craft ever to have moored here was a floating shed made from driftwood by the artist Sara Rees, for Locws 2007, the 'Arts Across the City' event, held every two years, that was established in 1999 by David Hastie and the internationally renowned conceptual artist Tim Davies. Anchored outside the National Waterfront Museum, the shed was intended as an arrival from some unspecified, but presumably dystopian, time in the future. It was the antithesis of the sleek chunks of millionaires' plastic moored nearby. Especially in

the early days, it was the focus on posh craft, in both senses, that tended to blinker the gaze to other aspects of the Maritime Quarter, reducing a complex and ambitious project to mere caricature. The 550-berth marina is only part of the scheme; by 1991, there had been established a new community of 2,000 council tenants, renters and owner-occupiers, only a small proportion of whom had anything to do with boats. But the high number of curtained windows speaks loudly of the council's biggest headache – second home owner-ship, which undermines the quarter's coherence as a community. The council was keen to avoid the creation of a moneyed (not to mention Tory-voting) ghetto. They also wanted to avoid a community that developed as a seaside kraal with its back to the city. Accordingly, the quarter has incorporated the city's refurbished Georgian-Victorian-Edwardian core; the Mumbles to Morriston bike-path runs through it; there are small businesses, studios, pubs, restaurants, workshops, museums, a theatre, galleries – keeping visitors and people from other parts of the city passing through.

Many come simply to walk, breathe the fishy-oily air and enjoy the place just for itself. In America, the private housing would probably come right down to the water's edge, excluding non-residents, but here a five-metre public walkway all round the yacht basin shows that people come first. The squares and piazzas, in summer, have brought a new conviviality to the city's heart, as lovers canoodle, people play boules, kids dive-bomb into the water from the top of the truncated blue swing-bridge. On a winter's day, you can be wonderfully alone on the cobbled quays, your head ringing with the Aeolian frenzy of the South Dock halyard orchestra.

While not all of the new buildings qualify as architecture, most make a worthy stab at a feeling of 'marine vernacular' in contempo-rary mood, using a wide variety of stone, brick and wrought metal. The more recent the building, generally the more adventurous the architecture. Although the developers often resented the extra cost, they were obliged by the council's 'per cent for art scheme' to join with them in paying for an unprecedented amount of what is known prosaically as 'enhancement' work, the numerous artistic grace-notes that are a crucial articulation of meaning and detail. A walk in the Maritime Quarter is an experience of delighted ambush – by carvings, plaques, statues, clocks, weather vanes, figure-heads, turrets, pavilions, sundials, lights, gates, towers and witty and arcane messages in stone. They've even erected rooftop perches for the seagulls. Here is art well outside the museum's confines – and not the ephemeral fizz of 'community art', but rooted, enduring works inspired by the labours, discoveries and sustaining knowledges that have made Swansea and the world what they are. Rarely, since the middle-ages, have as many as ten artists – of the standing of Wendy Taylor, Rob Conybear, Ian Hamilton Finlay – been employed on a single building project.

Much of the stonework here, particularly the relief carving, is the work of Phil Chatfield, who set up studio and home, while he was working on the development, in a capacious lean-to shed behind the Assembly Rooms. The sculptor's boyish enthusiasm for model planes, boats and trains saw him give a large model railway the run of the lean-to; it would chuff through his kitchen as he made his breakfast and rattle past his pillowed head at night. Phil was aboard the ill-fated barque *Maria Asumpta*, a regular visitor to Swansea Marina, when it was wrecked off the Cornish coast on 30 May, 1995, with the loss of three lives. "One of the saddest things for me," he said, "is that we had been anchored off Mumbles the night before and it was my duty to wake the people on board. I was the one that woke my friends on the morning of their deaths."

On a wall just round the corner from Llys Jernegan, where Phil had his shed, and opposite Robin Campbell's innovatively designed Environment Centre, is a Chatfield carving – the single word 'youuuuuuuuuuu' – that often intrigues or baffles viewers. Its author, the Llangollen-based concrete poet Peter Meilleur (pen name Childe Roland), a trilingual Quebecois (French, English and Welsh), explains: "The work is about the personal pronoun 'YOU' going on a pilgrimage across the page in search of a new identity which is found in the sound of the letter 'U' which serves as an abbreviated form of the pronoun while still retaining some vestige of its former self." A memorable performer at the Mission Gallery and elsewhere, Peter has fond memories of the city. "Often when taking a bus from the Quadrant towards some suburb, I have been entertained by the repartee and humorous banter between the driver and the passen-

gers, which would have everybody on board laughing. I like Swansea because it reminds me of Quebec City which has, like Swansea, a lower town by the docks and an upper town – up and down like the language of the bus driver and passengers. I have visited Swansea many times but I still have not managed to visit the house of Dylan Thomas, "Never mind, cariad," says an elderly lady on the bus, "I been yur all my life and I never seen the place neither. Knew his dad, though!" Uplands next stop."

The Maritime Quarter in recent years has come to look a little tired, and has suffered from a certain soullessness, partly because of the unrepresentative social mix – chiefly retired people and young professionals – and the absence of children. But the opening of the National Waterfront Museum in 2006 has sent a fresh surge of energy through the area, and it's hoped that new penthouse apartments on the old Spontex site, combined with the SA1 effect from over the river, will help revitalize the quarter. Less welcome has been the construction at the south-west corner of the marina of the 29-storey, 106-m Meridian Quay skyscraper – Wales's tallest apartment block, phallically out-gunning anything in Cardiff. Plaid Cymru and others who fear this could be the beginnings of Swansea becoming a concrete-towered Benidorm have been pressing for a tall buildings policy. The name of the company responsible? Earthquake.

STORMING THE MARINA

Thursday, they warned, Thursday's the day …

And Thursday is: a force twelve and rising
by dawn's upon us: those with hatches
batten, as hoardings explode
and boughs like battle-dead strew the parks.
We are unaccustomed in the cool, fed north
to such rages of wind:
even industry hesitates.

But a kid loves it, scudded down the quayside
– squat-n-leap – like a flap-wing crow,
his yelps for joy
gobbled by the banshees blown in from Eire
and raving woe through the yuppies' halyards.
I can remember
the shiver of strength down that boy's spine
as slates from a warehouse splash across his path
and unsinkables drown in the teacup marina –
the hug of tragedies not your own.

We are closer to the news than some of us know.

Thursday's advice is to stay indoors.
Indoors I stay, typing on a sheet
that even here, in this pre-stressed concrete
weather-tight room, quivers in the wind.

THE QUEEN'S HOTEL

The launch in 1990 of my new book of poems at the Arts Workshop[6] in Gloucester Place – followed, I'd hoped, by a quiet drink in the Queen's with a few pals – has been remembered ever since as an arresting occasion. I enter the pub to find Swansea's leading crumhorn player in not so much a fight as a lurch with the landlord. Losing ground to the landlord, Swansea's leading crumhorn player, staggers backwards against the food counter and manages to demolish – smashing it to smithereens – a bulky, glass cabinet. I waste no time apprehending the crumhornista, propelling him outside onto the pavement and advising him to piss off home. Then I turn, with some stragglers from the Arts Workshop, to rejoin our friends in the Queen's. But the door is barred to us – we're all banned.

We wander off to find a pint where we can, and it's not until the following morning that I catch up with subsequent events. It was fortunate for Swansea's leading crumhorn player that he took my advice and pissed off pronto. He was well out of the way by the time the police arrived on the scene, but they had plenty of other artists to choose from. They helped themselves to one of Swansea's leading sculptors, who had had nothing to do with the shattered food cabinet,

and carted him off to the cells. When his artist girlfriend and her musician friend, who had been with a splinter group banned from the pub, eventually heard of the sculptor's arrest, the two women made for the police station to protest his innocence and demand his release – whereupon they too were arrested and slammed in the cells for the rest of the night. There followed months of tedious legal shenanigans –

while Swansea's most forgetful crumhorn player claimed to know nothing of the whirlwind he'd sown.

With most of Swansea's artists banned from their favourite pub, the close-knit artists' scene centred on the Queen's soon unravelled, and the city's makers reverted to more atomised ways. After about eighteen months, with a change of landlord, the ban lapsed, and some of the artists drifted back, the Queen's being one of the few real pubs – as opposed to big-screen, disco-blasting booze factories – in the city centre.

> she turns on long legs
> away from the bar: not
> as beautiful as feared

It's a warm August evening, and I'm sitting in the Queen's with Sandfields-born Helen Eriksen ('vodi and sodi'), daughter of a Methodist lay preacher, who was landlady here in the mid 1980s, and the artist Uta Molling (also 'vodi and sodi'), who came from Mannheim in 1985 on a six-month artists' exchange and has been here ever since. Vivacious, raven-haired queen of the Queen's, actress, musician, high-class dancer, famous for doing the splits on the bar and for her long, mascaraed eyelashes ("too short-sighted to put them in straight these days"), Helen was so popular as a barmaid that when her boss moved on to another pub the locals signed a petition calling for her to be made landlady.

"Every day was fun," she says. "We just could not stop having fun. The Roman evening, everyone in togas, the limerick evening, the sculpture evening, using half moons of ice from the ice machine. Thanks to one of the fishermen, we had a large crab walk in through the door one day. There was quite a gay scene for a while, with the boys camping it up in dresses from my huge wardrobe, my feather boas and stilettos. In those days, we had to close at 3.30 (like hell!), so the party would often continue upstairs. There were some crazy happenings, but we had a policy of sorting out any trouble on the night – I'd throw anyone out, if need be – and no post mortems the next day."

Partying has a long tradition in this part of town. In the eighteenth century, in a field on the other side of Gloucester Place, the infamous Burrows Fair used to be held, until drunken mayhem forced its closure. The Queen's, now on the corner of Gloucester Place and Cambrian Place, was first established a few doors further west along

Cambrian Place. It moved to its present position in 1892 and became notorious as a snuggery for doxies. The pub is said to be haunted by the ghost of a prostitute who hanged herself there, and inexplicable sobbing at night time has occasionally been reported. In 1973, the Queen's closed for a few years, but the regeneration of the Maritime Quarter gave it a new lease of life; in 2005, the immediate Queen's locality enjoyed a few seconds of fame as 'Victorian Cardiff' in an episode of Dr. Who[7] (which is scripted by Swansea-born Russell T. Davies, who likes to give his home town a cameo role in each series). And in July 2007, the bar was an ideal grandstand for watching Kylie Minogue and David Tennant coming and going from the Exchange Buildings opposite as they filmed the Dr. Who Christmas special *Voyage of the Damned.*

The pub has always enjoyed a mixed clientele: sailors, fishermen, builders, office workers and business people, reporters and printers from *The Evening Post* round the corner, pre-clubbers, actors from the Dylan Thomas Theatre, residents from the many old people's homes in the area – and, in the 1980s, old heroes of the hop such as Togo and Gormley from SASH, the shelter next door for single homeless people (when a prosecuting solicitor told Swansea magistrates that Gormley had a drink problem, the accused famously protested "I do not have a drink problem – I love the bloody stuff"). One of its less appealing 'characters' is a mangy stuffed bear, with bones protruding at feet and snarling snout, and a Welsh flag draped around its midriff. They claim it's the bear from the No.10 pub in Union Street, but few who remember the No. 10 bear recognise this sad ursine wreck.

Still the artists come, although in smaller numbers these days. Regulars in the 1980s included the painter Jack Jones, the Hafod's answer to L.S. Lowry; potter Jan Davies; architect and painter Robin Campbell; sculptor Rob Conybear; the stained glass artists Amber Hiscott and David Pearl, who still have a studio above what's now the Mission Gallery; the poet Huw Half-Ear, allegedly a protégé of literary impresario Keidrych Rhys. Frequent out-of-town visitors were Jon Dressel, the 'Yanklo-Welsh' poet who divided his time between Trinity College, Carmarthen and St. Louis, where he ran just about the best pub in America[8], and the Cardiff poet John Tripp. John particularly enjoyed bank-holiday weekends at the Queen's. On one of these visits, we invented bardic tennis: John spotted a Dylanesque phrase on the one-arm bandit, 'When the cherry bonus light is lit', and lobbed it at me, in anticipation of my lobbing back some comparably sonorous line of instantaneous nonsense, such as "and the aldermen, moon-wise, rack the bloater" ... and so the game proceeded, until some earnest fellow drinker would muscle in with a line of apparent sense – in which, in Queen's mode, we had no interest. It was a great place for spontaneous poetry, music and comedy, particularly during the Swansea Fringe, when a young Paul Merton and his foil John Irwin first strutted their stuff. Paul still visits Swansea, although, says his friend Uta, the last time he came he'd grown a beard to hide behind, Anne Robinson having recently made her anti-Welsh remarks on his *Room 101* show.

While Helen reigned behind the bar, it was the louder-than-life septuagenarian Maude Davidson – a Carmarthenshire-born high-society journalist with a frightfully pukka accent – who held forth on the customers' side. She would sometimes 'sing' a ditty of her own composition:

> I'm tired of whisky, I'm tired of gin,
> I'm tired of perpetually living in sin.
> I'm tired of rumba, big apple and trucking,
> And after last night – O GAWD – am I tired.

Maude would perch on a high stool, ready by the end of a night's drinking to topple backwards – Maude, bar stool, pink bloomers and all – without, apparently, ever hurting herself. It would be the job then of one of the gentlemen present to walk her safely home.

DUSK AT THE QUEEN'S

> Sundowner. Great beams of the hot stuff
> shout down through the Queen's
> high bowed panes, unreceived

by the bigshots and slinkies, lush
Dafydd on his back in a clearing of legs
– "which way, Iesu mawr, which way is up?" –

the Sultans, the swing, the
love deals fixed and a spat raging
when – what the hell? – there hales in at the door

an old comrade of the vine
who stands to deliver, in a lull between discs,
an intelligence hot from his own front line.

"Appertaining," he says, stubble to the stucco
as the wisechat wanes ...
"Appertaining to the per-pen-dic-ular ...

... I have nothing further to say – "
and he bangs back out, our eyes now ushered
to the street, the sky: this airborne thing, an

ambitious umbrella – no – a cormorant sailing
the officious length of Gloucester Place,
dusting all with silence as she scrapes the moon.

THE DYLAN THOMAS CENTRE

"*Wales on Sunday* has asked me for an article on the Old Guildhall,"
I say over the phone to Michael Rush, chief executive of West
Glamorgan County Council. "May I have a peek inside?"

"Not convenient just now," he replies.

I'm not surprised. It's May 1989, and "the noblest classical building in Swansea"[9], abandoned to vagrants and the elements since
1982, is not in a condition that its council caretakers want exposed in
the press. But I find it only too convenient to amble through an ever-
open rear gate and hop in through one of many broken downstairs
windows. Swansea's fourth town hall, from 1848 until 1934 – after
which it served successively as a youth employment centre, a techni-
cal school for boys, a college of further education (the 'bottom tech',
as opposed to the 'top tech' in Mount Pleasant), and finally an annexe

to Dynevor School – is in a scandalous state of seemingly purposeful neglect: shrubs rooting in its classical, Corinthian-mode façade, some of it shored up with scaffolding; brambles gliding up the pitted Bath-stone walls; yawning holes in the roof; the vestibule dome peppered by vandals' missiles; two classical pillars in the great hallway flayed to the lathwork; mould, slime and weeds taking root in dripping, cavernous chambers.

There's much extravagant talk about a new role for the Grade II* listed, riverside building in Somerset Place but precious little action. Then along comes the UK Year of Literature and Writing 1995, "the biggest festival of literature the world has ever seen". One of a series of government-sponsored, year-long festivals, in which selected British cities celebrated a chosen art form, it was the brainchild of Kevin Thomas, the then director of the Welsh Academy, the national association of writers[10]. The festival was initially offered to Cardiff – which turned it down. "What writer of note, apart from Dylan Thomas, has Wales ever produced?" an elected sage in the capital was said to have remarked. Then Kevin turned to Swansea, which leapt lustily into bed with the Academy, and by early 1992 it had won the bid to host the year.

Central to the plan was the creation of Tŷ Llên (literature house), a national literature centre for Wales. An international competition was held to find an exuberantly contemporary design, and the icono-clastic architect Will Alsop won it. The local press whipped up a storm of contempt for Alsop's 'lego on sticks', the council lost its nerve, the Alsop design was dumped – and the Old Guildhall was seized on as Plan B. All that remained after its rapid 'refurbishment'

were two splendid outer walls; the once grand interior was scooped away in its entirety, and an office block, tarted up with marble, cherry wood and assorted 'period' features, put in its place. Some of this office block, with restaurant, lecture theatre and bar, had a confer-ence centre-ish feel, and it was this bit that purported to be Tŷ Llên. Tŷ Llên was 'the National Literature Centre for Wales' because Swansea City Council

"Once it was the colour of saying"

Dylan Thomas 1914 - 1953

said so; because unless Tŷ Llên remained 'the National Literature Centre for Wales' for a set number of years the council would not be entitled to the 3.6m Eurobucks they'd spent on saving the Old Guildhall. It was widely predicted at the time that the Tŷ Llên name and idea would be dropped as soon as they could get away with it[11]. What they really intended calling the place, Dylan Thomas Centre / Canolfan Dylan Thomas, was already writ disproportionately huge, around a gigantic coat of arms in iodised bronze, at the rear of the building – which had now become the Tawe-facing front.

No one these days talks of Tŷ Llên – or Tŷ Dan, as Swansea's artists dubbed it, after the then leisure services director Dan Minster, a somewhat dour American whose previous job with his country's Trident missile programme evidently qualified him as just the creative sort to nurture the arts in Swansea. During the run-up to the Year of Literature, writers and artists were disastrously alienated from the project by Minster and co. The idea that Wales, with Swansea at the hub, should host the Year of Literature had come from the nation's writers; but, with Swansea City Council attempting to hijack the whole thing, initial enthusiasm curdled into anger, then finally, for many, indifference.

About fifty local artists formed the Swansea Writers' and Artists' Group (SWAG) in order to "participate actively in the planning, setting up and running of the Year of Literature". We held meeting, wrote letters, threw wild parties, spawned 'the Pentrechwyth secessionists'[12] (a demented splinter group of boycotters; no festival is complete without its boycotters), published a magazine, staged readings and jam sessions, issued spiky press releases – but failed utterly, after two years, to achieve our prime objective.

At its lowest ebb, in 1993, the embryonic Year of Literature was, even by Swansea standards, a bigger comedy of municipal errors than the acidly deriding pen of a Kingsley Amis could have devised. The *Post* declared it "a saga of disasters". When its first director, the poet Maura Dooley, arrived on the scene funds were so low that her fridge of an office (in what would later become Morgan's Hotel) was supplied with neither heating nor so much as a typewriter. She got pregnant and left.

Into this carnival of follies stepped a new director, Sean Doran, fresh from various arts admin. triumphs in his native Northern Ireland. Things at this eleventh hour looked bad, Sean agreed, but he reckoned he could turn the whole thing round. We wondered where he kept his leprechauns.

But turn it round he did. With a Stakhanovite team of a dozen full-timers, and considerably less than £1m to spend on programming, Sean and co. staged over 1500 events during a remarkable year which brought many of the world's greatest wordsmiths to Swansea: Allen Ginsberg, Seamus Heaney, Denise Levertov, Sorley MacLean, Yehuda Amichai, Miroslav Holub, Kenzaburo Oe, Rita Dove, Amos Oz, Irena Ratushinskaya, Michael Ondaatje, John Berger, Van Morrison, R.S. Thomas – to name only a tiny fraction. The Year's president, Jimmy Carter, presided at Tŷ Llên over the formal inauguration of the Welsh branch of PEN[13].

Tŷ Llên itself was opened officially on St David's Day, 1995. The writers of Wales having been specifically excluded from having a say in what a national literature centre should be and do, it seemed a most unwriterly place, with its smartly uniformed staff and Hiltonesque ambience, and obvious design flaws, such as the cramped seating in the theatre and the miserly proportions of the (expensive) bar. In the self-consciously grand restaurant – so popular for receptions that already people were calling Tŷ Llên 'the national wedding centre for Wales' – there were sandwiches, municipal vinegar, and speeches, including one from an ungracious, bearded SWAGerer who proposed that if writers couldn't take over the running of Tŷ Llên they should blow it up.

A writer did eventually take over the Dylan Thomas Centre's varied and lively literary programme, which continues to this day. The Plymouth-born poet Dave Woolley (1958) came to Swansea to join the Year of Literature team, and has been here ever since – no doubt the festival's greatest (if only) living legacy. In addition to staging literary and musical events, including the annual Dylan Thomas Festival, the building houses a major, and permanent, Dylan Thomas exhibition, an art gallery, a restaurant and a cosy bookshop café. It plays a crucial role in the artistic life of Swansea and has done much to persuade more sceptical, prim or official elements to embrace Dylan Thomas as a son of Swansea deserving of celebration (if only because the 'Dylan Thomas effect' is said to be worth £3.6m a year to Swansea). Even the council's white van fleet is in on the action, with a range of Dylan Thomas quotations, with his signature beneath, on the sides of over two hundred vehicles.

THE SWANSEA JACK

What used to be the London pub, on the corner of what is now West Way and Oystermouth Road, changed its name in 1979 to the Swansea Jack, in honour one of Swansea's favourite sons – a dog. His claim to fame is summarised on the stone that was raised over his grave, about 1.5km further west, on the sea front opposite St Helen's cricket ground:

ERECTED TO THE MEMORY OF
SWANSEA JACK
THE BRAVE RETRIEVER WHO SAVED 27 HUMAN
AND 2 CANINE LIVES FROM DROWNING
LOVED AND MOURNED BY ALL DOG LOVERS
DIED OCTOBER 2ND 1937 AT THE AGE OF SEVEN
YEARS
NE'ER HAD MANKIND MORE FAITHFUL FRIEND
THAN THOU
WHO OFT THY LIFE DIDST LEND
TO SAVE SOME HUMAN
SOUL FROM DEATH
OWNER AND TRAINER W.M. THOMAS

It's commonly assumed that this black Labrador retriever gave Swansea people their familiar nickname; but the expression 'Swansea Jack' came before the dog, and the reverse is the case. The term 'Jack' was applied in many parts of Britain to sailors – so a 'Scouser Jack' was a sailor from Liverpool. It is hardly surprising, therefore, that Swansea's famously skilled and hardy Cape Hornermen – whose reputation could win them a job on a ship in any port in the world – should have come to be categorised universally, from the nineteenth century onwards, as 'Swansea Jacks'.

Don't expect to find out about Swansea Jack by visiting the Swansea Jack pub. There used to be plenty of Swansea Jack memorabilia on the walls, but when the council-owned free house re-opened

in 2006, after a spell behind
shutters, the Jack mementoes
were swept away, to be replaced
by faded newspaper photos and
cuttings about football. As in
dozens of other Swansea pubs.
And at precisely the moment
when football, with the closure
of the nearby Vetch, was moving
from the Sandfields to Landore.
What's left of Jack is just his
name and his fading image on
the sign outside.

The dog started life as plain
Jack. He belonged to an illiterate haulier and jack-of-all-trades,
William Thomas, who lived in rough-and-ready accommodation –
basically a stable – at Padley's Yard, North Dock. Impatient with his
young retriever's water-shyness, Thomas reputedly threw the dog into
the North Dock to 'cure' him of his aversion. It seemed to work.
Before long, in June 1931, Jack pulled off his first accounted rescue.
A 12-year-old boy, who couldn't swim, fell into the dock and was in
danger of drowning: Jack hurled himself into the water and dragged
the child to the dockside. More rescues followed in quick succession –
a drunken sailor in the dock, a swimmer in the bay, a sackful of
puppies thrown in the Tawe to drown. In no time, the dog graduated
from Swansea star to international canine hero, with headlines in *The
Daily Mirror*, exhibition tours, a guest spot at Crufts, and a stream of
honorary diplomas, badges, medals, cups, collars, shields, tankards
and trophies. He remains the only dog to have been twice awarded the
National Canine Defence League's bronze medal, the 'canine V.C.'

Quitting Padley's Yard in 1933, soon after Jack's earlier triumphs,
Thomas lodged for a couple of years at the Victoria Hotel in College
Street, while Jack made himself useful about town, helping children
to cross the road and looking out, as ever, for drowning creatures to
save. Thomas retired from the haulage business in 1936 and went to
live with his daughter and family at 3 Roger Street, Treboeth. Jack
went too.

But in early September 1937, Jack was taken ill at Treboeth. The
vet diagnosed delayed phosphorous poisoning caused by the acciden-
tal ingestion of a poison called Rodine. It took Swansea Jack weeks to
die, as the poison slowly eroded his liver, kidneys, heart and brain.

When the end came, on 2 October, a distraught and angry William Thomas wrapped his dog in a blanket and buried him in the back garden at 3 Roger Street.

Within a day or two of Jack's death, a campaign started in the press to find Swansea's canine hero a more honoured resting place, and the council eventually agreed to rebury the dog on the promenade. Having been buried for eighteen days, Jack was duly dug up and, unwrapped from his blanket, was "discovered to be absolutely dirt free with no deterioration what-so-ever". The local undertaker made a coffin for him, and he spent a day or so lying in working-class state in the *parlwr* at 3 Roger Street, surrounded by floral tributes and the mementoes of his heroism. A stream of mourners came to pay their last respects and, no doubt, to wonder at the novel sight of a dog in a coffin.

The municipal burial was followed nearly a year later – on the anniversary of Jack's death – by the unveiling of the monument by the mayor and a service of dedication conducted by the Rev. Leon Atkin. The head depicted on the monument is not that of Jack, but of one of his offspring said to have resembled him. The far from inexpensive monument was the gift of its maker, the monumental sculptor J Cecil Jones of Oxford Street. "It was partly sentiment and partly a business venture," he said at the time; it couldn't have done any harm to the business, which survived into the present century at 212 Oxford Street, before gliding round the corner into Dillwyn Street.

William Thomas did not long survive his renowned dog. He died five months after a bomb, falling on open land at Treboeth on the evening of 2 August 1940, blasted him from where he was standing in the back doorway of his home and threw him headlong into the back garden. He is buried in the churchyard at Llansamlet.

SWANSEA PRISON

"I'm going to prison today." "I'm going to the prison today." What a difference a 'the' can make. I've said both, at different times, and done both. I said the first one breakfast time in September 1988 when I knew that my refusal to pay a fine imposed for 'criminal damage' of the perimeter fence at the US Naval Facility, Brawdy – as part of a CND protest – would lead to Swansea magistrates sending me to prison later that morning. This they duly did, sentencing me to seven days which, in the event, were reduced to four, thanks to 'good behaviour'[14].

Few know what goes on behind the louring walls of 200 Oystermouth Road, or Cox's Farm as Her Majesty's Prison Swansea is often called, after William Cox who was appointed its first governor in 1829. He farmed a small plot of land (to supply the prisoners) adjacent to the House of Correction, official title of the first prison to be built on this site, in 1826-28. The site was later enlarged, displacing Glamorgan Street westward to its present position, and by 1861 a completely rebuilt prison – the "half-hearted attempt at the architecture of menace"[15] that confronts us today – was banging up its first inmates, women included. Grim as conditions were in that forbidding pile (and the place is no holiday camp today), they improved considerably on those in Swansea's earlier prison, a set of four rooms (one for women) in the ruined keep of the castle, with no furniture, no glass in the windows, and no fuel permitted even in winter.

A harsh regime based on punishment, deterrence and reform was characteristic of the Victorian institution. The tread wheel, which today would be condemned as an instrument of torture, was used as a form of 'occupational therapy'. Then there was the 'crank', a large box full of sand and gravel, through which a paddle had to be churned by means of a handle projecting from the side: a prisoner might have to 'earn' his lunch by turning that handle 5,000 times. A warder could increase the pressure by tightening a screw on the side of the box – which is why warders to this day are known as 'screws'[16].

Although the prison offers among the most expensive accommodation in Swansea – £112 a night[17], compared with £100 for a room at the five-star Morgan's Hotel – and although £6m has recently been spent on modernisation, ending at last the foul routine of 'slopping out', conditions are far from ideal. Cells measuring twelve feet by seven, which the Victorians thought adequate for one person, have usually to accommodate two. Swansea is at times the most overcrowded prison in Wales and England: with an official capacity of 248 inmates, in 2006 it was running at 171% of its capacity, with 428 inmates. It's a category B local prison, serving an area stretching roughly from Milford to Merthyr; about three-quarters of the inmates are Swansea and west Wales men.

The last time I entered Swansea Prison was through its main wooden portals, in the internal cage of a police van with half a dozen other law-breakers convicted that morning. Four in their twenties, accomplices in some financial scam, had been sent down for years, and were loud with frightened bravado, boasting of their criminal exploits and previous jail terms; a younger man – who would be my cell mate – sat in stunned, ashen silence. Today, I wheel my bike in through a side door for 'processing': I'm photographed, electronically finger-printed, questioned … but the procedure's curtailed when the receptionist seems to recognise my name and voice. "You're Martyn Jenkins's brother, aren't you? We can skip the rest of this …" I'm taken upstairs to the administration corridor to meet my guide, Helen Davey, passing a large, framed photograph of the queen – well, it is her prison. And it's the queen's language that rules here: now, as two decades ago – in spite of the many Cymdeithas yr Iaith[18] activists who've done time here – there's hardly a word of Welsh to be seen on any public notices.

The biggest change architecturally is a new building – in the yard to our left as we leave the administration block – known as the Rotunda, whose garish green parapet sticks out above the prison walls. The Rotunda gives access to the main prison blocks and contains the kitchen, the visiting hall and the reception area. Also new is a high-security fence topped with rolls of razor wire, which makes a prison within the prison of the main blocks. Helen, like her colleagues, is a-jangle with keys, there being countless doors to unlock and re-lock as we make our way around. It's only early April, but it's stiflingly warm everywhere.

Reception as I remember it – in 'C' wing, at that time, the oldest prison building (1848) – was a cold, brusque affair, presided over by a severe Englishman in a white coat and half-moon glasses, and a team of cons doing his bidding and bossing the new arrivals about. (Most of the warders, as distinct from the prison's upper management, are locals. I was impressed by their generally friendly

attitude and the extent to which they were intimate with the prisoners' histories and home circumstances. It might explain why Swansea has never seen the unrest and rioting that's been experienced in other overcrowded jails – although violence against staff is increasing as the prison population grows.) There are still, as then, the usual questions about drugs, alcohol, physical and mental health, and suicide attempts (the more overcrowded a prison, the higher the number of suicides – usually by asphyxiation, and most commonly at night). But there seems to be more emphasis these days on identifying those with racist, violent or disturbed dispositions. "Some old lags manipulate the system and say they're racist just to get a cell to themselves," says the reception officer. "We know they're blagging, but we have to take such claims seriously."

For a first-time offender the initial twenty-four hours can be the most stressful, he says. "It depends on things like the length of sentence. We have lifers for a while, but they are usually sent to Cardiff. Sentences longer than ten years are rare." New admissions are kept in a special induction area, 'F' wing, for seven to ten days, where staff look out for negative responses such as self-harming.

When I chat later to the governor, Phil Taylor[19], he explains how the prison's reformatory efforts are hampered by a sentencing policy driven by (often misguided) public opinion. "Sentences are either too long or too short," he says. "You can do very little with someone in two months or even six months. A fourteen-day sentence is irrelevant. It does nothing to address the problem. Nine to twelve months are needed to complete the 12-step alcohol and drugs programme. Prison works, given time – but not too much time."

Alcohol and drugs, particularly heroin, have become the biggest challenge facing the prison system. But the number one obsession of almost everyone behind bars is tobacco; along with skins and matches, tobacco is a vital unit of prison currency. Shortly after I'd settled into 'A' wing, a burly hulk of a con who'd heard about the CND action on the radio, surreptitiously pressed into my palm, as we passed in a corridor, about a quarter of an ounce of tobacco – as a token of his support for CND. This generous gift was no use to me, a non-smoker, but it was a boon to my cell-mate Billy[20], a jittery twenty-year-old who had expected to be back in time for lunch after his court appearance – and was shocked to find himself bundled off to jail for a fortnight, for smashing a shop window and helping himself to a pair of trousers he needed to get into a club on The Kingsway. Billy later traded a little of the tobacco for some skins. He'd thought he could make do with a single match, by splitting it into four. We tried to do this with our fingernails, a staple from the prison regulation booklet, a hard flake of paint – but got nowhere. Later, he managed to trade a rollie for five matches.

Sex, of course, is another obsession, most cells being plastered with garish pages of girlie flesh ripped out of magazines and stuck to the walls with toothpaste, mashed potato or spunk. This tradition hasn't changed, but the brightly decorated cells are a little sweeter these days – smelling mildly of soap – now that the reviled slop buckets, with their foul ammoniac stench, have been replaced by stainless steel toilet and washing units.

The daily routine seems much as it was. Cells unlocked at 7.50 a.m. Breakfast collected from kitchens on a metal tray, and eaten in cells, which are locked until 9.00. Then work (cleaning, cooking, building, horticulture), for about 40p an hour, or education. Swansea's plumbing course is a big hit with prisoners. Key skills, such as maths, are often taught by tapping into prisoners' experiences. Many are interested in cars (not necessarily their own): the maths teacher encourages them, for instance, to compare the speeds of different models (speed = distance divided by time) as a way of exploring the mathematical basics. If the weather's fine, there's likely to be an hour's perambulation of the exercise yard, and at weekends especially there could be a visiting hour. After 4 p.m., prisoners are confined to their cells. The last meal of the day is served at 4.30 and a mug of tea at 7.00. So stretched are Swansea's resources that at any one time half of all prisoners are confined to their cells; inmates can spend between 18 and 22.5 hours a day there. It's known as 'warehousing' people.

The kitchens, where twenty-two prisoners work, provide the prison's most sought-after employment. When the poet and pacifist Waldo Williams served six weeks in this 'college for criminals' in 1960 – for refusing to pay tax to the warfare state – he declared that Swansea jail made the best brown bread in the whole of Wales. The prison was still baking delicious brown rolls in 1988 – but not any longer. Porridge, though, remains on the menu, and highly popular it is, too. Over 1200 meals a day are provided and all sorts of diets have to be catered for – veggie, vegan, Muslim, diabetic. Easily the favourite food is chips. "But they're only available every other day," says the head chef, who has a mere £1.41 per day to spend on each prisoner's food.

A tablet set in the prison wall marks a swathe of lawn beneath which are buried, in unmarked graves, the fifteen men who were executed at Swansea between 1858 and 1958 (the death penalty was abolished in 1965). These convicted murderers, denied burial in consecrated ground, include two Greek sailors whose hanging in 1858 – in the sand dunes, roughly where the Marriott Hotel stands today – attracted a huge crowd of 20,000. The execution in 1866 of

18-year-old Robert Coe, on the same spot, was a similar spectacle, with showmen and stalls, and profiteers charging a fee for a grandstand view. Unsettled by such degrading circuses, the authorities called a halt to public executions, and subsequent hangings at Swansea took place within the prison walls. The last to go to the gallows in Wales did so at Swansea in 1958: Vivian Frederick Teed who murdered a sub-postmaster in Carmarthen Road, Fforestfach in a bungled robbery.

Four days in Swansea prison, mostly spent reading, was no great hardship. But four months, let alone four years, would be altogether a different matter. The jail seems cruelly sited, with fragmented vistas of freedom on all sides. From my cell on the fourth floor, I could see yachts sailing in the bay and children playing on the beach. The friends and girlfriends of prisoners, dressed up for a night on the town, would scramble up the grassy bank outside County Hall to wave, blow kisses and shout messages to the men behind bars – just as lately, on the northern side of the jail, prisoners' wives and girlfriends have been clambering over the roof of the abandoned Vetch Field football ground to hail their men. For decades, prisoners would have had the roar of the Vetch crowd ringing enticingly in their ears and, once in a while, the music of such as The Who and Stevie Wonder, when the ground was used for rock concerts. Those who derive any benefit from a prison sentence seem few in comparison to those, on the one hand, whose sentences are so long that they abandon all hope, and those, on the other, who are in jail for only a few months, which may be just long enough to lose their home, family and job. The whole failing system is antiquated and barbaric. There must be a better way.

notes

1 It is thought that Giraldus Cambrensis, on his tour through Wales with Archbishop Baldwin in 1188, when they were preaching the Second Crusade, addressed the people of Kilvey at the chapel. It was here too, in 1321, that the Welshmen of Kilvey succeeded – if only for a short period – in stalling an attempt by Edward II's representative to take possession of Gower for the English king. The incident ignited the revolt of the barons which ended in Edward's murder and the restoration of Gower to the de Breos descendent John de Mowbray. What remained of the chapel and its sea-encroached graveyard disappeared in the early nineteenth century when George Tennant brought his canal through to the river and laid the foundations for what became known as Port Tennant.

2 He was the steel industrialist Captain H. Leighton Davies.

3 LMS: London, Midland and Scottish.

4 The artist who kindly lent me her studio was Beate Gegenwart.

5 The Iveys took their name from Ivey Place at the entrance to High Street station.

6 Now the Mission Gallery.

7 *The Unquiet Dead.*

8 Dressel's in St Louis, now run by his son Ben.

9 John Newman, *The Buildings of Wales*: Glamorgan, Penguin, 1995

10 The current chief executive is the Cardiff poet Peter Finch, whose experimental installation (with Maggs Harries), featuring a dozen vacuum cleaners 'exorcising' people's demons, was one of the first events at the Dylan Thomas Centre.

11 Lloyd Rees caught the mentality in his poem 'Town Planning, 1971': 'Tŷ Llên was far too Welsh for visitors to enter, / so now they call it the Dylan Thomas Centre.'

12 A local poet, her boyfriend and the boyfriend's mother.

13 PEN is the international organisation that campaigns for freedom of expression. The Welsh branch seems to have been moribund ever since.

14 For a fuller account of the protest and my spell behind bars see 'A Snowball's Chance' and 'The Diary of Prisoner WX 067' in my book of essays *Footsore on the Frontier* (Gomer Press, 2001).

15 John Newman.

16 For a fuller account of the tread wheel and the 'crank', and the prison's history in general, see Peter Goodall's *For Whom the Bell Tolls* (Gomer Press, 2001).

17 Swansea prison costs the taxpayer £10.5m a year.

18 The Welsh Language Society.

19 Phil Taylor was succeeded as governor, in June 2006, by Durham-born Andrea Whitfield.

20 Not his real name.

CENTRAL

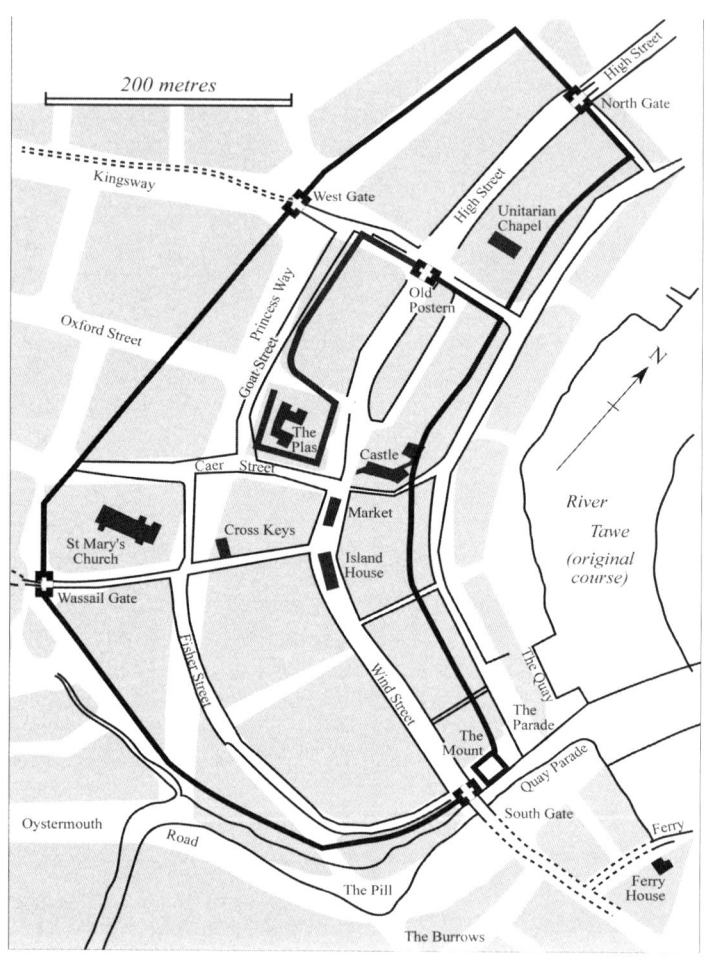

Medieval Swansea's streets and walls superimposed on the modern city street plan.

CASTLE SQUARE

It's a warm summer's night and – cut-offs on, sandals off – I'm wading knee-deep, with my friend David Pearl, in the pool surrounding Amber Hiscott's leaf sculpture in Castle Square. We've had a drink or two in the No Sign, it's true, but we're not up to the usual post-pub capers of those for whom the pool and its cascade is a toy to be flooded with dye or washing detergent, or, if they can find the plug, drained of its water. When Amber designed the sculpture – which was inspired by a Dylan Thomas quotation she's had inscribed around the retaining wall, "We sail a boat upon the path paddled with leaves down an ecstatic line of light" – she made sure that its glass planks would withstand the weight of an army of revellers. But sometimes the funsters manage to dislodge the silver tube that plays water over the leaf's upper surface – as they have recently done – and it's our job tonight, as Amber looks on, to fix it. We manage to do so without attracting the attentions of the law and without cutting our feet on any broken bottles lying in the murk.

Castle Square is Swansea's attempt at a European-style central piazza, an empty space with no particular function, in which you can simply linger, observe and enjoy whatever might develop: street theatre, buskers, free pop concerts, political demos, caterwauling winos, lovers canoodling under the light-spangled trees, strutting pigeons and swooping gulls, ball kickers, frisbee hurlers, newspaper readers, lunch-break picnickers – and skateboarders. Ever since the herbaceous Castle Gardens became the stone and concrete Castle Square in the late 1980s, the area has become a magnet for skate-boarders. It's claimed they cause over £20,000's worth of damage to the stonework every year, but nothing seems to deter them, from bylaws and prohibition signs to the installation of hundreds of skateboard-unfriendly studs and metal plates.

Winos

Always under summer
the bottle-glass through privet,
raised twitching image
of the sun at their mouths

and always I
am passing through, one for them
with the suits and skirts
trotting nine-to-five
down the regular paths.

We are closer than we know,
a thirst on us both
for waters wetter
than these sufficient times
can bring to dry mouths.

You have seen, retreated;
and I have seen.
Your way is silence,
a drowning of the voice
in large pink toothless smiles.
I am not for this garden.

It's the clean articulation of
    white cherry/blue sky
that draws me on through

though I am drunk sometimes,
blind drunk and speechless,
just as you sometimes, as you
stumble through the pigeons
baying out obscenities, will
infiltrate a truth to deafened ears.

The square is dominated, to the east, by the castle (or what's left of it) – with the Cross Keys pub, it's Swansea's oldest building – and, beyond it, the mirror-clad British Telecom tower (1970) (which used to be more darkly imposing before its 1992 glassy makeover). The poet Tony Conran, visiting Swansea as part of his research into Welsh castles[1], expected to find an "ignorable" or "very little castle", but he found, on the contrary, that "It is not very happy / But it is not small." Built in the 1330s to control the eastern entrance to the lordship of Gower, it was a ruin by the late sixteenth century. All that remains today are the castle's north block connected by a curtain wall to

the impressive southern range, with its distinctive arcaded parapet of dressed Sutton stone, said to have been designed by Bishop Henry de Gower (?1278-1347) whose palaces at Lamphey and St David's bear similar features. If the castle, inevitably, attracted the ire of the dispossessed natives – Owain Glyndŵr, for instance, seized both town and castle in 1406 – it seems for much of its history to have been largely unloved by the denizens of Swansea. Having fulfilled various post-defensive roles over the centuries, from glassworks to prison to workhouse, it was threatened with demolition in 1957 by a body distinguished to this day for its cavalier insouciance towards Swansea's heritage – the local council. Its members, describing the castle variously as "a shambles" and "a shocking thing", wanted to clear the site for development. It was thanks largely to a campaign by the Gower Society and a stern directive from the Ministry of Works that the castle was saved.

Such was the clutter of buildings pressing in on the ruins at that time that it was difficult to see much more of the castle than its southern tower. The most prominent of these buildings was the old general post office which had been taken over by the local paper in 1901 and which – surviving the three-nights blitz that destroyed almost everything around it – housed *The South Wales Evening Post*'s offices and presses until 1968. I served a sort of unofficial cub reporter's apprenticeship in those dark and dusty offices, owing to my father's acquaintance with the then chief reporter, Len Goss. Dad persuaded long-suffering Len to look over various practice articles his pimply boy was concocting between writing letters to newspapers throughout Britain in an effort to land a trainee reporter's job. There was a

seedy romance to the place – not least, of course, because Dylan Thomas had worked there. So too had the novelist, biographer and investigative writer Paul Ferris (1929), whose wedding – to my mother's cousin, the literary agent Gloria Morton – I had attended as a cringing pageboy. Other Swansea-born writers to have worked at the *Post* include the poet and filmmaker John Ormond (1923-90) and the journalist and broadcaster John Morgan (1929-88). I remember John telling me, when he was chairman of the Welsh Union of Writers in the 1980s, that he'd been walking down High Street with Dylan Thomas in the early 1950s; passing the *Evening Post* building, John had mentioned that Ormond was working there as a sub-editor. "Ah, John Ormond," remarked Dylan, "the *enfant horrible* of Welsh letters".

A neighbouring building that also survived the bombs was the Castle Cinema, built c.1913 as the Cinematograph Palace, its fruity, baroque, colonnaded, Bath-stone frontage somewhat wasted on its cramped corner of Worcester Place. A novelty introduced here – in time, I remember, for the Beatles' film *A Hard Day's Night* (1964) – were the back-of-house, two-person 'cuddlers', which were much sought after by snogging youth. No films (or snogs) have been seen at the Castle for years. Known these days as Laserzone, it's where you go to play virtual war games. How much longer the Grade II listed building will survive the developers' amnesiac ambitions remains to be seen. The buddleia hovers, vulture like, on its roof.

It was some years after the *Post* decamped to Adelaide Street before the castle grounds were cleared of clutter and grassed. In the late 70s, there were still some lean-to sheds towards the rear of the site and an iron-spiked gate to keep people out. This posed a challenge one night to the guitarist Brian Breeze who, lurching up Wind Street after a gig at the Coach, decided he'd like to have a look around the castle. He wobbled his woozy way to the top of the gate, but as he was stepping over the spikes at the top and onto the asbestos roof of one of the lean-tos, the gate started to swing away and he lost his footing. As he fell, a spike ripped through his trouser-leg and lodged firmly in the seat of his trousers, leaving Brian hanging there, waving his arms and legs, but otherwise immovably impaled. He jiggled vigorously up and down in the hope that his weight would tear the trousers – which it did, and he plummeted to the ground. Deciding to take home a souvenir of the evening, he relieved the castle wall of about half a hundredweight of its fabric. The semi-trouserless guitarist with a block of stone in his arms managed to find a taxi to take him home to Clase, where he presented his sleeping and unimpressed wife Mabe with her medieval takeaway. They kept the 'Breeze block' in their fireplace for years. But one night, during a party to celebrate Brian's appearance on *The Old Grey Whistle Test*, their chunk of Swansea castle went missing and has not been heard of since.

The square itself was the site for at least 500 years of Swansea's grandest house, Plas Newydd (New Place), with its irregular court-yard and outbuildings. It was the home of local magnates such as the Cradocks and Herberts and various stewards of the lords of Gower. A model in Swansea Museum shows how the dilapidated mansion, abandoned after about 1800, looked shortly before its demolition in 1840.

Also destroyed in the blitz was Swansea's biggest Victorian store, Ben Evans, which had been built on the site of the Plas in 1893. Ben's enjoys still, in the minds of older Swansea people, an almost legendary reputation for its endless variety of household goods, clothes and services, including a full-size model horse for trying out new riding attire, and a hairdressing salon in whose curtained cubicles the ladies of Swansea would sit beneath huge electric perming contraptions. Destroyed with the rest of the Ben Evans block was the Three Lamps pub, which was rebuilt on the other side of the (now pedestrianised) slope that links Princess Way with Castle Bailey Street. Known as the Office these days, it's a popular live music venue.

It's usually assumed that Caer Street on the south side of the square is a straight rendition into Welsh of Castle Street. But histori-ans argue that its original name was Carr Street, as this was where Gower farmers used to park their carts – 'cars' or 'carrs', as they called them – on market day. The town's first 'carr park' is perform-ing a similar role today, being a busy taxi rank for the skimpily clad Wind Street carousers.

The 'Jacobethan' Beau Nash House that runs the length of Caer Street was built in the style of the building that stood here before the bombs fell (it's named after Richard 'Beau' Nash (1674-1762), 'director of pleasures' at fashionable Bath, who was born round the corner, in a house next door to the Cross Keys). The woodwork of this half-timbered building came from oak and teak taken from the luxury liner *Reina Del Pacifico*, which was scrapped in the 1950s. The main business on this side of the square was the outfitter Sidney Heath, who specialised in 'clothes for gentlemen' and school uniforms: black blazers for Dynevor, maroon for Bishop Gore, navy blue (with harp on breast pocket) for Craig-y-Nos (or Lloyd's, as it was known). Bombed out in 1941, Sidney Heath moved to temporary accommodation in Walter Road, but returned after reconstruction, eventually selling out to the luxury knick-knacks emporium Treasure. By the turn of the century, the good-time industry of Wind Street had turned the corner into Caer Street and – in the form of Yates's – had established itself as the booze-king conqueror of Sidney Heath's half-timbered, genteel realm.

Beau Nash House is distinctly at odds with the modernist, glass-and-concrete pretensions of the rest of post-blitz, rebuilt Swansea. The building that houses McDonald's at the western end of the square – a popular milling ground for Swansea youngsters, especially 'Goths' and 'Emos' – was clearly intended to reflect contemporary architectural trends when it opened as Boots in the 1950s. It looked, according to Kingsley Amis, like "a tool-chest with flagpoles / Glued on, and flanges, and a dirty great / Baronial doorway, and things like port-holes …"

Boots, which later gave way to Halford's bicycles, had the usual medications and cosmetics on the ground floor; upstairs was a lending library, chiefly of light fiction (I remember working my way methodically through all of its 'Famous Five' books), and a record department with the ultimate in individual listening booths, where we adolescents sampled – pre-Stones, pre-Beatles – the latest 45s: the Shadows, B. Bumble and the Stingers, the Tornadoes, Trini Lopez, Peter, Paul and Mary. Music to have dreamy crushes to. Today's youth are more 'hands on', as the graffiti on the light-bases and flower stands outside McDonald's suggest: 'Sophie slag', 'Caroline is a fuckface', 'I LUVZ IOAN', 'Alec Hazel is a hobit – and he's cowin' sexy', 'Ryan is ghey' (a common spelling), 'I'm a Welsh noodle miner – look at me dance'.

HIGH STREET

High Street, with its continuation into Castle Street, Castle Bailey Street and Wind Street, has been the town's spine since medieval times. If you understand High Street, you understand Swansea. And if you mess with High Street – by, for instance, displacing the retail heart of the city to the Quadrant and out-of-town shopping centres – Swansea as a whole loses its balance.

Boarded up businesses, charity shops, abandoned theatres, empty upper storeys, pigeons nesting in attics, buddleia rooting on parapets, gangs in tracksuits and baseball caps, drunks and bums getting louder and more aggressive as darkness falls – such are the symptoms of a street that has been in decline for decades. While incidences of violence have tended to fall throughout the city, the violent crime in High Street was reported in 2006 to have increased by nearly 80 per cent. But with the station forecourt receiving a chrome-and-glass makeover, the Grand Hotel being restored to its original elegance, and plans in the pipeline for a £22m 'urban village' scheme for the area, the street may be on the verge of a come-back.

> quick march down High Street,
> new strimmer at the slope:
> a man with a lawn

High Street, the northern gateway to Swansea, begins at Dyfatty whose name – literally 'sheep house' – evokes the area's long association with the sale and butchery of livestock. There was a succession of slaughterhouses here, the last (1887) – behind high walls on the western side of Dyfatty Street – serving as Swansea's main abattoir until the late 1960s.

The area is best known these days for the Dyfatty flats, four fourteen-storey blocks which dominate the upper High Street area and which generate many a tall, implausible tale. One of the most persistent (probably based on some news item from the 1970s) relates to the flat-dwellers' reputed penchant for equestrian pets and how visitors should not be alarmed to find themselves sharing the lift with a pony. In recent years, the antisocial behaviour of alcoholics and druggies – break-ins, vandalism, syringes on the landings and stairways – has made life hell for many of the residents. There's speculation that the only solution to the problem is to demolish the flats.

Two aspects of city centre hedonism are reflected by signs on opposite sides of the road as you enter High Street, one advertising Swansea Limousine Hire, the other reading 'Alcohol control area – it is an OFFENCE to DRINK ALCOHOL HERE if you have been warned not to by a police officer. Failure to comply may lead to arrest.'

> winos a-tiptoe
> on midday streets, trying
> not to wake us

The alcoholic mayhem of Wind Street, to which High Street – with its own seedier, more down-at-heel booze culture – transports hundreds of young revellers of an evening, is nothing new in the life of the city centre. Swansea a hundred years ago was a far wilder place than it is today, with over thirty pubs in High Street alone (compared with nine in 2007) and some of the town's most deprived and lawless inhabitants living in squalorous alleyways and courts off it, with their *cwrw bach*s[2], brothels, criminal networks and riotous behaviour. Drunken women, then as now, would hurl themselves into punch-ups. W.C. Rogers describes how regulars at the White Swan, women included, would pour out of the pub to round off an evening's entertainment with bare-knuckle fighting.

Not far from the Swan on the other side of the road, just north of the Old Duke pub, was a mound known as Crug-las where the renowned evangelist Howel Harris (1714-73) came close to assassination. A drunk, in the largely hostile crowd Harris was preaching to,

aimed a pistol at him, but the gun misfired and Harris was unscathed. The drunk ran off, fell asleep in a limekiln and was killed by the fumes.

Another giant of Nonconformity, the one-eyed preacher Christmas Evans (1776-1838), did not survive the last of his many Swansea visits. He died at the minister's house in Tontine Street after the Sunday evening service at Bethesda Baptist chapel, which is just off High Street in Prince of Wales Road, and is buried in Bethesda's graveyard. Although a Grade I listed chapel (one of only sixteen in Wales), Bethesda suffered years of neglect and seemed to be disappearing in a jungle of Japanese knotweed, until it was taken over by the NSPCC, who made it their new Swansea headquarters in 2004. The knotweed, in spite of regular dousings with herbicide, and the nylon membrane and gravel that have been spread over the grave-yard, has by no means given up the fight. Knotweed covers over 100 ha of land in the Swansea area, and is a seemingly intractable problem, particularly along railway embankments, on wasteland and in cemeteries. Not even concrete and brick walls can halt its march.

The crimson fingers of resurgent knotweed are an insistent presence in the graveyard of another recently renovated and historic church, St Matthew's in High Street, which was founded by the Knights Hospitallers in about 1165 – well outside the town walls – as the Church of St John's-juxta-Swansea. Its £800,000 conversion into a dual-purpose building – church in the eastern half and, in the western, a drop-in centre run by the homeless charity Cyrenians – is regarded as a ground-breaking scheme for Wales, there being so many churches and chapels bereft of a contemporary role[3]. Although the Cyrenians centre (managed by Conrad Watkins, son of the poet Vernon Watkins) is entirely independent of the church half of the building, it perpetuates a mission of hospitality pursued by the church's founders nearly 900 years ago. It was for many pilgrims their last stop before boarding a ship moored on the Tawe and sailing to Santiago de Compostella in Galicia. At St John's, they'd be fed and watered, and have their ailments treated, just as today the needy can get breakfast for 75p, lunch for £1, as well as access to a nurse and a doctor, help with drugs and alcohol problems, and advice on such matters as housing and jobs.

The church, the fourth on this site, changed its name to St Matthew's when the Vivians, Swansea's leading coppermas-ter dynasty, insisted, in the 1880s, on naming their new church in the Hafod after St John. 'Copperopolis' has left its mark here in other ways too. The coppermaster Sir John Morris, founder of Morriston, is buried with his wife Dame Henrietta in two copper coffins beneath the floor of the church, and in the graveyard there are to be seen the strange yet unmistakeable outlines of three copper coffins protruding a couple of centimetres above ground level. It is apparently a property of copper that if it's buried in the earth it will eventually work its way to the surface. The coffins are open – presumably because as soon as they broke the surface, their valuable copper lids were stolen. Other notable graves here include that of Julia Ann Hatton (the poet 'Anne of Swansea') and Fanny Imlay, Shelley's step-daughter, who killed herself in the Bush Hotel in 1816. Shelley came to Swansea to arrange her funeral. "Misery – O Misery," he wrote after reading her valedictory note, "This world is all too wide for thee!" It seems curious, in such a built-up area, to find behind St Matthew's a tree-shaded field. This, in fact, is a mass grave – with the bodies buried twenty to thirty feet deep – of those who died in three mid-nineteenth-century cholera epidemics. The land can never be built on.

Almost as invasive as knotweed in this part of town is buddleia. Among the guttering and parapets colonised by buddleia are those of the flat-iron-shaped Palace Theatre, at the junction of Prince of Wales Road with High Street, which has been steadily deteriorating since its closure as a gay nightclub in 2004. A Grade II listed structure and one of Swansea's most winsome buildings, it opened in 1888 as the Swansea Pavilion Music Hall, becoming the Swansea Empire Music Hall in 1892 and, in 1904, the Palace of Varieties. Swansea's first ever film show was held here in 1896, the rise of film – at music hall's

expense – proving ultimately unstoppable: in 1908, the theatre was converted to a cinema, the People's Bioscope Palace, although there would still be periods when it was used for variety and drama, until it became a bingo hall in the 1960s and finally a club. Among the stars who appeared at the Palace in its heyday were Charlie Chaplin, Lily Langtry, Dan Leno and George Robey; in 1960, Anthony Hopkins made his first professional appearance here. As one of only two purpose-built music halls left in Britain, with perfect acoustics and an interior more or less intact, from leather seats in 'the gods' to fully operational scenery-flying gear, its importance has been recognised by actors such as Edward Fox and Ruth Madoc who have been campaigning anxiously for its restoration. In the meantime, the buddleia tightens its corrosive grip and the rats and pigeons flourish.

A similarly stricken old cinema – and subsequent bingo hall – is to be found in lower High Street, the 1400-seat, long boarded-up Elysium. I remember seeing *Lorna Doone* there in the 1950s, and in the 1970s I gave my first ever WEA lectures – on poetry and drama – in the Labour Club established in the basement. Once upon a time, the Elysium played a significant role in the political life of Swansea. Lloyd George orated there, and in 1917 a meeting that had been called by brave socialists and soldiers' delegates to denounce the war and to argue for a negotiated peace was violently terminated by pro-war thugs. I was inspired and often humbled by the intellectual acumen of my little WEA gathering, but otherwise – in those flaking and smoke-yellowed basement rooms, surrounded by fading photographs of bechained aldermen and Labour worthies, and posters advertising the annual Easter bonnet competition[4] – I felt little continuing connection with the venerable local traditions of anti-war campaigning, internationalism, and social and industrial radicalism. The Elysium represented not so much old Labour as ossified Labour.

Although much of High Street survived the Nazi bombs, some of its most appealing features were obliterated by the council in the 1960s. The self-consciously postmodern Mackworth Court block preserves the name of the 112-bedroom Mackworth Hotel (1880s; not to be confused with an older Mackworth in Wind Street). One of Swansea's most opulent hotels, it was demolished in 1967, at about the same time as the nearby High Street Arcade, which was as elegant as the finest of Cardiff's arcades and renowned for shops such as the

two music suppliers, Snell's and Duck, Son & Pinker, and Madame Foner's (ladies' underwear and corsets). In its place stands the monumentally oppressive thirteen-storey office block Alexandra House. High Street's other main architectural monstrosity – even more ambitiously ugly – is Tŷ Bryn Glas near the railway station, the crude, red-brick fortress of the Land Registry.

There are, nevertheless, plenty of interesting buildings in High Street, in a pleasingly anarchic variety of styles, from mock Tudor, to Teutonic (with sunflower reliefs), to art deco (with stylised elephant heads). Two of Swansea's oldest pubs are sited here: the late Georgian Bush (now a gay complex, renamed Creation and Eden) and the King's Arms (an important music venue in the 1960s – Spencer Davis was a regular performer here).

One of the street's oldest buildings is the Unitarian church, founded in 1698 as a Presbyterian chapel, rebuilt in 1847 for the Unitarians, and rebuilt again, on a two-tier design, after a fire in 1987 destroyed everything but ten iron pillars and the walls. Children at the Joan Williams Stage School, which is based here, are belting out 'When the Saints Go Marching In' as I enter through the double frontage and cross to the rear door that opens onto a graveyard overlooking the Strand, some ten metres below. Here, on top of a huge retaining wall, you appreciate the vastness of the infilling operation that was necessary to make the High Street area level – and amenable, therefore, to development. Beneath the largely overgrown gardens at the rear of buildings on the east side of High Street, and under the buildings themselves, there are likely to be extensive architectural remains of an earlier Swansea. And a close examination of the street's older buildings could yield evidence of the Georgian and Victorian passageways and courts that were typical of the housing in this part of town until the slum clearances of the earlier twentieth century.

Swansea Housing Association's 'urban village' scheme for High Street is intended to bring residents back to the area, and will involve

200 apartments, arts studios, shops, cafés and bars. Let's hope, therefore, that High Street will reassume something of the focus and purpose it had for centuries, as the defining street of Swansea.

The language of love, in a High Street pub

walkin down this fuckin street
I spies this fuckin bar
an feelin fuckin thirsty
I goes in for a fuckin jar

it's pretty fuckin lonely
for a Friday fuckin night
me an this fuckin woman
the only fuckers in fuckin sight

so I buys meself a fuckin pint
an her a fuckin stout
an we drinks for fuckin hours
till they kicks us fuckin out

then we takes this fuckin taxi
to this block of fuckin flats
an we rolls into her fuckin bed
as pissed as fuckin rats

what next? you're fuckin thinking
well yes of fucking course
we took at last to her fuckin bed
an ad sexual intercourse

WIND STREET

Considered, in 1821, "the handsomest street in Wales" for the "general breadth and the peculiar width of its flagging", Wind Street today is notorious throughout the land for its riotously festive nightlife. Blitzpop blasting from disco-bars; funereal bouncers chewing gum and checking IDs; pasty beggars skulking in doorways; and the sequinned, bling-decked, tattooed, perfumed, high and high-heeled prospectors of night descending in their thousands, especially

at weekends – as minimally clothed in December as they are in July
– to preen and parade, dance and drug, yowl and carouse, and – if
they get lucky – to pull.

Dafydd ap Gwilym Goes To Town

Same Saturday night low expectations.
Why bother indeed
to powder the cock and pocket the lens case?
I don't even figure with the bus conductor
who stares right through me with his one good eye
and misses my fare.
Ah well, another quid
for the Double Dragon …

Too much boozing brings on dandruff.
Rosemary shampoo, they say, is a cure.
But I can think of a better one, cariad,
I can think of a better one.

Weaving through this squawking, gob-mouthed frenzy are the lone
sellers – quiet people from poor countries – of red roses wrapped in
cellophane. The police glide by every few minutes, and at times of
heightened festivity, such as Christmas and New Year, there are
medics on hand in field hospitals to tend the binged out and brawl
battered. Wind Street's got a reputation, alright, but my daughters
love it, and I think I would too if I were their age. Violent crime there
is supposed to have rocketed, with 180 punch-ups in 2005, compared
with only 20 in 2000. But I've never felt unsafe there. Unhinged
exuberance rather than menace seems to be the dominant mood.

One of the city's oldest streets, and a rare survivor of the blitz, it
was laid down in medieval times as a main thoroughfare through the
walled town, with the South Gate into Swansea at its southern end.
Its name – pronounced 'wined' – is a puzzle. Like its namesake in
Neath, it can hardly be said to 'wind'. Some have proposed that
strong winds blowing up from the river gave the street its name –
after all, it wasn't until the eighteenth century that the modern
pronunciation of wind, to rhyme with 'sinned', became common;
others have suggested that, as a street of wine merchants, it was originally Wine Street.

Commerce and shopping were certainly, for centuries, its main business. Swansea's ancient market, initially a street market and then an open-sided hall, was held at its top end, in the middle of the street, until 1830. The town's classiest hotels in the eighteenth and nineteenth centuries, the Mackworth Arms and the George (later the Metropole), were situated in Wind Street, as were the first theatres and circulating libraries. Nothing remains of them. But there are many survivors of another major Wind Street pursuit, banking. The first bank in Wales opened in Wind Street in 1771, and more (increasingly grandiloquent) establishments soon followed.

I came close, once, to buying one of these temples to Mammon. By the later 1980s, the revolution in information technology had rendered such banking halls obsolete. It was time, the council declared in 1997, to give the street a new identity – as Swansea's Continental-style café quarter, with art galleries, lunchtime theatre, jazz combos, chamber orchestras, and alfresco wining and dining on sun-dappled pavements. An opportune moment, thought the Swansea Writers' and Artists' Group (SWAG), for us to acquire (with grant support) a Wind Street bank and turn it into a much needed arts centre, along the lines of Cardiff's Chapter. We put in an offer of £250,000 for Barclays at number 57, but we were beaten to it by one of the big booze chains with ready cash. The building, within months, became the Bank Statement, one of the biggest of Wind Street's industrial drinking factories, and the café quarter of municipal delusion was well on the way to becoming Booze Boulevard. Swansea's night-time economy, with Wind Street at its heart, is said by now to be worth over £200m a year.

Although only 250 metres long, Wind Street contains some thirty pubs and bars (discounting restaurants), only four of which are not owned by big international chains likes Yates's and Que Pasa; its total bar-only capacity is 14,000. The street still has enormous architectural character, but its boozy makeover has resulted in the loss of much variety and distinctiveness in its pubs and shops – indeed, there's only one shop left, Cogger's newsagents at the entrance to Salubrious Passage.

The street is best experienced, my daughters tell me, from the bottom up. My youngest, Branwen, therefore talks me up Wind Street – with unflinching subjectivity – from the revellers' drop-off point near Frankie and Benny's.

One of my favourite shops down here, Emmanuel Perera's Continental Stores, became La Prensa café-bar. Two neighbouring businesses, the tiny Borough Arms and a newsagent's, were engulfed

by La Brasseria, a great place to go for an infusion of Spanish *duende* in the depths of a gloomy Swansea winter. "You were taking visiting writers there two or three times a week in the Year of flamin' Literature," says the youngest, "but you've never taken me there once."ext birthday, Bran, I promise. A newer Spanish-style restaurant on the other side of the street is La Tasca – "You've never taken me there, either" – which I'm pretty sure is built on the site of the Star Theatre (1869), the most popular of Swansea's music halls. I looked into this in 2006 when Swansea's Fluellen Theatre Company revived the famous Victorian melodrama *Maria Marten or The Murder in the Red Barn*, which was premiered at the Star in the 1880s.

Opposite La Tasca is the first of the nightspots, Revolution: "Classy, moethus, strict on ID. Nice cocktails." Why, with its pseudo-Russian reversed 'R', is it called Revolution? Because when Lloyd's bank owned the building they installed a turntable for bullion vans using its rear entrance in The Strand – to avoid hazardous manoeuvres in the street. The plan was to make the turntable a central feature of the club, but it didn't catch on; the turntable was smashed up and carted away.

A couple of doors up is a long-established live-music venue, the Adelphi. The pub's Marciano bar and restaurant lays claim to an incident during the Second World War when the American boxer (and milk drinker) Rocky Marciano is said to have been taunted in the Adelphi by a hard-drinking Australian soldier; one dig from Marciano knocked the Australian out cold – and led to the arrest of the future world heavyweight champion[5]. Opposite the Adelphi is SoBar: "Full of chavs and mingers. Fun music, not techno. Absolutely the most disgusting toilets of any club I've been into in my life." The Bank Statement is "Popular with Saturday-night people, very busy, mixed ages, people walking round with pitchers of cocktails, and a straw, to themselves."

The granite-columned, Neo-Baroque Idols on the corner of the cobbled Green Dragon Lane has "dancers on the bar" and the music's "a little old school – power ballads, men singing along to Queen's 'Don't stop me now'." It's the most magnificent building in Wind Street. Built on the site of the Mackworth Arms and opened in 1901 as Swansea's head post office, it's faced with Bath stone and green Quarella sandstone from near Bridgend; it has the air, as John Newman says, of "a late medieval Flemish Town Hall." Ice Bar[6], on the other corner of the lane (whose roadway stones are grooved by generations of steel-shod carts passing over them), is "Cheap as chips. Lovely people behind the bar. But the people who go there are mingers, mingers, chavs beyond belief."

The Pitcher and Piano opposite – "classy, tends to be for older[7], business people" – used to be known as the Coach House, and probably served as such for the Mackworth Arms. With the Mond Building in Union Street, the Coach was very much a student haunt in the 1970s; it was popular too with bikers. The house band in its cramped but atmospheric cellar was the Trembling Knees (still going strong) whose arm-flailing singer, Plum Howells, used to take the piss out of flower power by wearing a cabbage on his head. The jam-packed cellar would get so hot that condensation would form on the filthy wooden ceiling – and then drip into your drink.

SA1[8], which used to be the Goose and Granite, is where you can get "shots with some dust in the bottom that scrapes the back of your throat, so it goes into your bloodstream quicker". The Goose and Granite's sprawling development in the 1990s obliterated one of Wind Street's most colourful pubs, the Duke, whose back bar – presided over by a landlord with a formidable Alsatian and political views well to the right of Edward I – was a favourite haunt of the Swansea left: Fred Fitton of the SWP, Ray Thomas of the CP, Paul Elliott of NUPE, Ian Bone and assorted anarchists, to name but a tiny selection. It was Bone, the butler's son who founded Class War and was described by one tabloid newspaper as 'the most dangerous man in Britain', who founded the Swansea scandal-sheet *Alarm* which exposed widespread corruption in the city and got several councillors and businessmen sent to jail.

Another magnificent building, the Edwardian baroque former Midland Bank (1910), houses Varsity: "Nice for a quiet drink on week nights – loads of seats, really comfortable and quite comforting." It's next door to what seems to be our critic's least favourite haunt, Yates's: "What a dive. Old[9] or desperate people go there, disgusting pervy men and boys who can't pull elsewhere. Rubbish music."

And her number one nightspot? Walkabout: "I full on love it. All sorts go there. Lovely staff. Absolutely fantastic music, everyone dancing, everyone really friendly." Another favourite 'honorary Wind Street' venue is Monkey in Castle Street: "Live music, good atmosphere, arty people." In the early 1980s, when the Walkabout building was home to the Royal Antedeluvian Order of Buffalos, there was the occasional poetry reading among its rafters. Pete Hodgkiss, editor of the internationally important and Swansea-generated magazine *Poetry Information*, would bring in experimentalists such as Opal L. Nations, and on one occasion in 1982, the Cardiff poet John Tripp's views on the Falklands/Malvinas war came close to provoking a punch-up; all ended cheerily enough with a local prostitute dancing on a table.

Having reached the top of Wind Street, the revels normally continue in Play, the big new(ish) establishment down in Salubrious Place, or in one of the voluminous clubs on The Kingsway. Most revellers totter the 200 metres to The Kingsway, but some will pay £3 for a taxi. "Lazy buggers."

THE NO SIGN

The curiously named No Sign, at 56 Wind Street, is the oldest wine bar in Swansea[10]. My father and his pals (and sometimes his two pop-quaffing, bored little boys) used to drink here in the 1950s, and it's still recognisably the same place, although it has undergone a certain simplification in recent years, losing its distinct 'compartments', and becoming, at eighty-five metres, the longest bar in Swansea.

Its 'traditional' ambience – bare wooden floors, reclaimed furniture, 'distressed' paintwork, glass cabinets, fireplaces, old bottles on dusty shelves, and no alcopops, no robotic dance music – relieves it of the nervy trendiness that afflicts most other Wind Street establishments, and makes it warmly welcoming of 'old' (those treasurable inverted commas) people like me (and younger ones too) who enjoy a chat or a read in congenial surroundings.

My father and his friends tended to refer to the (then) men-only bar as Munday's, after the wine-merchant family that had run the business – with branches all over town – since 1837. Their wives called it the Gluepot – because their men tended to get stuck there. (I've also heard it referred to as Dante's Inferno, after the charming and anything but infernal Dante Molfetti who was the No Sign's head

barman for many years.) The
front compartment, with two
easy chairs either side a
fireplace, was the off-licence. It
was presided over by a large
portrait, still hanging over the
mantelpiece, of Clark Williams,
a pre-Munday's owner (who
looks uncannily like an
approachable version of Dan
Minster, Swansea's leisure
services director in the 1990s).
The next compartment was
the proprietor Gerry

Munday's office, later made into a bar at which the drinkers stood on
duckboards; and then came the back bar. This was more or less the
No Sign which the owners believe is fleetingly mentioned in Dylan
Thomas's late short story 'The Followers' as "the wine vaults", with
the adjacent Salubrious Passage becoming "Paradise Alley" and then
"Paradise Passage".

First referred to – as a "no sign custom house" – in a document of
1690, it's been in turn a brew house, a brewery, a wine and spirits
merchants, and a public house. When licensing was introduced in
Wales and England, every public house had to be registered with a
name and a sign; but number 56, being a bar at that time, not a public
house, was categorised as a 'no sign' establishment. When the need
for an official sign eventually arose about a century ago, the Mundays
plumped – like Magritte captioning his painting of a pipe 'Ceci n'est
pas une pipe'[11] – for a sign that read simply 'No Sign'.

The No Sign's hidden glory is its capacious and – especially by
candlelight – atmospheric cellar, whose initial mustiness reminds me
of damp public buildings in India. It's great for parties, dancing and
live music, but it excels as a venue for spoken word events: perfect
acoustics and no distractions from dishwashing, jukeboxes, bass
guitars and buses: the word is all. Allen Ginsberg was among
dozens of writers who read here during the 1995 Year of Literature.
His official reading at the university's Taliesin Theatre was over-
subscribed and the poet felt sorry for those who'd failed to get in.
"Find me another venue," he told the organisers, "and I'll do another
reading." So they found him the No Sign cellar, and a raptly atten-
tive full house heard him deliver a long new poem. Most thought as

they applauded him – Ginsberg being in anything but robust health – that that was the end of a wonderfully historic occasion. But no. "Give me a little break," he said, "and I'll do some more." The second half, an hour's worth of some of his 'greatest hits', rounded off one of the most memorable nights I've known in Swansea – thanks in no small part to the magic of the No Sign's cellar. Sadly, for a pub that likes to flaunt its Dylan Thomas associations, there's been no poetry there for a decade or more.

OXFORD STREET

Due for obliteration as this book goes to press are the last remaining lines of the ill-fated Oxford Street poetry project. In 1992, the council invited three poets (David Hughes, Menna Elfyn and myself) and two artists from the planning department (Robin Campbell and Brenda Oakes) to produce poems celebrating "the magic of place", along with sculptures and street furniture to present them. The idea was to give the newly pedestrianised eastern end of Oxford Street, with its post-war, clone-town stores, a stronger local identity.

We came up with micropoems, poems for benches, poems for finger-posts, poems for bollards, poems to run along the pavement and up lampposts – in English, Welsh and Swansea dialect. To sing and celebrate Swansea, in a range of equally valid voices, was the aim. One of Dave Hughes's micropoems – 'Ambition is critical' – found its way to paving outside High Street station. The first in Oxford Street itself was another of Dave's – 'Boldness before princes' – angled to address the castle, ancient seat of alien power. At the other end of the precinct were Menna's 'Mae saint a satan yn symud ar y sement'[12] and, nearby, some wooden benches carved with her words. Midway between them, raying out from a lamppost, was my 'Swansea Toast':

> To every burgess a burgage, to every Jack a Jackette,
> Jacs bach, good ground from which to soar.

> To all Jacks their acres beyond the wood,
> The sun's green song and a fishy rain.

> To each his nine, her ten holes[13], a care
> For the sea, and sewin muscling their moons upstream.

> To all Jacks their seven hills, peace in their homes,
> South westerly winds and salubrious passage.

At around the time the poems were becoming part of the streetscape – and when, simultaneously, Swansea was bidding to host the UK Year of Literature and Writing 1995 – Swansea appeared, superficially, to be a confident, cultured city. Thanks largely to changes at the top, and a lurch rightward among the elected members, that confidence evaporated and Swansea lost its nerve. It seemed to want to be an art-free city, or one prettily spruced up with classroom ceramics and schoolkid murals (to say nothing of ack-ack guns). Art was not to be trusted. This was, after all, the city that banned Monty Python's *The Life of Brian*[14] and Howard Brenton's *The Romans in Britain*.

A sculptural feature we had planned was a 'stage set' fragment of a Roman arch framing the words, in Swansea dialect, 'Seezer avenaclew wotsgowin on'[15]. The plan got no further than the maquette stage, after a mole in the engineering department leaked a crude sketch of the arch to *The Swansea Herald*, an advertising freesheet.

It was the *Herald* that now led a general press attack on the poetry project. Our use of Swansea dialect, it averred, was "in extremely bad taste" and amounted to "taking the mickey out of the local patois". Out came the municipal hacksaws and screwdrivers, therefore, and away went every word in the language spoken by tens of thousands of Swansea people. A bilingual fingerpost near the church – 'Cofiwch yfory / Remember tomorrow' – was irrational, declared the *Post* on a Saturday. By Monday morning, therefore, the offending micropoem had been removed. Whatever the local press or individual 'poetry fans' at the Guildhall took exception to, the local authority obediently removed, unable or unwilling to support the art works it had commissioned.

It was one thing to introduce art to the maritime playground south of Oystermouth Road, and quite another, we soon learned, to attempt to unleash its energies through the money-making heart of the city, especially if humour and politics were involved. Only a fraction of what we had planned for Oxford Street, and associated streets, was installed. By the spring of 2008, all of what was not 'censored by freesheet' will have vanished.

THE KINGSWAY

Only two buildings were left standing in Gower Street and Heathfield Street (now The Kingsway) after the 1941 blitz – the proudly classical Mount Pleasant Baptist Chapel (1826 and 1876) and the Plaza cinema (1931). The chapel, with its golden Bath-stone façade and four Corinthian columns, is still with us, angled to the trajectory of Gower Street rather than that of The Kingsway, but the Plaza – a people's picture palace in sublimely confident art-deco style – fell victim to the rampant 'improving' vandalism of the 1960s, which cemented (literally) The Kingsway's appearance as the most architecturally humdrum street in Swansea.

The Plaza stood – where Jumpin Jaks and Time&Envy now stand – largely in isolation for much of the 1950s, with nothing but a bomb-site car park stretching from its western wall as far as Dillwyn Street, and the new, dual-carriageway Kingsway (1950) passing in front. The Kingsway was supposed to have been part of a grand processional boulevard linking the town centre with the Guildhall, but the plan was abandoned because scores of buildings in the St Helen's Road region would have had to be demolished. There was, nevertheless, the occasional procession. In the 1950s, we'd pull into the pot-holed car park and sit on the roof of our father's Morris Oxford to watch Chipperfield's or Billy Smart's or Bertram Mills's circus parading through town, the elephants and camels padding by so close that we could smell them.

Of Swansea's dozen or more cinemas, the Plaza was by far the grandest, with its spacious foyer, broad stone staircase, and first-floor, cane-furnished restaurant. Perhaps its greatest novelty was the auditorium's huge glass light, of a floral design; it was set into a shallow dome which changed colour, almost imperceptibly, as the light changed colour.

There's nothing imperceptible about the gunning strobes and razoring lasers on today's Kingsway. The Plaza's long gone, but The Kingsway has been for decades the club-land capital of south-west Wales, with its dozens of nightspots and pubs attracting over 20,000 people on a busy night – although its crown has slipped lately in the direction of Wind Street, leaving some of the venues struggling to fill their dancefloors.

We'll do an east–west tour, with, again, my daughter Branwen as our club-critic guide. Claiming an honorary Kingsway place is Swansea's oldest nightspot, Baron's in College Street, which closed suddenly in 2006. Known first as the Embassy and then the Townsman, it's where Bonnie Tyler was 'discovered', accidentally, by a talent scout who was looking, on the wrong floor of the Townsman, for one Vic Oakley. More recently, Baron's featured in the famous pissing scene in the Swansea-based *noir* fantasy *Twin Town* (1997) and it was popular with soul fans for its 'Funked Up' nights.

The dominant building at the Kingsway's eastern end, with its face tilted away from the street in the direction of some non-existent focal point, is the post-war and self-consciously posh Dragon Hotel. Its ground-floor brasserie used to be the Griffin bar, popular with 'sixties youth, who'd two-time across The Kingsway – in disorderly surges – with the Griffin's arch rival, the Hanbury ('dive'). Branwen and co. often begin their nights on the town at Café Mambo ('nice people run it, and nice people go there'), before heading for the livelier western end of The Kingsway, which begins at its junction with Union Street. Here, opposite a tweedy gentlemen's outfitters called Calders (now an optician's) and upstairs from what's now the Bank of Scotland, used to be the bourgeoisie's premier restaurant, the Burlington, run by stylish Italians who introduced Swansea to wine bottles in raffia baskets, flambéing at the table and veal *à la crème*.

Just off The Kingsway, behind the multi-storey car park, are two clubs "full of pill-heads": Escape (which used to be the Valbonne) and Crow Bar. Opposite, on The Kingsway proper, there are Jumpin Jaks ("Good on Sundays, oldies on Saturdays") and Time&Envy, two distinct venues joined by a door. Time is "full of chavs, spice boys[16] and mingers" while Envy boasts "hotties, good music, strict bouncers". It's on this site, when the Plaza was demolished, that the Top

Rank, surmounted by the Odeon cinema, was built in 1966. It had a glass dance-floor[17] and a revolving stage: while one band performed, the next would be setting up. The Top Rank (later Ritzy's), with its notoriously violent bouncers, was Swansea's biggest rock venue, featuring acts such as the Swinging Blue Jeans, the Merseybeats, The Spencer Davis Group, Amen Corner, Badfinger, Geno Washington and the Ram Jam Band, Police, Squeeze, Siouxsie and the Banshees, Ginger Baker and Rod Stewart, among scores more. There were annual student rag balls there, invariably with half a dozen named bands on the bill, and activities such as 'grab a granny night' and amateur boxing.

The Rank is remembered by many for the tragic death, in 1972, of Les Harvey, lead guitarist with the blues-based Glasgow band Stone the Crows. The electronics on the rock scene in the 'sixties and early 'seventies were often lethally unsafe, and what happened to Les Harvey was all too typical of how a rock musician could suffer electrocution: if you had a guitar in one hand and you made contact with an unearthed microphone with the other, you'd go into spasm and, incapable of letting go of either, your body would be a conduit for the full 240 volts. The trauma to Alex Harvey of his younger brother's death in Swansea seems to have galvanised him like nothing else to revive a faltering career. The manic energy it inspired in him – erupting with astounding, desperate force on the Sensational Alex Harvey Band's second album, *N.E.X.T.* (1974) – made the SAHB the foremost touring band in Europe in the mid 1970s. Alex's own appearance at the Rank in 1974 was reportedly a difficult, emotional occasion for the 'tough guy' from Glasgow[18].

One of the newer, 'honorary Kingsway' clubs at its western end (actually in Dillwyn Street) is Sin City. It opened in 2006 to cater for various tastes. Funked Up, via Baron's and Monkey, gets 'funky and soulful' on Wednesdays. Then there's Face Off ("lots of Emos[19], lots of dope, really good music, sweaty"), imported from Escape, which has "an Indie room, for Indie music, and a metal room for heavy metal: long-hairs, leather, piercings, tattoos" and a mosh pit in which excitable dancers flail their arms, thrash their hair, and shove each other with two-hand shoves, so that people go crashing into each other: "You can be pushing someone like you hate their guts and then dancing with them the next minute."

Opposite Sin City is the last boozer on The Kingsway proper, the music-free Potter's Wheel, popular with those who like to shout their conversations and, like most Wetherspoon houses, as bland as an international airport bar. It was on the pavement outside the Potter's Wheel, in 2004, that one-legged Kalan Kawa Karim, a Kurdish refugee who had survived torture under Saddam Hussein's regime, met his death in a racist attack that later brought thousands of people onto the streets to take part in a massive anti-racism rally.

> windy demo –
> swatted in the face
> by a 'Peace' flag

His killer, a drunken, unemployed panel beater from Bonymaen called Lee Mordecai, was jailed for five years for racially aggravated manslaughter. The attack focused attention on a seam of racism in Swansea which those in authority appear reluctant to acknowledge, but which has sometimes made life a fear-ridden misery for members of ethnic minorities[20] and the small number of refugees who have been granted asylum here[21].

Another serious cause for concern has been the menace of boy racers who have used The Kingsway as a race track, screeching round the roundabouts (now demolished) at either end of the street and sometimes causing serious accidents. The parents of popular nineteen-year-old student Geraint Flynn, from Tycoch, who died after being hit by a car in The Kingsway in 2005, have campaigned, with a petition signed by over 14,000 people, for the street to be closed to traffic at night.

THE WINDSOR LODGE HOTEL

Allen Ginsberg (1926-97) comes to Wales to take part in the UK Year of Literature and Writing 1995. Festival director Sean Doran is driving him out to the exclusive Fairyhill Hotel in Gower, where the staff, on the instructions of Ginsberg's management, have been preparing for the poet a strictly macrobiotic regime.

"Where you taking me?" asks Ginsberg.

"A lovely country hotel on the Gower peninsula," replies Sean.

"I don't want no country hotel, man," says Ginsberg, "I want downtown Swansea."

So downtown Swansea it is. Sean turns the car round and they head for the Windsor Lodge near the bottom of Mount Pleasant, where many of the festival's writers have stayed – but where, Sean fears, there'll be no macrobiotic food on the menu. He needn't have worried. Within minutes of booking in, Ginsberg is tucking into a plateful of cod and chips at the greasy-spoon Pantry café in Swansea market.

Wanting to know about Welsh poetry, Ginsberg invites a few poets to join him for (a surprisingly carnivorous) dinner at the Windsor Lodge. It's lamb for the Geordie poet Tom Pickard, venison for me, veal for Dafydd Rowlands – and steak for Ginsberg. He's heard, vaguely, of *englynion* and *cynghanedd*, and has the names of a couple of poets – Ceiriog and Dic Jones – he'd like to meet. The Beat wizard of free-wheeling open form is curious to find out what these Welsh strict-form guys are up to.

Dafydd, the twice-crowned *prifardd*[22] from Pontardawe (and future Archdruid), explains to Ginsberg that it's a little late in the day for a meeting with Ceiriog (John Ceiriog Hughes; 1832-87), but as for Dic Jones (1934), *dim problem* – and away, the following morning, the bardic carnivores zoom in Dafydd's crimson racer. Dic is not to be found mucking out the cows on his Blaenannerch farm – he's up the road in Aber, in deep session with the *cynganeddwyr*[23]. So on they go to Neuadd Pantycelyn where, you may be sure, a memorable day of *ymryson y beirdd*[24] is had by all. On their way back to Swansea, they swing by Dylan Thomas's grave at Laugharne, where Ginsberg falls to his knees and recites a mantra, while Dafydd keeps an eye out for the police.

That juicy, bloody, fillet steak of Ginsberg's had me puzzled. I'd expected him to be a veggie. "It's true," he said, "that most Buddhists are vegetarians but I adhere to a minority path and eat meat, and we Buddhists who eat meat believe that by taking the flesh of a dead animal into ourselves we enable that animal, through us, to do all sorts of things – make music, write poems, meditate on the cosmos – that on its own it wouldn't have a chance of doing."

One of Swansea's relatively few Georgian houses, Windsor Lodge was built as a villa in the late eighteenth century – in what would then have been an Arcadian setting – for one Edward Hughes, a burly, well-to-do carpenter who was a renowned bully. His many enemies were delighted, therefore, when the man who built the villa for him, one David Burfoot, gave Hughes a thrashing after Hughes attempted to cheat him out of his share of a joint lottery win. Hughes's son Edward, an even bigger thug, was notorious as the British Navy's most formidable cutlass fighter; Nelson invariably chose 'Gallows Ned', as he was known, to lead his cutting-out and boarding parties. A later, more peaceable occupant of Windsor Lodge was Dr William

Hewson, a vicar of Swansea.

It was opened as a hotel in 1970 by Pam and Ron Rumble, hoteliers of vision and flare. "It had been in multiple occupancy and was a wreck," Ron told me. "Although it was one of the most historic houses in Swansea, the council just didn't want to know – we could have driven a bulldozer through it for all they cared. All they wanted listing was the bay tree by the front door." When the council later saw what wonders the Rumbles had worked, they changed their tune and had the building listed as a Grade II.

It was a natural choice as a billet for writers during the Year of Literature. Jimmy Carter (and his two taciturn minders) stayed here, as did, among many others, Count Nikolai Tolstoy, Louis de Bernières, John Heath-Stubbs, Larry Adler, Martha Gellhorn, Adrian Mitchell. There were many loud (or quiet and intense) literary dinners, and hungover literary breakfasts.

One of Pam's most treasured souvenirs is a sketch by Ralph Steadman of Dylan Thomas's daughter Aeronwy. Following an anarchic double-act by Ralph and Adrian Mitchell at the Dylan Thomas Centre during the 1998 Dylan Thomas Festival – to launch their joint publication *Who Killed Dylan Thomas?* – Aeronwy, Ralph, Adrian and friends were stood a meal by festival director Dave Woolley at the Windsor Lodge. While the rest of us were content with the house red, Ralph – who can afford to like good wine – ordered for himself, at his own expense, a £100 bottle of the best red in the cellar. During the meal, Ralph doodled – in biro, red wine and brandy – a caricature of Aeronwy on his cloth napkin, an angular, if hardly flattering, likeness. Then he ordered a second £100-bottle of wine

and, to the waitress's confusion, offered to pay for it with the hotel's own napkin on which he'd been scribbling. The owner was called, but Pam had no hesitation in exchanging that bottle of wine for an original Ralph Steadman.

Wanting to retire from the hotel business, the Rumbles put the Windsor Lodge up for sale. It was very nearly bought as a centre for the Swansea Buddhists (who would doubtless have looked askance at their co-religionist's juicy steak), but it was sold in 2006 to Shelley Ashworth, owner of the Alexander Guest House, Uplands. It continues as a hotel, carnivorous Buddhists welcome.

THE MANSION HOUSE, FFYNONE

"We are making theatre, different theatre from that which we made before," says Paul Davies, co-founder of Swansea's internationally acclaimed Volcano Theatre Company. "How different this is, or where it is leading, may not be questions that we can now answer."

With this restlessly experimental company – pioneering exponents, since their formation in the mid 1980s, of 'physical theatre' – you never know what to expect, apart from the unexpected. From Tony Harrison's *V* to an irreverent deconstruction of *Under Milk Wood*, from a version of *Macbeth*, foetid with the stench of the West murders, to – of all things – Noel Coward's *Private Lives*: by 2006, Volcano had produced twenty-five shows and toured thirty-eight countries, tirelessly stretching the definitions of physical theatre, and occupying territory – with their energy, anger, class and sexual politics, anarchy and occasional histrionics – that is usually startling and uncomfortable.

Tonight, Volcano have taken over the Mansion House in Ffynone, the official residence of the lord mayor of Swansea, for an event whose title, *Reasons to be Silent*, suggests that this may not be the roller-coaster ride of loud, sweaty excess that many have come to expect of the company.

It's yet another damp November night as Margot and I squelch beneath umbrellas up past the soughing pines of St James's Gardens (1897) – a renowned cottaging location – skirting on our left some of Swansea's most opulent nineteenth-century houses, many of them converted to flats, bedsits or offices. Grand town houses give way in Ffynone Road to even grander edifices, fully deserving the appellation 'pile', too big these days for individual ownership and converted to private hospital (the Sancta Maria, formerly the Brunswick), religious institution (the Church of the Holy Name, Mission to the Deaf) or old people's home. Llwyn Helyg, now burnt out and vandalised, is where Margot – Swansea born, New Jersey raised, theology student and jazz-singer-to-be – spent some of her teenage years, living as family in the household of the distinguished poet and

scholar Pennar Davies (1911-96), an old friend of her minister father's. The house was not only the Davieses' home, but the Swansea Memorial College, of which Pennar was principal until his retirement in 1981.

Ffynone is where upper-crust Swansea decamped to after the Burrows were overwhelmed by industrialisation. The area is named after an imposing, early nineteenth-century mansion called Ffynone (demolished c.1960), where Ffynone Close was later developed. The name, from *ffynhonau*, means springs, and the area once abounded with them. Most have been piped and culverted out of sight. But opposite the sad wreckage of Llwyn Helyg, just inside the entrance to the Mansion House's steep and sinuous driveway, is a bushy gap and a cockleshell path that leads to one of the old *ffynhonnau*. It's clogged with vegetation now, but there was clearly a pool here and it's wet enough to host irises and other water-favouring plants.

The asymmetrical and vaguely Gothic Mansion House (1863) was built – as Brooklands House – by William 'Coppernose' Richards for his builder brother, Evan Matthew Richards, who was mayor of Swansea in 1855 and 1862. William Richards was the architect of various prominent buildings, such as the Music Hall (1864), later renamed the Albert Hall. Brooklands became the Mansion House in 1922 when the corporation acquired it as the official residence of the mayor.

Monkey-puzzle trees, palms, cooing pigeons, sloping lawns: in summer, it's known for garden parties and fundraising dos, with strawberries and cream, chilled wine and Bucks Fizz. There's a sundial on the terrace and two six-pounder brass cannon. These weather-greened guns were commissioned by local merchants and ship owners, in 1804, to defend the harbour against possible attack by the French.

Other functions at the Mansion House include business breakfasts, coffee mornings, afternoon teas, cheese and wine evenings, municipal receptions and VIP banquets. But the lord mayor rarely chooses to reside there these days. It's a distinctly unlived in, rattling shell of a building. All the more suitable, therefore, for Volcano's purposes. They want us to explore the house, calling up our own memories of the places we have lived in, and populating its rooms and corridors with ghosts of our own.

The front door is opened to us by a softly spoken young Irishman who tells us he's the butler. It's true, he says, as we fifteen or so punters gather in the cloakroom, that the lord mayor is not in residence, but 'Sir Toby' is having a dinner party, and he'd like us all, therefore, to remain silent throughout our visit. The cloakroom, where each of us picks up a plan of the house, a head-harness torch and a CD walkman, is the only lighted part of the building. We are to make our way round the house from one numbered location to another, in any order we like, listening to corresponding numbered track on our CDs. We have an hour.

In the dining room, a very youthful Sir Toby, in fustian tweeds, sits alone and statuesquely still, half way down a long table set with white cloth and gleaming cutlery and glasses. At his side, a maidservant languidly polishes a silver knife. They are still thus engaged when we drop in on them an hour later.

In the drawing room, there's a grand piano, an ornate silver elephant and various works of art on loan from the Glynn Vivian, including two distinctive views of the bay by Grant Murray. Next door, a bunch of students, each plugged into a walkman, are silently dancing. Of more interest is a rogue's gallery, in caricature, of past mayors, several of whom, such as Gerald Murphy and Sidney Jenkins, passed many a moon behind the bars of a rather less distin-guished Victorian pile, for various municipal 'misjudgements'.

We pass through the kitchen to the cellar door. The voice on the walkman reminds us that, for many, 'cellar door' is one of the most beautiful sounds in the English language. Down in the cellar, which is entirely devoid of clutter, "we do not need words, however they sound …" But we get them anyway, live, from both Paul Davies and Volcano's mercurial co-founder Fern Smith, she of the captivating sea-deep eyes. No blue eyes tonight, though. Fern, in a long, filth-dusted dress, and Paul, in a similarly dishevelled naval jacket, are both blindfolded, the prisoners of a corpsed marriage, "our twenty-five years of misery", locked in a Strindbergian dialogue of torturous circularity.

On then towards the first floor, up the mahogany staircase dominated by a huge stained-glass window celebrating the Richards family. In a twin bedroom there's a film, projected onto the carpet, of a child's hand drawing houses, while various children's voices fantasise about their dream homes. We are barred by 'no entry' signs from some of the rooms, but one, numbered 14, with a sign specifically forbidding entry, is not quite closed. I push it open and enter. This seems to be more intimately the lord mayor's living room, with photos on the mantelpiece of the current incumbent Chris Holley and family.

When our hour's done, we return the torches and walkmans to the cloakroom. The butler presents each of us with a souvenir – a nugget of fire-blackened brick, which he says is a fragment of the building's foundation stone – before he bows us out into the drizzling dark.

notes

1 Conran, Tony, *Castles*, Gomer Press, 1993.
2 A *cwrw bach* was a drinking den to which you brought your own beer.
3 Another dual-purpose building is Mumbles Methodist Church, with a café and tourist information centre on the ground floor and a chapel above.
4 At least women were allowed into the Labour Club at the Elysium. The Labour Club in Wind Street maintained an all-male rule until the 1980s.
5 This (unsubstantiated) story has also been associated with the Garibaldi and the Builders.
6 Subsequently renamed Bar,Co.
7 Older = 18 to 35.
8 Renamed yet again, after our walk, as Reflex The 80's Bar.
9 Old = 40+.
10 The oldest pub is the Cross Keys.
11 "This is not a pipe'"
12 Both saint and satan are moving on this cement.
13 "What's this holes business?" I've sometimes been asked. Count yours, starting with the eyes and working down.
14 Lasting from 1980 until 1997, it was the world's longest-running ban on the film. On hearing that the ban had been lifted, the Pythons' Eric Idle commented mischievously "What a shame. Is nothing sacred?'
15 Caesar hasn't a clue what's going on.
16 Spice boys:"one diamond earring, perfect hair, vain, tight jeans, shoes not trainers, tight shirt, pink polo shirt'.
17 Said to be the first in Britain.
18 Alex Harvey died in 1982, a day short of his 47th birthday.
19 Emos: "peroxide blonde, side-swept hair, skinny jeans, dark eyes, dope-heads, tend to cut themselves, suicidal despairing music".
20 The English, of course, constitute Swansea's largest ethnic minority, but they seem not to be included in official statistics that show that less than two per cent of Swansea's population come from an ethnic minority.
21 In the 2005 general election, 770 people in the Swansea East constituency voted for the BNP.

22 Literally 'chief poet', a title bestowed on winners of the chair or crown at the National Eisteddfod.

23 Poets who write in Welsh strict metres.

24 Bardic contest.

EAST

KILVEY HILL

"The town and harbour are overhung by a lofty green mountain," George Borrow (1803-81) observed of Kilvey in the mid nineteenth century. It would not be green for much longer. The fumes belching from the industries below – some 2,325,000 cubic feet of sulphuric acid a day were being released into the air – soon poisoned its vegetation and turned its western flanks more or less black. Although black and barren they have seemed to remain, that appearance from down in the town is deceptive. Climb Kilvey's modest (for a 'mountain') 200 m – which few Swansea people have ever attempted – and you'll be astonished not only by the finest panoramic views that the city affords but also by the wealth and variety of the hill's flora and fauna. On Kilvey's relatively uncontaminated eastern half there are well-tended fields on which horses, sheep and cattle graze – within less than a mile, as the red kite flies, of the sirens and snarl-ups of the city centre.

Before the authorities clamped down on the dumping and burning of old or stolen cars, you used to be able to drive bumpily to Kilvey's summit using Morris Lane, one of Swansea's most ancient thoroughfares. Once known as Heol Meuric, and established possibly two thousand years ago, if not earlier, the track is thought to have been used by the Romans as a route through what is now Bonymaen. Although barriers these days deny four-wheeled access to Morris Lane, it nevertheless offers pedestrians the most straightforward route to the top. Stretches of it have been concreted in recent decades, shoe prints and graffiti having been inscribed in the cement before it dried. You can make out, for instance, 'Fern child' and 'Budgie', the latter suggesting a date for the concreting in the early 1970s, when the Cardiff heavy-metal band were at the height of their popularity.

But, as Heol Meuric implies, Kilvey has a venerable history. There are three Bonze Age tombs on its summit; in 1968, a fragment of Iron Age or Roman era pottery was found in a small defended enclosure; and – as Cilfái – the hill in medieval times was at the heart of an extensive Welsh lordship lying outside the Norman town. Hopcyn ap Tomos of Cilfái, whose great library was praised by Dafydd y Coed, one of the last of the Poets of the Princes, made bitter complaint here in the fourteenth century that the Welsh were "suffering pain … and exile in their native land".

One of several pedestrian routes up Kilvey – which Margot and I take one overcast August afternoon – involves, initially, following an east–west track which begins in St Thomas, where Headland Road meets Granville Road, and which runs parallel with Fabian Way. It was once the line of the railway that was constructed to carry Pennant sandstone from quarries along the southern face of Kilvey to build the new harbour piers in the early years of the nineteenth century. It descends to intersect with St Illtyd's Crescent in Danygraig, before

veering uphill, rough and rubbly, through the forestry. We zigzag steeply upwards, now and then cutting straight up along foot-worn pathways through the heather; there are butterflies everywhere.

Tithe maps of the 1840s show the entire hill divided into fields. Some remain, although many, with their jumps, makeshift stables and jacketed hunters, have become horsy playgrounds. We climb up past the fields of Dan y Beacon farm on a plateau halfway up the hill and emerge through scrub at the summit. Here, in a grassy clearing surrounded by firs, is a *twmp* topped with ruined stonework. This is all that remains of the *bigwrn* or beacon which for long was assumed – wrongly, it seems – to have been a tower windmill. It was erected probably in the seventeenth century and must still have been a landmark in the early twentieth when the poet Edward Thomas (1878-1917) made the climb: "… some money has been spent on making the old round windmill tower, towards the seaward and green end of Kilvey Hill, impervious to weather, boys, and the few dirty-faced cows of those pastures," he wrote. "The seats round the windmill tower are a little worn, but I never saw anyone there, nor met anyone who had been there."

The beacon – once visible to mariners from the Tusker Rock to Lundy – has been usurped as a landmark by three telecommunications masts situated a short distance to the west, adjacent to a viewpoint which is where today's visitor will find seats. Approaching the viewpoint through the hilltop's soughing firs, we realise at last what has been the source of the heavily amplified pop music wafting our way on the climb up: pre-match music at the brand new White Rock stadium (shortly to be renamed Liberty) under the lee of the hill. By now, the match is well under way. We can hear the crowd cheering. One particularly thunderous roar as we reach the viewpoint surely betokens a goal for the home side. We learn later that the Swans, desperate for a win in the inaugural match at their new home, have beaten Tranmere Rovers 1–0, in front of some 17,000 fans.

Because of the fir trees, Kilvey's panoramic splendours cannot be savoured in their entirety from any single spot – unless you're an engineer up one of the masts. You have to move around. From the viewpoint itself, you can look east to Baglan and Port Talbot (where, they say in post-industrial Swansea, every cloud has a sulphur lining); south over St Thomas, the docks and the Severn Sea to the Devonshire coast and Exmoor; south west to Mumbles, the headlands of Langland, Caswell and Pwlldu, and Gower's defining ridge of Cefn Bryn; west to Carmarthen Bay, the Pembrokeshire coast and the Preselis; and north west, over the retail sheds of the Lower Swansea Valley, the terraces of Landore and the DVLA monstrosity at Clase to the Bannau of Carmarthenshire. For the view to the north east, you need to stand at the eastern edge of the forestry, near the beacon's ruins. Crymlyn Bog is hidden from view by the grassy brow of the hill, but the estuary of the river Nedd is to be seen, and then, further inland, peaks such as Fan Gyhyrich, Fan Nedd and Fan Fawr stretching towards a horizon which, in the nineteenth century, would have been hazy with columns of smoke pouring skyward from Merthyr Tydfil and Dowlais nearly 40 kilometres distant.

There's the low hum of generators as we pass by the masts behind their spiky stockade and head west towards the steep, quarried edge that overhangs the river, the Hafod and High Street station. The vegetation here, struggling to reassume the blighted, slaggy land, is scrubby grass and heather. The ghost of a long-abandoned field is marked by low, degraded banks which were once hedgerows. Nearby is what is surely a shallow bomb crater. This could have resulted from the first occasion – the afternoon of 27 June, 1940 – that high-explosive bombs landed on Kilvey, or from subsequent attacks when bombs intended for the town or the docks fell harmlessly on the hill.

It was reportedly during the third of the 'Three Nights Blitz' – 21 February, 1941 – that local Home Guardsmen noticed a hand torch being used as a signal from the brow of Kilvey, apparently to guide enemy planes towards the docks. By the time they reached the top, they could make out the fifth-columnist running away down the northern incline. The guardsmen opened fire, but he managed to dodge their bullets. They obviously scared him, though, as no further signals were seen from Kilvey.

We descend gradually along the western and apparently blackest side of 'black' Kilvey, passing through a lush density of mainly deciduous trees – which might surprise those below who see only gaunt, post-industrial aridity when they gaze up at the hill. Thousands of these trees, however, have been reduced to ashen phantoms by recent fires, vandalism being a major threat to Kilvey's wildlife. Conservationists have recently lamented the "wanton savagery" of those responsible, in separate incidents, for beating badgers to death with spades, digging foxes from their earths, killing the vixens and throwing their cubs to dogs, and shooting buzzards and red kites. In the summer of 2005, someone's pet dog was tethered to a tree on Kilvey and left to die; it was reported to have "melted" in the heat.

Kilvey seems oddly unloved by the people of Swansea. Off-road (and usually unlicensed) bikers in their flashy helmets, deafened and deafening as they hither and thither blatter and blare, appear to be the hill's only regular visitors. Plans surface now and then for making more of the hill. Why not, for instance, a cable car from St Thomas to the summit? An interpretation centre? A revolving restaurant? In 1994, some bright spark of a graphic designer proposed for the summit a huge and hideous statue of Swansea's supposed founder, Sweyn the Viking, which would be as tall as the Statue of Liberty and "put Swansea on the map". Frequent calls since then for us to have our own Angel of the North may yet see Swansea – given the habitual aesthetic insensibilities of the city fathers and mothers – claiming a conspicuous place on some map of monumental follies.

CRYMLYN

Two very different natural habitats – bog and burrows – are neighbours here, separated from each other by a 600m-wide strip of firmer ground which has been consolidated by human activity: the Tennant Canal, railway lines, industry, housing, oil storage tanks (until recently) and Fabian Way, the A483 dual carriageway that's the eastern gateway to the city (it used to be known as the Jersey Marine). All three distinct environments are founded, nevertheless, on a single prehistoric peat bed.

The boundary between Swansea and Neath Port Talbot runs roughly down the middle of the 280-ha bog, ceding to Neath Port Talbot, as it approaches the coast, most of Crymlyn's human settlement, despite the fact that many people living in the community of Crymlyn Burrows tend to identify primarily with Swansea. The area's Swansea focus was highlighted in 2005 when the 47-year-old twins John and Huw Thomas opened their ambitious 1940s Swansea Bay Museum in a former Shell Oil office block at Baldwins Crescent. Four years in the planning, the museum's purpose is to tell the story of the impact of the Second World War on Swansea's civilian life. The air raids, the blackouts, the devastation, the rationing, the end-of-war street parties – including the experience of rock cakes, dried egg, Camp coffee and Spam sandwiches – are regularly recreated at the Thomases' museum.

Crymlyn Burrows people have often considered themselves 'forgotten Swansea', having had to put up with the sewage works, sulphurous smells from the oil tanks, the Tir John rubbish tip, the troubled waste incinerator plant and a depot, on the old tank-farm site, for tens of thousands of pipes for the controversial Milford Haven to Gloucester gas pipeline. But two hundred years ago fashionable Swansea would flock to Crymlyn Burrows for the Swansea races which were held on a two-mile long, circular course – on land where the Visteon car parts factory now stands. Swansea's first cricket matches were played here too, from about the 1770s, and in hard winters the skating club would take to the ice, to perform slithery quadrilles to the strains of the rebeck.

If Crymlyn's attractions seem curiosities of the past, it's probably because few of those bowling urgently along Fabian Way have ever thought of getting out of their cars to take a closer look.

The burrows, south of Fabian Way, are a significant fragment of

the 35km belt of golden dunes that, prior to the industrial revolution, fringed Swansea Bay, from Blackpill in the west to Ogmore in the east. An extraordinary quantity of sand is on the move here. One tidal cycle, in stormy conditions, can shift over 230,000 tonnes of it, contributing in time to the relentless seaward expansion of the dunes. A hundred years ago, the sea came right up to the road's edge. But now it's over half a kilometre away – and invisible from the road. The burrows are a Site of Special Scientific Interest bordering a magnificent, if largely ignored, four-kilometre stretch of beach.

It was sand, during the great sandstorms of the thirteenth and fourteenth centuries, that finally shut the sea out of the 4.5-km marshy inlet that became Crymlyn bog, which is flanked by Kilvey Hill to the west and the 26-m Lousy Hill to the east (so called because it was once 'lousy' with rabbits). From a distance, the 1.5-km wide basin's vegetation, uniformly blonde in winter, apart from the odd alder copse, looks like a heath you could walk across. But you'd soon be in trouble. What might appear from a distance to be bleached couch grass is composed largely of shoulder-high reeds in a treacherous swamp, negotiable only by those with expert knowledge. With the adjoining Pant-y-Sais basin, it forms the biggest expanse of lowland fen in Wales, and is a National Nature Reserve rich in natural treasures, among them rare sedges, a rare species of raft spider, *Dolomedes fimbriatus*, and rare birds such as the water rail, Cetti's warbler and the reed warbler.

The closest you can safely get to the bog is a kilometre-long, circular trail established on its western edge at the interpretation centre just off the Pentre-dŵr–Port Tennant road. Bog Road, as it's known, is the domain of two rather different classes of rider: the Bonymaen scrambler-bike boys, roaring around in full robot-like gear, and an aspiring equestrian class, with their horsy homesteads, blanketed steeds in muddy paddocks, and makeshift stables. A couple of inquisitive, mud-caked nags follow us as we slip, squelch and slide – wellies essential in winter – around the trail.

The fen is basically a raft of vegetation over deep, soft mud. Upon an ancient foundation of prehistoric peat, a secondary thickness of peat has accreted – to a depth of up to 4.5 m. Some of the peat feels grounded underfoot, but some of it wobbles ominously, like a jelly. Surveyors have described sticking poles in the fibrous crust, only to find them meeting no resistance after about 30 cm.

No place to visit alone, the bog is an eerie, mysterious environment. A hundred or so metres off our trail, and half submerged, is an abandoned stone shed. Sticking out elsewhere are the remains of piles which once supported a railroad carrying stone from Kilvey for the construction of the King's Dock. To build anything here would seem a futile ambition, but still to be traced is the line of the Glan-y-wern (or Red Jacket) Canal built in 1790 to ferry coal to the river Nedd. Our trail takes us over its northern end. Later, we walk along the towpath – from Jersey Marine to Port Tennant – of the Tennant Canal (1854), with which the Glan-y-wern merges at the southern edge of the bog.

Odd fragments of stonework protruding from the reeds tend to fuel the legend that the bog hides the engulfed remains of a great city – the first Swansea. Once a river valley, much of the basin was probably a lake before it clogged up with silt and vegetation. In the late eighteenth century, it was known as Cors (bog) Crym Llyn (lake), with Crym (from *crymu*, to bow) suggesting that it may once have been a site of druidical worship. Certainly, some of the names around the bog are evocative. The low promontory on its east side known as Gelli'r Allor (promontory of the altar). Pwll Conan (Conan's pool), where a warrior grandson of Rhys ap Tewdwr, king of Deheubarth[1], was drowned in the eleventh century. The ruins of the ancient Capel St Margaret (to the east of Gelli'r Allor), where hiring fairs were held before they were moved to Neath.

It seems incongruous that such a numinous and internationally important wetland should be dominated at its southern end by the plateau of a massive municipal rubbish dump. The 40-ha Tir John 'landfill' operation splurges over the site of the former Tir John North power station (c.1935-76) whose generating capacity – 40 megawatts – was so formidable for its time that it was known throughout Britain simply as Sir John; it produced the cheapest electricity in Britain. The city's only dump, Tir John was closed in 2005 by the Environment Agency, owing to water pollution concerns. The council was then forced to spend an extra £2.5m a year[2] transporting nearly 120,000 tonnes of Swansea's waste to Pwllfawatkin at Pontardawe, Trecatti near Merthyr, and Withey Hedge in Pembrokeshire (a further 31,000 tonnes of waste being recycled in Swansea). But in 2007, the Environment Agency case was overturned and the council prepared to carry on dumping at Tir John for another ten years.

DOCKS, EASTSIDE

There are three linked docks on the east side of the Tawe – the Prince of Wales, the King's and the Queen's, each one edging progressively seaward – whose construction, from 1879 onwards, obliterated a natural inlet known as Fabian's Bay. It's ironic that Fabian Way, Swansea's noisy and polluting eastern approach, should have been named after what must once have been an idyllic spot, comparable to one of rural Gower's inlets.

The bay took its name from the family of one Daniel Fabian who came from Llanrhidian in 1639 to farm at Glanybad Farm (or Tir Lan y Bad) at St Thomas. Their farmhouse, a useful landmark for vessels making their way to the natural 'harbour of refuge', soon became known as Fabian's house; it was demolished in 1850. Another local landmark, towards the eastern extremity of the inlet, was the Salthouse, where salt was evaporated from sea water (as at Port Eynon's Salthouse, still partially extant). It was from here – Salthouse Point – that Swansea's first eastern pier was constructed, in a westerly direction, between about 1805 and 1809. A shorter west pier was constructed towards it, from Black Point on the other side of the bay (roughly where the South Dock would later connect with the Tawe), the two piers converging in a pincer-like movement. Apart from a 70-m gap between the pier-heads, Fabian's Bay was now an enclosed and sheltered lying-up place for ships, although its operation as a harbour was still severely constrained by the tides. With today's very much longer piers thrusting straight out to sea, it's difficult to imagine the shape of the long-vanished Fabian's Bay – until you take note of a cracked, house-sized platform of dressed stone sitting forlornly in the river a short distance upstream from where, until late 2006, the Swansea–Cork Superferry used to dock. This, remarkably, is the original, 200-year-old east pier-head, its tip facing west and suggesting therefore the very different direction of its thrust from that of the modern piers. Stranded by a Victorian slipway that cut through the old pier, the pier-head served, until the 1920s, as a platform for the harbour's one-o'clock gun.

Had the Swansea Harbour Trust, anxious about the growing incapacity of the westside docks, co-operated with George Tennant and developed his 'shipping place' at the eastern end of Fabian's Bay, they'd have found a fitting site for eastside expansion. But by the time the trustees were ready to act, much of the site had been sold to the Lambert family for a copper-ore smelting plant, and there was almost

no space left. The new dock, therefore, would take up much of Port Tennant and the whole of Fabian's Bay, some of which had already been reclaimed by material excavated when the Tawe was redirected along the New Cut.

Work started – in 1879 – much later than it should have, with the specifications being based on data that were almost ten years out of date. It was, nevertheless, a formidable undertaking. Crowds flocked daily to watch the three hundred men who were employed round the clock – with four great 'steam navvies' and a crane grab – to scoop out vast tonnages of earth, stone and clay. A temporary dock-building culture was established on site, involving coffee shanties and religious services in a meeting house provided for the workers. It was officially opened as the Prince of Wales Dock on 18 October 1881 – by the Prince of Wales, with the Princess of Wales at his side (they would become King Edward VII and Queen Alexandra): Swansea's entire population of 76,000 turned out for the event. (Later that day, the princess gave her name to Alexandra Road.) The dock wasn't ready for shipping, however, until June 1882: the first vessel to use it was a scrap-metal smack called the *Atlas* which, certain wags opined, should have been called the *At Last*, in keeping with the inordinate amount of time it had taken to complete the project.

An easterly extension finished in 1898 increased the dock's capacity by fifty per cent, making it one of the largest in Britain, with 180,000 sq m of warehouse capacity and 32 km of railway track surrounding it. The 11-ha Prince of Wales Dock enabled Swansea – crucially – to export tinplate directly to America, without needing to send it via Liverpool: by 1913, Swansea was shipping out more

tinplate, terneplate and blackplate than any other port in the world. Other cargoes at the Prince of Wales included pig iron, scrap iron, pit props, timber, grain and general merchandise. Coal was exported from the northern quay, where there was also a sand and gravel wharf. The coal hoists were dismantled in 1987, and by 2006, when the dock's SA1 transformation was well under way, the sole, occasional visitor to the Prince of Wales was the *City of Cardiff* dredger, with sand for United Marine Aggregates.

As industry boomed and steamships grew ever larger, it was clear that Swansea needed yet more dock space. July 1904 saw Edward back in town (this time as king), to lift the first sod, on the foreshore, of the 28-ha King's Dock. About 160-ha of Swansea Bay were reclaimed to build the dock which, opening in 1909, more than doubled the port's capacity.

A further bulge into the bay resulted in the biggest of Swansea's docks, the Queen's. It was opened by Queen Mary in 1920, primarily to serve British Petroleum's oil refinery at Llandarcy[3] 8 km away, Britain's first major oil refinery (it opened in 1922). With facilities to pump oil directly to or from the refinery, the Queen's Dock gave a much-needed boost to the post-war port's fortunes.

Access to all three docks is through a lock that links the river mouth to the King's Dock, with communication passages 21 m and 30.5 m wide respectively leading to the Prince of Wales and the Queen's docks. The port can no longer receive the world's largest ships, as the lock cannot accommodate vessels much over the 23,000 gross tonnes mark.

In Swansea's maritime heyday, there could be scores of ships massed in the bay, waiting to enter the port. Often enough, these days, there isn't a single freighter to be seen in any of the docks. The Queen's decline began after 1970, when Llandarcy's crude-oil imports were transferred to Milford Haven, with a pipeline connecting both places. Now, following the recent cessation of BP's activities at Baglan (as well as at Llandarcy), the Queen's Dock is bereft of both ships and plans for the future.

Jon Rees, Associated British Port's safety manager, drove me one afternoon from his headquarters near the lock all the way round the King's and the Queen's docks to the east pier, site of one of Swansea's newer landmarks, a wind 43-m high turbine – which, say its critics, is incapable of powering more than a few kettles. It's a 5.6-km journey that takes you, on the southern side of the Queen's, along what is probably the straightest stretch of road in Swansea: there's no other vehicle in sight in this post-industrial wasteland, but a strict 30 m.p.h. still applies. Jon points out a curious wedge-shaped chunk of wall made of copper-slag blocks: a preserved section of blast wall from a refuge bunker erected in the Second World War. Dotted along the sea wall at regular intervals are three well-preserved wartime pillboxes. I clamber up onto the roof of one of them to take in the magnificent

length of virgin beach that stretches four kilometres from the docks to the estuary of the river Nedd. Gone, since 2005, are the dozens of oil storage tanks at the eastern end of the dock that used to lend such an acrid tang to the air as you drove past Crymlyn Burrows. This area now, with its spectacular panorama, is surely ripe for development. An extension of SA1, perhaps? An additional or replacement site for the university, which seems to be so short of space that there's been talk lately of it moving to Llanelli or thrusting out, Dubai-style, into the bay? Watch this space.

The last of Swansea's dry docks closed in 1999. The only dock with any significant commercial activity is the King's. This afternoon there's just one ship moored there, the *Atsuta*, loading coils of Port Talbot steel for China, but there are other cargoes awaiting transportation: coal from Tower and Celtic Energy; timber for Finland (strangely); a twinkling mountain of recycled glass for Spain (surely I recognised one or two old Rioja bottles?); used plant from BP Baglan on its way to India. A huge timber warehouse has just been completed at Robert's Road (its long, silvery roof becoming another landmark) and ABP have just invested in a £1.8m fertilizer warehouse on the Graigola Wharf – which is also where Swansea's 200-tonne lock gates are overhauled.

There are six gates in active service in the main lock, and four spares, each gate having to be removed for refurbishment every five years. That this is a mighty undertaking for the crane barge *Mersey Mammoth* – which recently failed, initially, to lift one of the gates – is all too apparent when you behold these magnificent, rust-red leviathans reclining in the sun on their wooden chocks. I tell my guide that their significance to the economy of Swansea prompts me to recast a famous poem by William Carlos Williams: "so much depends / upon // a red lock / gate …" "Everything," says Jon, "absolutely everything."

At the eastern end of the King's Dock, near a protrusion known as the Mole, is a compound which, from Fabian Way, looks like a giant toddler's playground, crammed with tops and toys of every hue. This, Trinity House's western headquarters (Harwich covers the east), is where, every five years on a rotational basis, the 484 warning buoys of southern Britain's western seaboard are brought for repair and repainting. Trinity House's 'west coast manager' is Andy Lamnea who was born a Swansea man thanks to a happy accident in the 1840s: a Greek seaman happened to be on board one of two ships that collided at Swansea, both of which were then confined to port for repairs; the Greek sailor, kicking his heels around town, fell for a Swansea girl – and soon enough life began to wind its way towards Andy Lamnea.

In addition to old-fashioned fog bells, most buoys – red for port, green for starboard ¬¬– are equipped with solar panels, lights and 'Raycon' radar systems, Andy explains. Many buoys carry the evocative names of wrecks or locations: Ten Feet Bank, Eel Point, Mount Mopus, Peverit Ledges, James Egan Layne, Prince Ivanhoe (the motor cruiser beached at Horton in 1981). In the repair sheds, across the way from the compound, the buoys are stripped of barnacles and old paint by high-pressure water jets, and their superstructures are blasted to the bare metal in an iron-grit bombardment chamber. Three green buoys are lined up outside ready for shipping to Sri Lanka, which lost many of its buoys to the 2004 tsunami. Moored nearby at the Mole is a divested lightship, awaiting a new lease of life as a floating restaurant, perhaps, or as a re-equipped lightship in some developing country.

The western seaboard, wilder by far than the eastern, has 54 operational lighthouses, which are looked after from Swansea (Harwich services 18). Maintaining the fabric of the lighthouses is the most demanding aspect of the operation, many of them having been built in the 1870s. Although serious, life-guarding work is Trinity House's *raison d'être*, it's gratifying to note that that sense of play suggested by initial 'tops and toys' impressions is not entirely misplaced. Most establishments desirous of augmenting their dignity with cannon generally plonk one either side of the main portico – not so Trinity House, Swansea, whose portakabin h.q. has a single canon trained directly on the front door, with a wooden mannequin poised to do the explosive honours and a dragon-design cowling over the cannon's mouth which reads 'Welsh and thirsty'.

Passing the coal wharf at the north-east end of the King's Dock, I note the names of Swansea's underemployed tug fleet: *Sea Endeavour, Garibaldo, Yewgarth, Hurricane H, Shireen S, Battleaxe*.

Few Swansea people get this close to the life of the docks. All traffic has to pass through a checkpoint near the eastern end of the Prince of Wales Dock, and if you don't have legitimate business in the docks, you don't get through. You'll catch a glimpse if heading for the Cork ferry or joining the *Waverley* or *Balmoral* for a cruise, but otherwise the docks are a no-go area – increasingly so since '9/11' and the ensuing 'war on terror'. Even the anglers who, until 2006, used to fish from the east pier and breakwater have been refused access – "for health and safety reasons", say ABP.

SA1

The £450m SA1 project – which makes a big fuss of itself at the eastern gateway to the city, with banners, fancy landscaping and a frenzy of building activity – will take until about 2014 to complete.

SA1 (the area's postcode) is at the forefront of the National Assembly's plan to boost the burgeoning watersports sector by 40%, increasing the sector's annual contribution to the Welsh economy to £224m by 2010. SA1's 400-berth marina, in the 11-ha Prince of Wales Dock, will nearly double the city's mooring capacity, bringing the total number of berths to over 1000, and making Swansea, in terms of capacity, the sailing capital of Wales and one of the largest sailing centres in Britain.

The 40.47-ha of land around the dock, semi derelict until recently or the site of light industrial concerns and building suppliers, are in the process of sprouting tree-lined boulevards, streets

and squares, with apartment blocks and houses, underground and multi-storey car parking, offices, businesses, bars, restaurants, a church, extensive leisure and marine facilities, and public art. "SA1 represents an extension eastward of the city centre," project surveyor Leigh Jenkins told me. "Everything you could want for living and working here will be provided, so that in theory you'd never have to leave, if you didn't want to."

By the late 1980s, Swansea's transformed Maritime Quarter was attracting international awards and setting a possible precedent for the increasingly run-down dockland on the other side of the Tawe, across which the spoils of freshly affluent Swansea had so far failed to find a way. The challenge was how to use the sea and the river to unite a city long divided between smug middle-class west and working-class east.

Nothing much happened until 2003 when, seemingly overnight, Swansea found itself with a startling new landmark, visible for miles, the architecturally exuberant Sail Bridge for pedestrians and cyclists. Designed by Wilkinson Eyre Architects (who gave the Geordies their famous 'winking eye' bridge in Gateshead) and crossing the Tawe just south of the New Cut Bridge, it surprised everyone and delighted most. What was all this about? Swansea didn't do 'modern', preferring the cosy familiarity of the outmoded, the second-hand and the make-do-and-mend. The £2m Sail Bridge, with its 42-metre mast, was intended as a fanfare of revolutionary intent, trumpeting the inauguration of the SA1 Swansea waterfront development, declaring the project's unabashed contemporaneity and proposing an end to the historic east/west divide.

Daring variety rather than harmonisation of style seems to be the guiding principle with some of the more adventurous architecture, although much of the development looks all too predictably like Swindon-by-the-Sea. Three historic buildings are being painstakingly adapted for new uses. The delightful Norwegian Seamen's Church, which moved from Newport in 1910 to a site at the entrance to the docks, has been rebuilt (2003-04) on a site at the heart of SA1. It was stored for a while in the second of these refurbished buildings, the so-called J-Shed (all dockside warehouses are named alphabetically), which has been a grain warehouse, a fish market and a general store. Its northern end was bombed in the war: repair work can be identified by discrepancies in the brick-

work and by the flatness of some ground-floor ceilings, whereas those in the undamaged portion are shallowly vaulted. Among the restaurant and bar businesses to move into the ground-floor is La Parilla, an off-shoot of Wind Street's La Brasseria. The upper floor has been converted into twenty New York-style loft apartments.

The third building, with its distinctive chimney stack, is the old Ice House, at the eastern end of the Sail Bridge. Earmarked as a fish restaurant, this unusual building – one of only two in Britain (Grimsby has the other) – is a reminder that fishing is the oldest of all Swansea's industries, apart from coalmining. It was built in the 1880s as an ice-making factory for the fishing industry, and it is believed that the freezing floor is still there beneath a later floor. Extended in about 1897, when Swansea was a major deep-fishing port, it became a chandlery in 1926 and then a flag-making factory.

There will be 65,000 sq m of business and office space to fill eventually, and the developers seem confident that the demand is there. They are similarly up-beat about the demand for SA1's 2,000 flats and houses. When Bellway's Altamar apartments first went on the market such was the demand, before even a pile had been driven, that prospective buyers camped out for three days in the hope of bagging a flat, at prices ranging from £125,000 for a one-bedroom property to £195,000 for a two-bedroom.

The rising prices of flats in SA1 are said to have driven up Swansea house prices as a whole – from an average of £55,000 in 2000 to £127,000 in 2007. Are the people of St Thomas on the verge of being priced out of their locality – as many have been built out of their views across the bay by SA1's higher risers, the tallest of which will be 19 storeys high? Or might SA1 succeed in dissolving the old east/west divide, only for the eastside to develop its own internal, north/south divide, between working-class St Thomas, Danygraig and Port Tennant, north of Fabian Way, and the chic moneyed enclave south of that thoroughfare? I asked a couple of St Thomas lads fishing in the dock what kinds of fish they caught here. "All sorts," said one, "but the fishing's not what it was, not since they started all … this," he sneered. "You don't approve of SA1, then?" "Certainly bloody don't. It's a place for rich people, innit? It'll just make more places for robbing and crime."

Like many Swansea people, I'm looking forward to drinking an espresso on the waterfront terraces of SA1, which seems likely to become the most attractive café quarter in the whole of Wales. SA1 may have become the city's trendiest address, but what may not be appreciated by many of those moving into its balconied duplexes is that they share a postcode with some of the poorest communities in Wales. It will take more than Swansea's belated saunter down the seaside path to cure the social ills of Bonymaen, Mayhill and Townhill, let alone those of similarly straitened communities beyond the confines of SA1.

Perhaps, in this time of global warming, those older communities on higher ground have got the best of it after all. The SA1 development is on a flood plain: it won't be much use after a few metres' rise in sea-level.

SEWAGE WORKS, FABIAN WAY

'No shit works here' was the ambiguous slogan on a placard once brandished near the site of Swansea's new sewage-works-to-be – or the Waste Water Treatment Works, as Welsh Water were keen to euphemise their 'no nuisance', 'flagship', 'odourless' plant. Having suffered for years the smells and filth of the Carbon Black works, the Tir John tip and, more recently, the incinerator, the coaling wharf and the huge cargoes of ammonia nitrate transported through the docks, the residents of St Thomas, particularly those of Port Tennant, were disinclined to take to their long-suffering bosoms the thousand or more litres-a-second of faecal gunge that Welsh Water were planning to funnel exclusively in their direction.

No one in Swansea wanted to see a continuation of the practice of pumping the city's raw sewage into the sea off Mumbles Head, and Surfers Against Sewage had been campaigning since 1990 for a full sewage treatment system. The campaign rallied massive public support and, as Welsh Water became the first water company in Britain to adopt a policy of full treatment for all coastal and estuarine discharges, Swansea was promised a 'space-age' treatment works, at a site near the eastern end of the docks, which would be second to

none[4]. But few in St Thomas believed Welsh Water's reassuring blandishments. They doubtless envisioned their maritime landscape being taken over by acres of sludge lagoons, filtration beds and men with forks pronging putrid mounds of bogroll, tampons, STs and condoms.

This, as things turned out, is not the sight that greets you at the city's eastern gateway. Fabian Way, rising from more or less sea level, yields a view, to the south-west, of the docks and the bay and Mumbles Head beyond. Immediately to your left, is a hill-like oasis of grass, flowers, shrubs and trees, surmounted by two futuristic white funnels either side of an observation pod like the bridge of a ship. This bosky ridge is the sewage works – or its roof. The works entrance, approached by a road running through the docks, is on the other side of the 'hill'.

That 'no shit works here' does indeed seem to be the case as I enter the deserted reception area. It was rumoured when the £90m plant opened in 1999 that a man with a laptop could operate the whole shebang from a car park ten miles away – a sensible distance for him to be, remarked my friend Richard Porch, who'd noted on a visit "a smell like a hundred dead tramps rotting quietly in a waterlogged ditch." I'm braced, therefore, for a pong. But there's nothing yet. Only, perhaps, the slightest of slight whiffs, like the hint of a fart lingering after a beautiful – if silently flatulent – woman has left a large, airy room.

I'm welcomed by Ray Carter, the team leader – his team being, certainly, a small one: just four operators and two fitters, to cope with the 'product' of 155,000 people, in addition to industrial effluent (about 25% of the total influx) and storm water. When, after heavy rain, the plant is working to full capacity, Ray and his team are responsible for 3,100 litres of sewage a second. "A lot of money had to be spent on it after it was built," says Ray, "and there are still things that need doing. But it's certainly one of the most technologically advanced treatment plants in the world." Although the plant can't be operated entirely by that man sitting in a car ten miles away, it's sufficiently automated to run unmanned at night and at weekends.

It's time to venture, as it were, into the bowels of the plant. There's a persistent hum, certainly, but it's more the hum of machinery than of what's flowing murkily around us. The smell can't be described as pleasant, but nor is it gaggingly offensive – more a defeated, leaden staleness. This may be partly because it's been raining, with the run-off from the roofs and streets significantly diluting the brown stuff. Air quality within the plant is monitored rigorously, to the extent, says Ray, that in spite of the smell the air quality inside is actually better than that on the unsmelly outside. Ray and co. like a little rain to keep things sweet, their least favoured weather conditions being a drought. When, as today, there's been a downpour after a long dry spell, tonnes of grit wash in from the streets, and we pass a skip, alongside the rag skip, almost full already with grit.

The sewage enters the plant at the western end where solids are screened for transfer to the rag skip: nappies, tampons, condoms, hair, dishcloths, tights, cotton buds, syringes, children's toys, tree roots, coagulated blocks of cooking fat. Grit and grease are removed in four large separator tanks, before the sewage flows into four primary settlement tanks, where 60% of the sludge is separated from waste water. This is then transferred to the aeration tanks where micro-organisms break down the sludge that remains: this 'activated sludge', pumped through with diffused air, is a grey broth popping busily with large, floppy bubbles. This liquid is then transferred to twelve secondary settlement tanks where any residual sludge is separated from what by now is referred to as clear water. Finally, the water is bombarded by powerful ultraviolet rays to destroy bacteria and viruses – and then piped out into Swansea Bay.

In the meantime, the sludge is thickened before being transferred to a digestion tank where bacteria work on it to produce carbon, nitrogen and methane. After 'dewatering', it's taken off site in a virtu-ally odourless 'cake' form, dried further at Afan and then used as farm fertiliser or on land reclamation and forestry schemes.

Billy Murphy, another member of Ray's notably convivial team, takes me up to the observation platform to show me the two buoys, directly ahead of us, that mark the end of the plant's 3.5-km pipeline, which was floated out to sea in 1996 and sunk into a wide trench dug in the sea bed. Within months of opening, says Billy, the E-coli content of Swansea Bay was virtually negligible. Like his team mates, he talks of the plant with pride and says it's a great place to work. "If only the public appreciated what an essential – and efficient – service is provided by this place. But people just look at their water bills and wonder why they are paying all this for what simply drops out of the sky. They don't begin to understand the complexities and expense of this huge operation." He points to a skip-load of 'cake' on the forecourt below us. "To treat, transport and dry that stuff costs between £300 and £400 per skip."

To be sure, there have been one or two significant mishaps. He points to a silver hopper-like structure to our left, one of two sludge digestion tanks. Its roof got blown off once by a build up of methane – and its contents spewed forth all over the yard. "Such incidents are rare," says Billy, "but they're all that the press want to know about."

The observation platform and a large room beneath it were designed as a visitor centre, with interpretative display panels, maps of Swansea's sewerage system and photos of the major works undertaken throughout the city in the 1990s. Ray would like to see parties of schoolchildren and ratepayers touring the plant. But few Swansea people seem interested in paying this remarkable facility a visit, or even know of its existence – in spite of the fact that a little of each of us passes through here every day.

ST THOMAS

The St Thomas–Dan-y-graig–Port Tennant region, hemmed in by Kilvey Hill, the docks, the Tawe and Crymlyn Bog, is about the only self-contained part of Swansea that can't expand or merge. Little more than two-and-a-half kilometres from west to east, its compact – and substantially Victorian – terraces seem from the docks or atop Kilvey to form a single entity, but the eastside's regions are considered by many who live there to be places apart in a world apart.

"I couldn't tell you much about Dan-y-graig and Port Tennant," says the seaman and poet Bryn Griffiths (b.1933) who, brought up in the Foxhole area of St Thomas, is taking me on a tour of his home patch. "They really were another world, and we had very little to do with them. And in St Thomas itself, of course, there was – and there still is – a sense of it being divorced from the main part of Swansea."

For centuries St Thomas was little more than a scatter of farms in the lordship of Kilvey, the hamlet's focal point being the ancient chapel of St Thomas the Martyr, which was largely destroyed by the (probable) tsunami of 1607. There's an eighteenth-century reference to the area as the 'Burrough of Bettws', which probably meant 'burrows' rather than 'borough', reflecting its then sandy location on the edge of Fabian's Bay. 'Bettws' or 'Betws', from the English 'bede house', meaning a 'house of prayer', referred to the historic chapel. The remains of the chapel and its graveyard were obliterated when a tidal harbour was built at the terminus of the Tennant Canal, which opened in 1824. The canal brought coal from the Nedd Valley to Swansea, and prosperity to the community that developed around its wharves – Port Tennant.

It was the foundation of Port Tennant that triggered the expansion of St Thomas and, later, that of Dan-y-graig (which, at the end of the nineteenth century was still a realm of country lanes, fields and farmhouses). The development of the docks, from 1852 onwards, accelerated the growth of St Thomas as a dockside, cosmopolitan and overwhelmingly working-class community, so that by 1891 its population, which had increased thirty-fold during the nineteenth century, stood at nearly 7,000 – more or less its population today. Linguistically, it's the most anglicized of Swansea's communities, with 87.07% of its inhabitants (in 2001) having no knowledge at all of Welsh.

We're walking along the western bank of the Tawe, adjacent to Sainsbury's car park, on a hot September morning, and Bryn is pointing out several St Thomas landmarks, the most prominent of which is the red-brick, four-storey primary school, built in 1897 to educate 1,200 children. It was known in his day as the elementary school. "Well named," says Bryn, who left school at the age of 14. "I never learned a damn thing there."

The approach to St Thomas from the Quay Parade bridge has been much 'simplified' by the removal, in the 1950s, of various railway lines that criss-crossed here. Where today there are bland patches of grass and broad expanses of traffic-congested tarmac, there used to be embankments, viaducts, the Midland railway station on its riverside *twmp*, level crossings and characterful establishments such as the Bridge Café, and pubs such as the Cyprus (roughly where today's Cape Horner stands), the Bottom Ship (roughly where the Ship stands, its adjective distinguishing it from the Top Ship in Foxhole), the Ivy Bush, where Bryn and friends would sing acapella of an evening, and the Red House. The Midland area of St Thomas is dominated these days by the chunky, flat-roofed Swansea Dockers Club, but in Bryn's day there was no official dockers' club. That was a role performed unofficially by the Red House. "As a seaman," says Bryn, "I hardly went in there. Dockers and seamen don't mix. Different cultures."

Another notable absence hereabouts, at the confluence of Pentre Guinea Road and Morris Lane, is the Scala, flatiron-shaped like the Palace in High Street, which was known to Harry Secombe's generation as the Pictorium or the 'Pic'. Behind the Scala was the St Thomas institution that was most influential in Bryn's life, the library.

Bryn was born in James Street, near the Grand Theatre, and his widowed mother and her three sons lived in various parts of Swansea – Pentrechwyth, Morriston, Bonymaen – before settling in Foxhole. Both his father and an older sister had died of TB; Bryn too contracted the disease and was sent before the war to a sanatorium in Llandrindod.

He remembers the early part of the war all too vividly. "After the bombing raids there'd be bits of human bodies all over the place. You'd lift up a piece of sacking and there would be a human head. After the third night of the blitz, I tramped into our house in Bonymaen with a live incendiary bomb on my shoulder – and everyone ran out of there screaming."

He was evacuated to a farm, Brohedydd, near Eglwyswrw in northern Pembrokeshire, where he stayed until the end of the war. It was, he says, the making of him, and the experience seeded in him an abiding love for the landscape and Welsh-language culture of the rural west.

In the meantime, the family had moved from Bonymaen to 186 Foxhole Road. "Coming back to that was a shock to the system. It was a crumbling slum. I'd had my own room on the farm and the food was magnificent. But here we were sharing a house with two other families. We had just two rooms. One for living in, in which all my mother had to cook on was the sort of coal fire you had in a bedroom, and a single gas ring. And one bedroom. Two of us slept in one bed, my mother slept in the other and my youngest brother slept in a drawer from a chest of drawers.

"We were at the bottom of the scale in terms of poverty. When you told other St Thomas people you were from Foxhole they went white. But we also had a lot of fun. Foxhole was a colourful community with lots of dramas. People looked after each other. They were certainly kind to us."

Nothing remains of number 186 or of any of the houses on the western side of the relentlessly busy Foxhole Road. All were demolished years ago, like so many of Foxhole's terraces. We pause at the railings where Bryn's home once stood and look over the river, way below us, towards High Street station and Mayhill beyond. A few months ago, there was a landslide here: the steep slope at our feet is pinned to the hillside with giant bolts, metal plates and a thick mesh of black nylon.

Immediately below Bryn's precipitous rear wall was a railway line (now the Swansea–Morriston bike path). "People would come out of the houses when the coal trains passed, and they'd swarm over the trucks, chucking coal down to the women running alongside with sacks to collect the lumps. The firemen on the trains would often throw down large lumps of coal for them, and after they'd cleaned out their engines' fire boxes in the shunting yards, the women would go scavenging for bits of burnable coal."

Many houses on the east side of the road have survived. Sitting on the raised terrace outside number 13 is Elwyn Stephens, who owned the butcher's shop in Bryn's terrace. He remembers Bryn's mother, Alice – or Gracie, as they called this noted clairvoyant who was also a fine singer – and many others from Bryn's time there. Elwyn agrees about Foxhole's distinctive nature. "It was a village," he says. "It was separate. If anyone was in trouble, people rallied round. The people were the social services."

On the hillside immediately above Foxhole is the distinctive little church of All Saints, which dates from 1842 and is an attractive Kilvey landmark as your train pulls into or out of High Street station on the other side of the river. It was built, like much else on this side of the Tawe, by the Grenfell dynasty of copper-masters. "Foxhole people didn't go there," recalls Bryn, leaning on the churchyard wall's coping of triangular slag blocks: "Gothic slag," he smiles. Its congregation was drawn mainly from the Avenues – the more recent, semi-detached housing built further up the slope – "posh people."

We loop back down to Foxhole Road, then turn left up Windmill Terrace, following the route Bryn took to school. We lean on a wall capped with semi-circular slag blocks – "Romanesque slag" – opposite a house labelled, with a piety that only slate can bestow, 'Llareggub' (try saying it backwards: it's the name Dylan Thomas gave to the fictional

village in his radio play *Under Milk Wood*; Dylan's mother, Florence Williams, was born in St Thomas – at 29 Delhi Street – in 1882). I take a few snaps of Bryn with his old *alma mater* in the background. The schoolyard, where he was regularly bullied, fell silent early in 2007, when the red-brick school (now awaiting redevelopment) was replaced by the £6.7m St Thomas Community School. Why the bullying? "Oh, the usual thing: being different, knowing the answers to questions – until I learned to shut up."

Knowing the answers, or working them out on his own, has served Bryn well in life. Apart from a year at Coleg Harlech, he has generally taught himself all he has needed to know: to navigate vessels across the seven seas, write journalism, make television and radio programmes, found the Guild of Welsh Writers (in London), edit influential anthologies such as *Welsh Voices* (1967) and run a small press in Australia – where he has lived much of his life and where, by now, he is probably better known as a poet than he is in Wales (although he has spent longer at sea than he has lived in Australia).

Other notable eastside achievers include the poet and editor Peter Thabit Jones (who was born and brought up at 10 Robert Owen Gardens), Peter's cousin the actor Richard Mylan, the painter Nick Holly, the rugby player (and church organist) Geoff Wheel, and the football players Tiger Morgan and Nigel Stevenson. A local world-beating institution is the famous Eastside Jazz Band, founded in 1950 by Percy Gilbert. With its drums, kazoos and tinselly regalia, this jaunty marching band, which has attracted over 3000 youngsters to its ranks over the years, has twice won the world title – in 1978 and 2003.

We pause for a pint in the Windsor Arms in Delhi Street, which has an intriguing selection of historic photographs in the lounge bar. No less intriguing are the comings and goings, between sun-drenched patio and dingy public bar, of a blonde thirtysomething wearing pink shades and, on her bronzed, toned, sinuously tattooed upper half, an almost invisible bikini top.

> she turns on long legs
> away from the bar – absolutely
> as beautiful as feared

Swansea, we agree, is disproportionately endowed with beautiful women.

"We learned about sex very early in Foxhole," he says. "In what is now the forest by the river, there was an anti-aircraft emplacement manned by American G.I.s – a place of great interest to local ladies. We used to sneak round observing the operations there of a summer's evening with considerable fascination, until the Yanks bribed us with chewing gum to go away."

From the profane to the sacred: our next port of call is the rather grand St Thomas church (1886-7) in Lewis Street, whose slender steeple is a defining feature of the eastside. This church too was built by the Grenfells. The blue plaque on its wall reads: 'Sir Harry Secombe CBE 1921-2001 Goon, Comedian and Singer who served here as a boy chorister.' The eastside's most famous son was born in Dan-y-graig Terrace, and lived also at 7 St Leger Crescent and 47 Grenfell Park Road, before bomb damage forced the family to move to the Uplands. He has written affectionately of St Thomas, describing this building as "a greyhound of a church looking haughtily down on the mongrel Nonconformist chapels of Port Tennant, its chimes both a reproach and a summons."

We round off the afternoon, having crossed the traffic-frenzied Fabian Way, at a café table on the edge of the Prince of Wales dock in SA1. We raise our glasses to St Thomas, burnished gold beneath the gorse of Kilvey Hill, and wonder how the eastside will fare as Swansea's latest fashionable quarter takes view-obscuring, inflationary shape on its doorstep.

BONYMAEN

It could be, in Swansea terms, an old rock star's[5] definition of the blues: having nowhere to keep a pint of milk cool in the sweltering Tawe Delta heatwave of July 2006. Not only is Spencer 'Keep on Running' Davis bereft of a fridge, he doesn't have a washing machine or anything else much in the house he has inherited from his mother in Mulberry Avenue, West Cross, and in which he finds himself more or less camping with a few sticks of furniture. Following her death three years ago, there was a somewhat 'uneven' (and acrimonious) division of the spoils, which resulted in the house being divested, in his absence, of all that was moveable and saleable – which is why we are meeting at 8 a.m. at the Baywash laundromat on the seafront at West Cross: he wants his wheelie-bag's worth of dirty washing done in time for a gig in Germany the day after tomorrow. In the meantime, he has arrangements to make at the Grand Theatre about a charity performance there in October for Macmillan Cancer Support (both his parents died of cancer), and he has kindly agreed to walk and talk me through Bonymaen[6] where he was brought up.

Spencer Davis (b. 1939; the 'e' was dropped as the result of a spelling mistake on the pressing of his first single) moved to the United States in 1970 and lives these days on Catalina Island (about 40 kilometres south west of Los Angeles), in the seaside town of Avalon which, he says, is rather like Swansea and whose name the locals mistakenly believe to be Spanish in origin; the Welshman knows better. Since the first rush of fame in the 1960s, with major hits such as 'Keep on Running', 'Somebody Help Me', 'Gimme Some Lovin'' and 'I'm a Man', he has toured almost constantly. In 2006, he played more than 70 gigs in countries such as Holland, Belgium, Denmark, England, Trinidad, the United States, Wales, Australia and, above all, Germany, where audiences delight in his fluent command of their language.

But no matter how packed his schedule, he has not forgotten his Welsh roots (he's a supporter and honorary member of Plaid Cymru) and he has always found time for Swansea. His mother's death at the age of 89, far from proposing any severance of the Swansea connection, seems to have reaffirmed his commitment to the area, in both practical and artistic terms. He's keeping on the former council house in Mulberry Avenue, having converted the loft into a spacious studio with a superb view over Swansea Bay, and he has campaigned on a number of local urban environment issues. His recently released 12-track album *So Far* marks a new departure, in that his writing has taken a distinctly autobiographical turn, with the home patch featuring on many of the songs: when he's not gigging "From door to door, coast to coast / Shakin' more hands than a talk-show host" we find him "Down in Wind Street on a Saturday night / When the glass is full and the moon is bright / Doing the Swansea shuffle".

The laundry deposited, we taxi up to Bonymaen, the dense traffic on Mumbles Road being a reminder of Swansea's archetypal folly of follies. "If they'd kept the Mumbles train, it would have contributed hugely to relieving the pressure of all this traffic," says Spencer, who pays fond homage on the new album to that "Rockin' and a-rollin' train to paradise".

On the crawl through the car-clogged city centre we talk of his beginnings. He was born in Mount Pleasant, at 71 North Hill Road. The family later lived at 13 Norfolk Street, which was destroyed in a bombing raid shortly after they'd left for Birkenhead and other towns in England, his father being in the army during the war. He was five when the family returned to Swansea and, eventually, a new home in Bonymaen. At Dynevor Boys School in the city centre – *alma mater* of other Swansea achievers such as Harry Secombe, Rowan Williams and Bernard Knight – he studied German, French and Spanish, and also did well at chemistry and English literature. "The music master was a man called Weber who, with Dewi Johns, the physics master, took great delight in physical punishment. Weber told me, "you will never do anything in music.""

Music, nevertheless, had him in its thrall from the moment in early childhood when his Uncle Herman called round with his mandolin. The "far-off lands and sights" of which his uncle sang sent young Spencer travelling too – on a journey that has never ended. Later, someone gave him a harmonica: "I never put it down from the moment I got it." He asked his parents for a guitar for Christmas, "but they gave me a piano accordion. Hardly the same thing. But I managed to pick up a few carol tunes and I went round Bonymaen, aged about 11 or 12, making enough money to buy shoes and trousers, which gave me the taste for being a professional musician." Four or five years later, he got his first guitar and was soon performing regularly at venues such as the King's Arms in High Street and Rob's (all-night) Café in St Helen's Road (a milieu in which he became friendly with the poet Bryn Griffiths, who sang with various local jazz bands). "I was playing with a harmonica bracket around my neck before I'd ever heard of Bob Dylan." The blues has remained a seminal influence: "Hooker and Leadbelly taught me how to be a man," he sings on a country-blues homage to the music that shaped his life.

Like many Welsh artists, he received unstinting support from his mother Mary. "But my father," says Spencer, "was a dick-head. He abused me physically and, unable to stand the beatings any longer, in 1956, at the age of 16, I got out." Eighteen months as a civil servant in London – "in a paper prison of my own design" – proved not the escape he could have desired, and "I nearly lost all hope / Till Elvis, Fats and Buddy / They tossed me a rope". Refusing a stint of national service "fighting for the queen", he returned to Swansea, completed his sixth-form education, went to Birmingham University in 1960 and eventually embarked on a teaching career that proved incompatible with his musical ambitions. "You're falling asleep, sir," his pupils observed one Monday morning after a hard weekend's gigging with

the band. So he gave up the day job; the Rhythm and Blues Quartette he'd formed in 1963 with Pete Yorke and the Winwood brothers became the Spencer Davis Group – and the story thereafter is known the world over.

"The land beyond Jordan" is how early nineteenth-century Swansea society used to characterise the bleak and god-forsaken Bonymaen area (as it was perceived), with its cockfighting, boozing and womanising. The cockfighting may have fallen out of fashion, but Bonymaen still has something of a 'reputation' – undeserved, locals insist – thanks to headlines that accentuate the antics of a minority (car theft, joy-riding, racism, badger bashing) while taking little account of the palpable warmth, good humour and resourcefulness of the majority.

After an extended tea stop at the family home, in Jersey Road, of Spencer's p.r., Helen Clarke-Woods, we head off, with her uncle and Spencer's childhood friend Keith Richards ("not the tree-climbing Keith Richard"), into deepest Bonymaen. We pass en route the burnt-out shell of the historic Capel y Cwm (1820s); destined now to be converted into flats, it replaced a chapel erected here in the 1780s deliberately to thwart the woodland-secluded activities of "the ungodly men of the area [who] would gather on a Sunday to play games, have cockfighting and every sort of merrymaking".

After the war, Spencer's father worked at the post office in Wind Street where he made boxes (he became known as Dai Box), and Mr and Mrs Davies, with their sons Spencer and Paul, moved into a prefab at 3 Cleddau Place, under the northern slope of a then treeless Kilvey Hill. The townspeople called the post-war prefabs "cowsheds", but to Spencer "We had arrived in the lap of luxury, with an airing cupboard you could live in. It had a huge fridge – I'd never seen one before – and my father used to make lollies for us out of government-issue orange juice.' The family lived here until about the time Spencer left for London, when they moved to 7 Gors Avenue, Townhill; they later moved to West Cross. Cleddau Place no longer exists, the prefabs having been replaced by brick-built houses.

"The scene here has changed utterly, and I wouldn't recognise the place if confronted with a photo out of the blue," he says, pinpointing 130 Brokesby Road as roughly the site of his old home.

Before Swansea's early twentieth-century slum clearance resettlements, Bonymaen – or Llanerch, as it was earlier known – was a stronghold of the Welsh language, many of the miners, copper workers, bargemen and small farmers of the area having migrated here from rural west Wales. "But most of the people in the prefabs were from the town, so there wasn't much Welsh," says Spencer. "The more Welsh parts were around Adulam chapel in Cefn Road and Capel y Cwm."

As we drift into Pentrechwyth and wander past Ogmore Place, he recalls making friends there, aged about 11, with a stamp collector. Still a serious philatelist, he has a collection worth thousands of pounds.

Next stop is the boarded-up, bush-sprouting wreck of Spencer's old Pentrechwyth Junior School. He's amused at a notice that reads 'WARNING ANTI VANDAL PAINT USED ON THESE PREMISES' – and at the signs all around us of the warning's ineffectuality: the roof tiles ripped off, the scorch marks, the graffiti, the airgun-pitted aluminium sheets over the school's windows[7].

At the heart of Bonymaen (Bôn-y-maen: base of the stone), on a grassy bank in front of the Bonymaen Inn, is the 1.3 metres high *maen*, the ancient standing stone that in coaching days was a landmark on the main road between Swansea and Neath. Spencer poses by the *maen*. "Why the fuck you taking pictures of that fuckin stone?" enquires a lad in a baseball cap. "It's very old," Spencer replies. "So?" "Older than you – older even than us.". "It's just a fuckin stone. Fuck. I'm going for a fuckin pint."

This seems like a good idea, and we follow him into the Bonymaen Inn, Spencer pointing out the space between the pub's inner and outer doors where, aged 13, he was allowed to busk with his "chest piano". "I was too young to go into the bar, but the drinkers would come out and deposit their coins." This afternoon's clientele, about a dozen men mostly of Spencer's generation, recognise him instantly – "Spencer Davis! What brings you back to Bonymaen?" – and he recognises many of them: old friends, boys he'd been at school with, a relative or two. He sits down with them and they settle into pondering the Bonymaen of their youth and the land he lives in now. "Big country, America," ventures one. "H'm,' muses Spencer, "big country, small minds."

It's from the Bonymaen Inn that the annual Kilvey Hill Cement Run sets out. Founded in honour of the late amateur boxer Nigel Page, the competition involves running nearly a mile up Kilvey Hill with a 50-kg bag of cement on your shoulders. Bonymaen's own Enzo Maccarinelli, the world cruiserweight champion, won the race in 2000, and was given even odds to win the 2007 event, which attracted a record 68 competitors (including women). But Enzo this time came in third, with a time of twelve minutes and four seconds.

We head finally for Cefn Road, for Spencer to tell me the story of the three-inch scar on the palm of his right hand. Ever on the look-out for means of raising cash, he had a paper round, he grew and sold lettuces, he went spud-bashing in Gower – and then there was the pop bottle scam. At Hopkins's shop in Cefn Road – closed now, but the shuttered serving hatch is still there – you could get money back on your empty bottles. The returned empties were stored in a yard at the rear, and Spencer would tiptoe round the back, help himself to an armful of bottles, carry them round to the hatch at the front – and get 'his' money back. All went well until one day his trespassing was rumbled by a yapping dog. He ran for the nearest wall, went to grip the top of it with his right hand – and gashed his palm on the jagged glass that had been set into the wall top. The wound should probably have been stitched, but he dared not tell his parents what had happened, and it was left to heal unaided.

His stamina undiminished, Spencer Davis keeps on running, but, as he sings on *So Far*, "I am not running from my past". With variety and inventiveness on this new album, certain ghosts are laid and positive influences celebrated: "It's been a good ride so far", the Swansea bluesman declares – yet, 67 years down the line, "I got so far to go".

notes

1 South-west Wales.
2 The total waste budget is £20m a year.
3 Llandarcy, unlike most other place names with a 'Llan' prefix, has nothing to do with a saint.

It embodies the name of William Knox D'Arcy, who founded what became the British Petroleum Company Ltd. *The Welsh Academy Encyclopaedia of Wales* describes him as "the only man to achieve 'Celtic' sainthood while still alive".

4 The plant has been managed since April 2005 by Kelda Water Services, a subsidiary of Yorkshire Water.

5 "I am not a rock star. I am a rhythm guitarist."

6 I am indebted to my former student Ceri Thomas, of Jersey Road, Bonymaen, for much of this section's local background.

7 The school was demolished three months later.

WEST

THE UPLANDS

"I love Uplands," wrote Jayney Rafferty, one of my writing students, in a fine haibun[1]. "It's like a big, dirty village full of delicious, crazy people …. One minute you're enclosed in rows of neat houses and the next you're plunged into shops and traffic and people, people everywhere …. I know the faces, I know the pubs and the women who work in the Spar and the skaters on the steps by Barclays …. Uplands is social. We never lock the door."

"Swansea's cosmopolitan / suburb hub," to quote another poet, Lloyd Rees, is named after one of those grand, nineteenth-century houses – such as Ffynone, Glanmôr and Pantygwydr – which no longer exist but which have inscribed their names indelibly on the city's map. A suburban villa which has survived is Brynymor House, enveloped by the horseshoe-like Eaton Crescent. It was built by the Quaker timber merchant Robert Eaton in the 1780s; it's now an Ursuline convent, known as Stella Maris. Most of the large, semi-detached houses here, built by Swansea's rapidly expanding professional class, are too big these days for single families. In the mid twentieth century, the nature of Eaton Crescent, and similar streets nearby, began to change, with properties being bought as guest houses or converted into private schools and old people's homes. Many have been divided internally to cram in as many students as possible.

Given the area's large student population, it's not surprising that Swansea's musical centre of gravity has shifted to the Uplands. Two of the most popular of Swansea's dozens of music venues face each

other from opposite sides of Uplands Crescents. The Chattery, a busy café of long standing, run by an Adelphi-era muso, Nigel Clatworthy, and his wife Margaret, and the Uplands Tavern, known to all as simply the Tav. Painted on the pink back wall behind the stage are the names of some fifty past and present regular Tav performers, such as The Amigos, The Squirts, Brian Breeze, Dave Tipton, Boys from the Hill, The Gutbucket Band, Micky Jones, John Rodge, Rag Foundation. Tonight it's the turn of local bass-guitar hero Martin Ace of the Man band, who's back from a temporary exile in Germany to perform with The Aces: guitarist Kevin 'Red' Ford, pianist Merthyr Tom and drummer Two Beat Pete. Rockabilly, rock-n-roll, r-&-b – the Aces chunk, chop, scythe and slice it: they're the hottest pub-rock band in the world. Everyone who can find some floor-space, be they pasty young 'emos' or bling-bedecked grandmas, is up dancing by the end of the night. 'That'll be the day', 'Rock around the clock', 'Carol', 'Reelin' an' Rockin', 'Johnny B. Goode' – these songs were the soundtrack to the youthful dreams and desires of every fifty- and sixty-year-old present tonight. And they know all the words, how yearningly they know those words.

"What's great about the Tav," yells my friend the lecturer Tom Cheesman, "is that the regulars have refused to let it get taken over by the students. It's a pub for all ages and all kinds of music. Walk in here any night, and you're sure to bump into people you know."

Rather less enthusiastic about the Uplands Tavern was the novelist and poet Kingsley Amis (1922-95), who taught English at the university between 1948 and 1961 (and whose younger son, the novelist Martin Amis, was born in Swansea in 1949). The Amises had several Swansea addresses, including 82 Vivian Road, Tycoch and, later, a three-storey house at 24 The Grove, Uplands. When they lived in Swansea, the pub was the Uplands Hotel (1880), and was divided conventionally into a lounge bar and a public bar. It had been Dylan Thomas's local, and indeed, there was a little-known meeting between Amis and Thomas in the Uplands Hotel in the early 1950s, according to the writer and broadcaster John Morgan, who was also present. John remembered that "Mr Amis was a bit miffed that Mr Thomas would not go back to his place for a drink, but went off instead with some Swansea boys."

Amis, who often spent his summers in Swansea, was not impressed by a kitsch make-over of the Uplands Hotel in the early 1980s, when it became known, briefly, as The Street: fake cobbles, fake shop fronts, fake (Cwmdonkin) park railings, king-size sun brollies, an old telephone kiosk and a Dylan-Thomas-themed pseudo-snug. He was not alone in declaring it the supreme example of 'a thoughtless and cultural vandalism' besetting Swansea in general. When it became the Uplands Tavern the more garish elements were removed, and in 2006 an attractive alfresco terrace was added (which in 2007 was commandeered by the smokers).

On the hillside above is Dylan Thomas's birthplace, the semi-detached 5 Cwmdonkin Drive. He was born, in 1914, in the front bedroom overlooking Cwmdonkin Park, and lived here until he was eighteen, writing about a fifth of his total poetic output in his bedroom at the rear of the house. You might expect that, like D.H. Lawrence's birthplace in Nottingham, it would be made accessible to visitors. But no. This is Swansea. It's owned by a Port Talbot solicitor who for years has let it out to students. The council leased it for a couple of years and ran literary events there, organised largely by Jo Furber of the Dylan Thomas Centre, who was living in number 5 at the time. The latest leaseholder is a Swansea businessman who plans to restore the house and run it as a holiday retreat. Or so he said in March 2005. Don't mistake the blue plaque by the front door for an instance of local piety. It was put there by the Cardiff-based television company TWW when they were making a documentary in 1963 to mark the tenth anniversary of the poet's death.

Cwmdonkin Park, which opened in 1874, having been developed as landscaping around a reservoir established there in 1854, inspired many passages in Dylan Thomas's work, most famously the poem 'The Hunchback in the Park', in which he evokes a "solitary mister"

> Eating bread from a newspaper
> Drinking water from the chained cup
> That the children filled with gravel
> In the fountain basin where I sailed my ship ...

The park is much as it was in Dylan's day. The cast-iron fountain is still there, although the chained cup long ago vanished, as did the bandstand and the reservoir, which was filled with rubble from the blitzed town, some gravestones from Cwmbwrla, and a few old cars, and grassed over to make a children's play area. In the water gardens near the fountain there's a dignified memorial, a block of Pennant sandstone from Cwmrhydyceirw quarry; its erection in 1963 was organised by the poet Vernon Watkins and the sculptor Ron Cour – who carved the inscription, the concluding lines of 'Fern Hill':

> Oh as I was young and easy in the mercy of his means,
> Time held me green and dying
> Though I sang in my chains like the sea.

Rather less dignified is another memorial nearby, a triangular, open-fronted, 'shelter', which might better be described as the Dylan Thomas memorial urinal. The vandals have been working on it for years – but not hard enough.

The Uplands has been a magnet for writers and artists, among them the Landore-born poet and playwright Graham Allen, who lives in Hillside Crescent, the Canadian-born painter Gordon Stuart, and the poet David Hughes, who captures the Swansea dialect so winningly in his collection *Tidy Boy*; both Stuart and Hughes have homes in Richmond Road.

The poet and translator Malcolm Parr, who lived in the Uplands for many years, remembers a disturbing encounter in the Uplands Bookshop one hot summer's afternoon in 1978. He was upstairs, browsing the paperbacks by the Smarties shelf, when suddenly he found himself swooped upon by a fully grown eagle.

"I wanted to scream," he told me. "I didn't know what on earth was going on and when the bird was going to start pecking my eyes out. It knocked me to the floor and was standing on my back. There were Smarties all over the place. Then suddenly a man – I later found out he was the eagle's owner – was hitting hell out of the eagle's back with a knotted rope, to get it off me."

It was a book promotion, apparently, that had gone wrong. Suburban Swansea the Uplands may be, but you never know, among its tidy terraces, what might happen next.

BRYNMILL

Where, exactly, Uplands ends and Brynmill begins few can say. They are like mutually sustaining conjoined twins, models of Victorian suburban planning. With a population density high enough to support a wide range of shops and amenities, it's all here, within walking or cycling distance: if you felt like it, you need never go to town (or Tesco) again.

The name Brynmill is much older than Uplands. It appears as

"Brynnemiskil" in a reference from the early fourteenth century, and it's associated with the two (at least) corn mills that were active for hundreds of years on the Bryn (or, later, Vivian) stream. Known also as Brynmill Brook or Brynmill Stream, and anciently as Saint David's Ditch, the stream marked the borough's western boundary in the early nineteenth century. It rises at Cockett and flows along the little valley below Hill House Hospital before disappearing behind Swansea College, to travel underground and through culverts beneath Sketty and the north-eastern corner of Singleton Park. It then puts in a brief, 400-metre appearance along the south-eastern edge of Singleton Park. Students bustling to their lectures cross the stream each morning on a footbridge near the junction of Park Place and Brynmill Lane. From the park, it's culverted under Mumbles Road and the Promenade, to debouch on the sands through the man-sized maw of an iron-and-concrete tube.

It was the stream that made possible Brynmill Park (1872). Wales's first town reservoir was established here in 1837, in reaction to the devastating impact of water-borne diseases – cholera above all – on urban populations, which had been reliant for centuries on increasingly polluted wells, springs and rivers. It was supplied largely from the Brynmill Stream. As a reservoir, it was a limited success – insufficient altitude yielding insufficient pressure – but as a lake, the focal point of the earliest and most delightful of Swansea's many parks, it was ideal.

> men at bowls,
> their bright spheres bustling
> among patient shadows

Brynmill Park was as near as Swansea got to having a zoo. As a special treat, our teachers used to troop us down in crocodile formation to ooh-and-ah at the monkeys, parrots, peacocks and other exotic creatures that were kept in a clutter of cages on the edge of the lake. By the 1980s, those cages were largely deserted, and by the twenty-first century the park as a whole had assumed a tired air. Swansea's oldest surviving public park is currently in the throes of a £1.3m restoration programme.

> park silenced by snow;
> a reeling scurry of gulls
> lost among the flakes

For much of the nineteenth century there were few houses in Brynmill. It was mostly farmland, dotted here and there with the villas of the well-to-do, such as Pantygwydr House, home of the ship-owning Richardson family. The house was situated near the bottom of Pantygwydr (literally, 'stream of glass') Road, which students and others baffled by Welsh love to mispronounce as "panty girdle". An unlikely survivor from that era is the even older Rhyddings House, a sadly neglected, pebbled-dashed ghost of a once commodious dwelling, on the corner of Bernard Street and St Alban's Road. It's possible that one of the finest poems in the English language was written in this three-storey house, Walter Savage Landor's eight-line lyric beginning "Ah, what avails the sceptered race" (see the section on The Promenade), and probable that Landor's first significant poem, *Gebir* (1798), was written here. Landor was one of several English writers shunted into Swansea exile by family or friends who, for various reasons, seem to have wanted them well out of the way[2]. Living on an allowance from his father of £150 a year, he spent most of the later 1790s in Swansea and lived for much of that time in Rhyddings House.

Hot on Landor's heels as a tenant of Rhyddings House was the Somerset-born physician Thomas Bowdler (1754-1825) who, for health reasons, spent his winters in Brynmill, from 1811 onwards. Here he embarked on the work that made him famous: removing from the plays of Shakespeare all the sex, violence and profanity that his prudish nose could sniff out; he similarly gutted Gibbon's *Decline and Fall of the Roman Empire*. How, without a modicum of push and shove, I wonder, did Bowdler imagine the Romans won their empire? Handing out bunches of grapes? His *Family Shakespeare* (1818) – "in which ... those words and expressions are omitted, which cannot with propriety be read aloud in a family" – was a best seller, ensuring that a new expression, 'to bowdlerize' (expurgate), entered the English language.

The great traducer of Shakespeare's art is buried at All Saints' church, Mumbles, the horizontal slab of his gravestone sandwiched between two splendidly phallic obelisks[3]. The epitaphs beneath which he elected to spend eternity have prompted many a wry smile:

PUTTING AWAY LYING, SPEAK EVERY
MAN TRUTH WITH HIS NEIGHBOUR: FOR
WE ARE MEMBERS ONE OF ANOTHER

and

ABOVE ALL THINGS, TRUTH BEARETH
AWAY THE VICTORY[4]

On the two hundredth anniversary of Bowdler's death, Kingsley Amis and the writer and broadcaster Wynford Vaughan Thomas (1908-87) honoured the expurgator's memory by placing on his grave a wreath of fig leaves.

Not to be confused with Rhyddings House is the nearby Rhyddings pub at the junction of Aylesbury Road with Brynmill Avenue. Its outside wall is an intriguing autograph book: every brick within human reach has been inscribed with a name or a set of initials.

The two- and three-storey Victorian terraces of Brynmill, like those of Uplands, Glanmôr and Mount Pleasant, are among the defining architectural glories of Swansea. From a boat in the bay or from Mumbles Pier you appreciate how wave upon wave of these sinuous terraces contour the rising ground, many with A-shaped gables atop two-storeyed bay windows.

at dawn, as at dusk,
the windows of Swansea
take fire and burn

Come closer and relish the details: the elegant finials crowning ornately carved barge-boards, the etched and stained-glass doors and top-lights, the harmonious tiling of front paths and hallways, the marble and cast-iron fireplaces, the ornamental cornices and light-roses, the serpentine banisters.

The careless decline of Rhyddings House is symptomatic of Brynmill's number one problem: HMOs – houses in multi-occupancy. Since the late 1960s, Brynmill's cohesion as a community has been progressively undermined by the 'buy-to-rent' brigade – profiteering, absentee landlords cashing in on the student market. Of the 12,000 students attending the university, only 3,000 are in university accommodation, while another 3,000 live at home; that leaves 7,000 to seek private digs. Brynmill, on the university's doorstep, is the obvious first place to look.

In the 1950s, in a street such as Waterloo Place, everyone knew everyone: there was Donald Anderson, future Labour MP; Frank Dunkin, who would drive the last train on the Mumbles railway; Ralph The Books Wishart, who ran a renowned second-hand bookshop in Alexandra Road. But by 2007, over half of the street's forty houses had become HMOs. In Bryn Road the ratio was even higher: seventy-three out of ninety-five houses were in multiple occupancy. Many Brynmill people have begun to feel strangers in streets where their families have lived perhaps for decades. If, as the university authorities insist, the rowdy, untidy element is a minority, it's nevertheless a sizeable one. While most HMO landlords seem content to let their houses go to rack and ruin, as long as they continue to rake in the rent, many of their tenants add to the general run-down impression by turning gardens into rubbish dumps, kicking cans and smashing bottles in the road, vandalising cars and caterwauling through the streets in drunken, vomitous gangs.

Many Brynmill students, of course, are no trouble at all, including the very young ones attending Ysgol Gymraeg Bryn-y-Môr, the Welsh-medium school for infants and juniors in St Alban's Road. The singer Cerys Matthews was a pupil here, when her family lived in West Cross, as were my own daughters, Angharad and Branwen. Such schools, especially in the more anglicised parts, give their pupils an invaluable sense of who and where, in Wales and the world, they are. No difficulty among these students in pronouncing Pantygwydr correctly – and knowing what it means.

KING EDWARD ROAD

No street better illustrates the fate of Swansea's once resplendent Victorian terraces than King Edward Road, which runs from St Helen's cricket and rugby ground to Brynymor Road. It's a dispiriting half a kilometre's walk through HMO-land: untended gardens piled with black bin bags, builders' rubble, old mattresses and broken furniture; peeling front doors, ragged curtains and bare light-bulbs;

house after house with its bay windows lopped off, as grotesque as a face deprived of a nose; ornate woodwork and sash windows replaced by crude, cheap-n-easy uPVC; slate roofs abandoned for tiles-of-all-sorts.

The street is like the architectural representation of a shrug. "Whatever," it seems to say.

The king it's named after is Edward VII, who came to Swansea in 1904 to cut the first sod for the King's Dock. It's had older names: St Augustin's Lane, Merry Fair Maid Land, White Ladies' Lane and, for long, Gors(e) Lane, after Gors Farm, which stood somewhere near the Cricketers pub (from *cors*, bog).

It was at the Cricketers that the poet and playwright Peter Read took exception to the cultural vandalism of renaming pubs. Some marketing joker had decided it would be a jolly jape to rename his company's pubs alliteratively after a 'suggestive' old word for barrel, 'firkin'. So, for a while, the Bay View in Oystermouth Road became the Foreshore and Firkin, while the Cricketers became the Fine Leg and Firkin. Peter, a former Baptist minister of serene disposition, has an extraordinary knack for getting himself banned from pubs. When he raised the name-change with the pub's manager he promptly found himself banned from yet another Swansea boozer. He went on to write his poem 'Firkin Pubs', a favourite at readings, which proposes other alliterating possibilities: the Frisk and Firkin near the cop shop; the Fester and Firkin near the hospital; the Ferkin and Firkin near the brothel.

> from the pub sways
> a choir, tied and suited,
> on a cloud of aftershave

I drop in at Dylan's Books to offer condolences to the owner, Jeff Towns, on his recent sad loss. For nearly thirty years, a wiry old gentlemen in a top hat, with his coat a collage of dust jackets, has bent to peer short-sightedly at the second-hand books in Jeff's window – both when the shop was in Salubrious Passage and later after it moved to 23 King Edward Road. But now, suddenly, he's been "taken out" and Jeff fears the worst. His finger has been found – by Jeff's colleague Tim Batcup on his walk in to work. "It reminds me of the ominous message accompanying some hostage's body-part in an American gangster movie," says Jeff. "If you want the rest, you'd better leave so many thousand pounds in a bin in the street."

We reminisce about this Dickensian, wood-carved figure, made for Jeff by a film-set designer, as we might about the recently deceased. "He's become lodged in Swansea consciousness," says Jeff. "All sorts of people phoned when they heard he'd gone. Boys used to act as if humping him from behind, thinking they were the first to have thought of that, and then the party girls took to doing it too." Jeff's only

hope is that come the end of term some landlord will find the old boy abandoned in a student flat.

Months pass; the silence is ominous. Then, to Jeff's delight, he's been found legless – as many before him – in an alleyway off Wind Street. "It will take a bit of work, and some graft," says Jeff, "but he will rise like a phoenix from the ashes."

CLYNE VALLEY

Carved out by the violence of colossal meltwater torrents at the end of the last ice age, Clyne Valley, with its extensive tracts of woodland either side of a meandering stream, would seem today to represent the essence of pastoral quietude. Few who visit the Clyne Valley Country Park stray much from the foot-and-bike path laid down on the track-bed of the old LMS railway line (which closed in 1964). But in among the trees you will find, if you know where to look, a fossilised industrial landscape, unsuspected by most locals, which is in a much fuller state of preservation than the more famous industrial environment of the Lower Swansea Valley.

Cut along the line of demarcation between the Lower and Middle Coal Measures, the valley was a crucible of industrial activity from at least the early fourteenth century until well into the twentieth, with – at various times – coal and iron mines, bell pits, quarries, canals, railways, cart tracks, leats (for water power), brickworks, iron and copper smelters, an arsenic works and wood-based industries for the production of charcoal, naptha and cellulose. Evidence of these

undertakings is still to be found, but many of them are swamped by impenetrable thickets of *Rhododendron ponticum.*

The rhododendron problem, I discover on a walk through the park one spring afternoon in 2006, is being addressed on an industrial scale. Margot and I head up Mill Lane and enter the forest opposite Clyne Castle, to follow a route along the valley's western rim. Huge machines with man-high wheels are parked here for the weekend, the mud motorway they've carved – to get at the rhododendrons – stretching northwards through the trees. We take, initially, a smaller track forking left and soon come to what looks like a castellated medieval tower. This was built as an exhaust stack for noxious fumes from the arsenic works a couple of hundred metres down the slope, and later turned into a Gothic pavilion. Looking for the arsenic works, we head directly downhill, crossing the mud thoroughfare and coming to a line of irregular holes – caved-in portions of the tunnel that connected the tower to the works.

The works' ivy-clad ruins are indeed substantial: the stump of another stack, flue labyrinths, the remains of furnaces encrusted with crystallised arsenic, a decayed office block, lengths of wall as high in places as six or nine metres. Built in the mid 1840s from Pennant sandstone rubble quarried nearby, the Clyne Wood Arsenic Works fell into disuse about fifteen years later, probably because of its proximity to the country mansions of members of the powerful Morris and Vivian dynasties. As "The only eighteenth-century or early nineteenth-century works in the former world centre of the non-ferrous smelting industry to preserve remains of its productive plant" – to quote John Newman – it's an important site; but Swansea, as usual, couldn't seem to care less.

We return to the muddy highroad, the woodland on either side of which has been so thoroughly unclogged of rhododendron that many old field boundaries, from before the forestation of the area, are visible in the form of shallow mossy banks. The track, with great wheel-rutted offshoots, sometimes passes between huge banks of rhododendron trunks and branches bound together like giant fasces, awaiting removal.

On reaching a clearing where bluebells have pushed up through the cindered remains of recently burned vegetation, we hear a loud metallic banging. We find a couple of lads with spades and a wheelbarrow working away at some earthy troughs and humps. They look like students on an archaeological dig. I ask

them what they're investigating. They're reluctant to be drawn, but Margot gets them to admit that they're building a series of ramps for their mountain bikes. In a few weeks' time, when the ferns have grown back, their switchback should be well hidden from prying eyes.

We press on past the isolated Keeper's Cottage and begin to descend through the bushes, passing another cindered expanse, mostly of singed birches, which is criss-crossed with old cart tracks. Here the bike boys have constructed yet more switchbacks. A cart track, which soon becomes a metre-deep holloway, leads us steeply downhill past the remains of a number of bell pits. Identifiable as mounds of waste on the lower side of shallow, basin-shaped sinks, sometimes water-filled, bell pits were primitive coal workings formed by miners digging a hole a little over a metre in diameter and three metres deep, then belling out at the bottom as far as they dared without bringing the roof down on top of them. There are over 250 of them dotted around the valley, particularly on the western side of the bike path.

Not far from the valley bottom we come to the most dramatic of Clyne's coal-mine sites, the collapsed mine-shaft of the Coed yr Ysgol colliery; the remaining conical pit is clearly much in use these days by the bike boys as a sort of plunge of death. Tall, thin trees are well established on the spoil tips round about, and sticking out of the undergrowth is an abandoned steam-powered engine which once hauled trams from an inclined entrance tunnel. A plaque on this rusting hulk reads 'J Wild and Co Ltd Oldham / 1891'.

Deciding on a pint roughly half way through our walk, we cross the stream, scramble up the embankment and head along the bike path towards the Railway Inn at Killay, about half a kilometre up the line, passing under a sturdy bridge, at either end of which lurks a Second World War pillbox. Strung out alongside the path, for most of the distance, are hundreds of metres of video tape.

The Railway, perched alongside the platform of the old station, is a proper pub: congenial locals and welcoming bar staff, a choice of three rooms to drink in (or an outside terrace), and quite simply the best beer in the world, Original Wood. It's available at only one other outlet, the Joiner's at Bishopston, where this nectar of the Celtic deities is brewed. That the Railway has survived the homogenising, profit-crazy mania that has destroyed so many pubs is a wonder – attributable, says the landlord, to two things: the beer from the Joiner's and the fact that the pub is council, rather than brewery, owned (and leased out on a monthly basis).

Savouring our Woods at a table outside, we wonder about that video tape. Easier by far, given the right equipment, to recover those images scattered and scrunched up along the bike path than to recall anything at all of the hundreds who toiled away their short lives in this valley – until well within 'living memory', as they say … except that 'living memory' seems to have forgotten everything about them. The homes they lived in, the food they ate, the joys and pains of their relationships, their exhausting labours, the diseases and accidents they suffered and died from. Gone, utterly; vanished as surely as the last puff of steam from that old engine in the woods. Once in a rare while, an historian or a poet will attempt to raise a voice for them. In 'An old lie out' the Swansea poet John Beynon (1943) commemorates the miners who were drowned when the sea broke into colliery workings under Swansea Bay. The owners, denying that certain men had lost their lives, refused their families compensation. But years later, a high tide caused the water level to rise up the old shaft in Clyne Valley, and the skeletal miners, as the poem has them declare, "were spat out, one by one, / The rank earth repelling all their lies / And our voiceless anger gloriously sown."[5]

The distorted seams of the 'South Crop' of the coalfield made it increasingly difficult – and unprofitable – to mine coal in Clyne, and the last of the valley's ten large collieries[6] closed in the 1920s, leaving brick-making as Clyne's sole industry. We drain our glasses, head back down the bike path and, soon after the bridge-with-pillboxes, veer left through the trees along the raised track of a former tramway leading to Rhyd-y-defaid colliery. The red brick road, we call the track, after the hundreds of locally made bricks embedded in its surface. We soon come to a tree-shaded pond and the site of the last of Clyne's brickworks which, shortly before it closed in about 1950, was producing 75,000 bricks a week. There are no buildings to be seen, but there are a couple of mounds of thousands of warped, bulbous, doubled, broken or otherwise misshapen bricks which have been rejected. They're stamped variously 'Evans-Bevan Ltd / Clyne Works / Killay', 'Clyne / Killay' or simply 'Killay'. I slip one into my knapsack for a doorstop.

The embanked tramway, passing straight as a Roman road through the trees, takes us to the Rhyd-y-defaid colliery site, where there's another pond, some fragments of wall, and extensive, wooded spoil-heaps. We turn right, on the main path from Killay to Sketty, in the direction of Olchfa Wood, hoping to find some sign of the racecourse, complete with grandstand, which was established in fields around here in the nineteenth century. But all seems to have been obliterated – either by dense, brambly undergrowth or by the huge (and hugely controversial) municipal tip that sprawled northwards for over a kilometre, from Ynys Newydd Road in Lower Sketty, during the 1970s and 1980s. The proximity of this tip, with its rats, flies and foul odours, to Derwen Fawr, one of the most 'select' areas of Swansea, always seemed a little curious. To the denizens of 'Dehn Vah', as many of them mispronounce the place, the dump was an affront and they campaigned vociferously against it, forcing its closure in the 1980s.

Anyone who remembers the gargantuan quantities of waste that were dumped here during those decades – and the noisy, fume-belching drama (beneath a constant cloud of scavenging gulls) of bulldozers, earth removers and huge tractors with iron-spiked wheels – would be surprised at the transformation of the dump into a bosky plateau, several metres high, of reeds, rushes, gorse, hawthorn, blackthorn, pussy willow, primroses and vast, impenetrable tracts of bramble. The plateau stops a few metres short of the ruined New Mill Farm and extends south, between the stream and Mill Wood, to a still busy collection point for garden refuse, dead furniture and defunct white goods.

The contents of the plateau seem well disguised until, here and there, a path gives way to a muddy puddle, through which protrude broken bottles, squashed cans and plastic bags. The tip itself has hidden forever both the site of Sir John Morris's Ynys Collieries (after which Ynys Newydd Road is named) and that of the Clyne Valley Colliery, which closed in the early 1920s[7].

The transportation of coal from Ynys was a main motive for laying down the Oystermouth (later, Mumbles) Railway. A branch of it curved sharply northwards from what is now Mumbles Road and followed a line taking it 100 metres up the present Derwen Fawr Road; it passed along the lane that gives access these days to a scattering of secluded houses – CCTV protected, spiky gates, stockade fencing, 'guard dogs loose' – on the eastern side of the stream, before veering away in the direction of the mines. Some sleepers were still visible in the 1970s, but the tip eventually obliterated the track into the colliery. The left side of the lane, as we head downstream towards Blackpill, is still banked and walled by the railway's high-quality stonework. Among dead leaves on the bank we find a contorted length of abandoned rail.

MUMBLES

If Mumbles is known in the wider world it's known, above all, for something it no longer has. In 2010, the historic Mumbles train, the world's first passenger carrying railway, will have been, for all of half a century, no more than a picture-postcard memory. "I got a ticket, but the station's hard to find," sings Spencer Davis on his 2006 album *So Far*, "The whistle's blowing, but it's only in my mind …. Bring back the Mumbles train." The railway's destruction in 1960 – described in 2006 as one of the worst instances of 'heritage homicide' in Wales – has always rankled with Swansea people.

One of my earliest memories is of the railway's 150th anniversary celebrations in June 1954. My parents took me, aged nearly six, down to Mumbles pier to watch a rail-borne parade of Mumbles trains, ancient and modern, process towards the buffers: a replica of the nineteenth-century horse-drawn coach, an old steam engine pulling a carriage, and, representing the modern era, one of the railway's thirteen red-and-cream electric cars – with crews and passengers in period garb. A ride on the Mumbles train, from Rutland Street (near today's Leisure Centre) to the pier – a 9-km, nineteen-minutes journey – was always a thrill, especially if you could bag a front-row seat on the upper deck and especially if the tide was in, which would seem to transform the swaying train into an impossible galleon. There was no higher currency for 'swapsies' at school than a halfpenny flattened out to the size of a penny by the wheels of the Mumbles train.

The original plan – for transporting minerals from Mumbles and

Clyne to the industries of the Lower Swansea Valley – was for an extension of the Swansea Canal. But a railway was eventually agreed on, and work began in 1804. It ran, initially, from the upper High Street basin of the Swansea Canal, along the Strand, across the Burrows to Blackpill, where a branch line forked up the Clyne valley, and on to Oystermouth, where it terminated (at the mini roundabout at the bottom of Newton Road); its extension towards Mumbles Head in the early 1890s led to the construction of Mumbles pier (1897-8). The railway, with its horse-drawn vehicles, was in business by early 1806, transporting chiefly coal from Clyne and limestone from Oystermouth. When it began to carry passengers in 1807, it became the first public-service passenger railway in the world – a record that Mumbles has traded on ever since.

Being a horse-drawn service for much of the nineteenth century (there was even an experiment with sails in 1807), the pace – as a guidebook commented wryly in 1870 – was 'not so rapid as to prevent observation'. The introduction of steam locomotives in 1877 made for a half-hour one-way journey and ushered in the golden age of the Mumbles railway, with as many as 3,000 passengers cramming aboard a single train at peak times such as bank holidays. The pace accelerated further in the 1927-9 period when the line was electrified and provided with its fleet of purpose-built thirty-tonne cars, with staircases at each end and entrances on the landward side only, to shelter passengers from driving rain and sea spray. In 1945, the line carried nearly 5 million passengers.

The railway closed in 1960, the bus company that owned it – South Wales Transport – claiming it was running at a loss (in fact, as revealed later, it was making a £5,500-a-year profit). At Swansea Museum's marina-side tram shed, you can see various mementoes, including a restored forechunk of one of the cars. Apart from the electricity sub-station at Blackpill (today's Junction Café), which is the railway's most significant relic, there are some traces here and there along the route. Against the more northerly of the Slip bridge's two span-bereft abutments, there's a pair of rusting 'power unit' boxes with the railway's insignia, and on the seafront at the Dunns, overlooked by three rusting traction poles that carried the overhead cables, there's an abandoned wooden shed which is all that remains of Oystermouth station. Harder to identify as a relic of the railway is a series of sleeper-slots which indent at regular intervals the low wall, on the north side of the promenade, in front of the Lal Quila restaurant; some of these indentations still hold fragments of weather-bleached sleeper.

But there's more to Mumbles than the ghost of its train. There's its Roman villa (hint of); its connection with St Illtud, who is said to have spent his old age in a cave here; its foggy associations with the sixth-century king, Urien Rheged, and the legendary poets Talhaearn and Taliesin; the bells from Santiago, Chile, of its Norman church, where Rowan Williams served as  chorister and altar boy; its Norman castle, with dungeon and 'whipping post', sometime home of the brutal de Breos dynasty; its former iron ore and limestone industries; its one-time fishing and oyster-dredging industries; the pier and the lighthouse; the heroic and sometimes tragic story of its lifeboat, and the annual anarchic raft race. Then there's the beer festival and the jazz and blues festival. The area is worth a Real volume all to itself.

I'm biased, I have to admit. I've lived in the village since 1979, when a friend's leaky asbestos shack came on the market, and I managed to rustle up the funds to fulfil a dream I'd had from childhood.

> long enough in one place
> to notice the people's
> ways of ageing

But what is meant by Mumbles – and by the seemingly synonymous term Oystermouth? Mumbles originally applied to the headland and its twin islets, although there's no agreement on the derivation of the word. A corruption of the Welsh 'man moel' (bare place), perhaps? A distortion of the French 'mammelles' (breasts)? This popular fancy has been dismissed by the scholar T.J. Morgan[8] as "quite precarious and unconvincing ... lucky-dip etymological speculation". Whatever its origin, the name has come to be inclusive of everywhere between Blackpill and Caswell, taking in West Cross, Norton, Newton, Langland – and Oystermouth, which these days is considered to be a limited area within a short radius of the old station square (although Oystermouth is also the name of the very much more extensive parish). Oystermouth has also been an etymological teaser, there seeming to be little correspondence with its Welsh equivalent, Ystumllwynarth (bend + grove + bear). The Normans referred to it as Ostremue, Ostremuere and Oestremutha. And the English antiquary John Leland (1506-52) rendered it as Estwilthlunarde in his *Itinerary*, seeming thereby to negate any association with the 'succulent bivalves' for which the place had been famous from Roman times. But the long-accepted Welsh form Ystumllwynarth is thought to be a corruption: it's based on a twelfth-century misreading of Ystinlumarch (in modern Welsh, Ystum-llymarch), which describes the place accurately enough – before pollution and over-fishing wiped out the bivalves – as 'Oyster bend' or 'Oyster curve'.

My continuing enchantment with Mumbles must have its roots in childhood. It was a place of magical things and happenings. Not only the Mumbles train, but the knickerbocker glories at Forte's ice-cream parlour in the Dunns, the festive lights in the summer, whirligigs and Mumbles rock at the Big Apple (c.1929), the delicious terror of the gaps between the planking on Mumbles pier, the paddle-steamer trips from the pier to Ilfracombe – and the Tivoli.

It was at the Tivoli, now a seedy gaming hall, that I had my first ever experience of cinema, aged about five. I enjoyed the film, *Three Men in a Boat* (1956), but I almost didn't make it to the opening credits, because in those days the film would be prefaced with sombre warnings about what to do if the cinema caught fire – and I was all for getting the hell out of there before the flames started licking the screen.

During the sixties, the Tiv was one of Swansea's most popular music venues. But, as with similar venues – maybe because of the cowboy films everyone watched – things could cut up rough. 'In most gigs there was a fight – or two – and some were very, very violent,' recalls the guitarist Brian Breeze. His wife Mabe, who was going at the time with one of the Iveys (who would later find international fame as Badfinger), remembers a frightening brawl at the Tiv.

While the band were setting up, she and two friends went to the Nag's Head. There they bumped into some Townhill boys who plied the girls with booze, and one of them gave her a scarf. The girls eventually managed to give their benefactors the slip and returned to the Tiv. But the Townhill boys, infuriated, followed them there and were incensed to see the scarf around the neck of guitarist Peter Ham. "A massive fight broke out," said Mabe, "during which the Iveys managed to call for reinforcements from other Swansea bands. Furniture was smashed, chair legs were wielded, someone arrived with a spanner flailing, and everyone got caught up in the horrendous violence."

Mumbles these days is an easy-going place for the most part, although Friday and Saturday nights along the infamously boozy Mumbles mile – which is a shadow of what it was, thanks to the stronger allure of the industrial partying of Wind Street and the Kingsway – can have their raucous moments, and woe betide the delicate sensibilities of any terraced sleeper requesting caterwauling, booze-addled youth to turn the gobby volume down as it can-kicks its way home in the early hours of the morning.

There's no denying, nevertheless, that Mumbles has undergone a degree of gentrification, with its café culture, fine restaurants and skyrocketing property prices. High-profile residents such as Mike Ruddock, Bonnie Tyler, Spencer Davis and (for a while) Lee Trundle draw attention to Mumbles as a desirable place to live – and no-one more so, of course, than Catherine Zeta-Jones who built a gated compound at Thistleboon for her occasional visits home and for her parents to live in (her father is known locally as Dai Hollywood).

The place might heave with visitors over a few weeks in summer, and *The Daily Mail* and *The Telegraph* might outsell *The Western Mail* and *The Guardian* by about fifteen to one in the moneyed outer reaches, but Mumbles is by no means, as some disdainful outsiders characterise it, "all tourists and Tories". It was a village, not so long ago, of quarrymen, fishermen and miners, and it still has a down-to-earth, welcoming heart – which beats most beguilingly in its alleyways, backstreets and terraced byways. There are delightful, out-of-the way pubs – with real beer, good conversation and not too much television – such as the Newton Inn and the nearby Rock and Fountain (where Mike Ruddock plays his guitar), and, in the village itself, the Victoria, and the Park, the Park being about as real a pub as you could hope to find.

the barmaid I once
craved – creased now, like me,
and double chinned

A regular at the Newton used to be the distinguished composer Daniel Jones (1912–93) – the first Welshman to write symphonies – who lived at 53 Southward Lane and who used to advertise his services in the local *Yellow Pages*, being the sole entry under 'Composers'. Other artists who have made Mumbles their home in recent times include the musician Mal Pope, the musician and stained-glass designer Jaroslav Mykisa, the harpist Delyth Jenkins, the painters Glenys Cour and Gareth Thomas, the tapestry maker Muriel Clement, the novelists Stevie Davies, Kitty Sewell and Grace Thompson, and the prolific author Alun Richards (1929–2004), whose novel based on the Mumbles lifeboat, *Ennal's Point* (1977), was adapted for television. The presence of so many artists – and the list could be much longer – suggests that Mumbles is an unusually congenial and inspiring place to live.

Binocular

From high upon this hill
the scene down there
is not one
of wasps, ice creams,
cigars, Radio One and Brummies whining
as a cussing husband casts off in his yacht –

but of white sails

inclining with hope
against a grey conspiracy of sky and sea.

SOUTHEND

Because houses along the Dunns to Knab Rock stretch of the Mumbles seafront were prone to flooding whenever a high tide coincided with a wind-driven surge, the council in the 1980s constructed a low, flood-defence wall along the landward side of the promenade, with recesses for benches.

If you look carefully at a run of nine of these benches roughly opposite the Conservative Club, you'll see drilled into the centre of the back-rest of each of them four neat holes, outlining the shape of a small rectangle. These holes are all that's left of a delightful, but unofficial, plan to give Mumbles some playful 'interventionist' public art.

In the early hours of 17 September 2004, nine members of the National Suburban Liberation Generation (NSLG) – mostly students at the West Wales School of the Arts, Carmarthen – arrived at the benches and began to affix to them small brass plaques hand-inscribed with intriguing messages such as 'For Miriam, whom I should have married', 'This seat is taken', 'Dedicated to Dafydd, who was conceived here in May', 'I gofio Angharad, a wnaeth byth eistedd yn llonydd' (In memory of Angharad, who could never sit still), and 'RIP all those who were lost before they ever found themselves'. As they busied themselves under cover of darkness, the NSLG activists failed to notice that Big Brother – in the form of a CCTV camera immediately above them – was observing every move. The police were quickly on the scene, and a representative member of the group, Jo Furnival, was carted off to the cells and charged with criminal damage and possession of an offensive weapon (a bradawl).

The offensive weapon charge was later dropped, but the police insisted – contrary to the council's position on the matter – on pursuing the case. While Jo consistently claimed to be innocent of the reckless vandalism implied by the charges, the prosecution consistently refused to consider a bind-over agreement – through a total of eight court appearances, as Jo organised his defence for a trial by jury in the crown court. Eventually, at Jo's ninth appearance in court, the Crown Prosecution Services decided to offer no evidence on the criminal damage charge, and Jo was simply bound over to keep the peace. Thus, a public art project which would have cost local people nothing turned into an anti-art 'happening' which, thanks to the protracted legal proceedings, cost the public purse £5,500.

At a party at Mozart's[9] in Walter Road, which was organised to thank the many Swansea artists who'd supported the NSLG cause, Jo Furnival stated: 'We're bored with the sort of ironic statements typical of post-modernist art. We think it's more interesting to make art that reminds people of what we have in common, and connects people with their own creativity. We want to be thought-provoking, but in a playful way.' The NSLG crew presented each of their core supporters with a slim box covered in black velvet. Inside were a screwdriver, four screws and a blank – but wonderfully provocative – brass plaque.

> the discos done,
> owl and sea help themselves
> to the night that's theirs

LANGLAND BAY

Langland is where the most serious of Swansea's serious money hangs out. Peer down on Langland and Caswell using Google Earth and count the swimming pools and tennis courts. It looks like suburban America.

Perhaps the most nouveaux of Langland's riches are to be found in Grove's Avenue, off Southward Lane, a privately owned cul-de-sac of houses with rootless names like Argent Lodge, Highgrove and Winterstoke House, which can sell for as much as £1m. High gates, high walls and high paranoia here – reflected in (English-only, of course) signs such as 'Private road NO PARKING unauthorised vehicles parking will be clamped / release fee £100' and 'Court action will be taken against owners of dogs fouling this land'. I fantasize sometimes about parading up and down this cul-de-sac with a large and very incontinent elephant.

The most ostentatious memento of a much earlier rush of money to the head is the turreted and towered High Gothic Revival pile that dominates the architectural landscape of the bay itself. Built in the 1860s as a marine villa for Henry Crawshay, of the Merthyr Tydfil dynasty of ironmasters, it overlorded the bay, with gardens sloping down to the seashore and a kitchen garden occupying the present car park. In 1893, it was considerably enlarged as a hotel of 'opulent splendour' for 150 guests. This lavish summer retreat from the realm of the industrial unwashed became, in 1922, a haven for the very class on which the Crawshays had depended for their wealth,

when the Club and Institute Union (CIU) bought it as a convalescent home and hotel for miners, steelmen and other workers. For over eighty years, workingmen's clubs from all over Britain sent their members here for subsidised sojourns by the sea. But in 2005, the 45-bedroom Langland Bay Workingmen's Club and Institute was sold for over £4m. As Langland Manor, it's reverting to private indulgence, being converted into 27 luxury apartments costing (in 2007) between £235,000 and £625,000 each.

Never having ventured inside the building or its grounds, I take advantage of the public auction of its contents, one December Saturday in 2005, to have a good nose around. It's a long, narrow building with – on its four storeys – rooms either side of stark, end-to-end corridors: brash carpets, uPVC window frames and artexed ceilings throughout, with an unembellished, two-star sort of ambience. The original rooms still have their Gothic-arch doorways. The bedrooms are much as the last guests left them. In one, I find a yellowing copy of *The Kenilworth Weekly News*; in another, a forgotten sponge bag. On the ground floor, serious buyers and the merely inquisitive drift in and out of the snooker rooms, bars and dining rooms picking over the 500 lots that have been assembled for sale: pianos, pool tables, potato peelers, Parker Knoll chairs, televisions, candlesticks, decanters, card tables, wine glasses, beer glasses, medical equipment, wheelchairs.

As the bidding gets underway, I wander outside, where the soughing of the sea and the presence of an undertaker's van on the forecourt quicken a poignant sense of fin de siècle. All the wooden benches out here are for sale too, lot numbers slapped alongside their donors' commemorative plaques: Greenwich Town Social Club, Kent Ladies Convalescent Home Fund.

I walk on then, skirting the golf course (once a farm belonging to Crawshay's estate), towards Snaple Point, the bay's western promontory.

> copper shafts
> through bundling grey, beaming up
> the Severn Sea

My mother remembers standing here as a teenager in the summer of 1940 and waving to the pilot of a low-flying aircraft bearing French markings. She was horrified to learn later that the presumed friend had been a foe in Gallic disguise. The plane had flown on unchallenged over Swansea where it dropped four high explosive bombs on King's Dock, killing twelve dockers. This enigmatic daytime attack was the third raid of the war and the first in which Swansea sustained casualties.

I return along the front, passing the distinctive row of 78 green and white beach huts beloved of weekend painters and visitors to what remains one of Gower's most popular beaches. Catherine Zeta-Jones, despite her nine homes in places like Bermuda and Majorca, claims that Langland is still her favourite beach, although I can't say I've noticed her and Michael disporting themselves here lately, or partaking at the Surfside Café of what is surely one of the most flavoursome mugs of tea in Wales. The wooden huts, which were built in the 1920s, are owned by the council and are let on alternate months, between April and September, for around £240 each. Periodic attempts by developers to demolish them and build flats in their place have been stoutly resisted, although in the summer of 2007 they came under attack – presumably for firewood – by the gangs of boozed-up boy racers that tend to take over the western end of the beach on weekend evenings. At about the same time, the council was proposing to demolish the weather-beaten huts and replace them with swankier, pricier versions (£10,000 for a 10-year lease).

> after the rain, more drizzle –
> this weather melts no jellyfish

Langland's all-weather devotees – when the waves are right – are the surfers. It was a visit to Langland in 1967 by the Australian surfing champion Keith Paul that inspired Pete Jones ('PJ') of Langland to his championship achievements in the 1970s – achievements emulated since then by surfers such as Swansea's Carwyn Williams and the long-boarder Chris 'Guts' Griffiths, also from Langland. With neighbouring Caswell, and Llangennith at the tip of Gower, Langland can claim to be the home of Welsh surfing.

> Whit Monday washout,
> red spade abandoned
> in the deluged castle

At the eastern end of the promenade is the delightful cove of Rotherslade (or Little Langland or, earlier, Lady's Bay) which, because parking is limited, is more of a locals' bay than Langland.

The entire landward width of the bay used to be taken up by the 'White Elephant' (1925), a colonnaded shelter surmounted by a roller-skating rink and café, with steps to the beach on either side. By about the 1970s, it had fallen into rusting, urinous decay. It was demolished in the 1990s and replaced by a lawn-flanked, canted decent to the beach, at the top of which is Rother's Tor Café, with its broad terrace for tables and chairs. The café is named after the large rock at the western side of the bay – also known as Rothers Skerr, Storr Rock or Donkey Rock – which is islanded when the tide is in, and from which generations of whooping youngsters have hurled themselves into the sea.

As the tide goes out, Rotherslade loses one island and gains another – Crab Island, a reef of jagged rocks to the south east, where, indeed, crabs are harvested. It's also, at about half-tide, a magnet for surfers, who need their wits about them to avoid being shredded by its serrated limestone.

Langland is a realm of vanished hotels. Next door to the CIU sanctuary there used to stand the Langland Bay Hotel which, as Samantha's disco and later Amanda's, was *the* Monday nightspot in the 'sixties and early 'seventies, featuring bands such as Love Sculpture[10], Dream, the Bystanders and the Eyes of Blue. The hotel stumbled mysteriously into the path of a developer's bulldozer one dark night in the early 1980s. And on the hilltop above, the Langland Court Hotel seemed so anxious, after lying empty for three years, to turn itself into 38 new flats that – one similarly dark night in 2005 – it burst obligingly into flames (city councillors proved less obliging, however, and turned the scheme down). The bay's other major hotel, the Osborne at Rotherslade, met its end in a more orderly manner: demolished in 2003 to make way for a louring block of 36 luxury investment squats. The project was masterminded by some conglomerate in Spain patently unconcerned to reflect anything of the spirit of place – a place honoured, for instance, in the paintings of the French Impressionist Alfred Sisley (1839-99) who spent his honeymoon at the Osborne in 1897, before dying of cancer just over a year later. The old Osborne (itself, eventually, an architectural shambles) proudly displayed along its main corridor faded reproductions of Sisley's superb views of the bay, together with a sketch of him sitting snugly in the hotel's kitchen.

Although ugly buildings continue to multiply in Rotherslade, the place is still honoured in all sorts of ways by those who love it: by the kids jumping off Donkey Rock; by the writings of the novelist Stevie

Davies who lives in Mumbles and swims here as often as she can (Tyrone O'Sullivan of Tower Colliery spends his summer holidays here too); by the splendid salon of bronzed and grey-haired amphibian 'old timers' whose habitual domain – for reading, talking, eating and drinking – is a suntrap in the cove's eastern corner. "I hope we can be like them when we reach their age," Stevie said to me once. I hope so too.

Poem found written at intervals in the snow on the Rotherslade to Limeslade sea path, 12.i.82

Oes heddwch?[11]

Love?

Poets?

Dyfodol?[12]

Or even a plumber?

GOWERTON

Tuesday was mart day. Every Tuesday, year after year, decade after decade, the cattle wagons and sheep and pig trailers would trundle through the streets of Gowerton to the livestock market built in 1927 between Gorwydd Road and the main Swansea to west Wales railway line. At the end of a raucous, crowded day, during which holes would be punched in the ears of every animal that went under the hammer[13], and blood would flow as copiously as the animals' shit and piss, the livestock would be ferried away, in different vehicles than they'd come in, to be turned into food, their fate sealed by the arcane mouth music of the auctioneers.

War, snow, flu pandemics – nothing, it seemed, could stand in the way of Gowerton mart. As long as the people of Swansea wanted to eat lamb, beef and bacon, the mart would open every holy Tuesday to provide their needs[14]. But then, as suddenly as if it had taken a direct hit from a Luftwaffe bomb, the mart came to an abrupt end. The foot and mouth outbreak of 2001 closed livestock markets throughout Britain, and Gowerton was among those that never reopened. It was the end of an era not only for Gowerton but for my family, who, as well as being farmers, had run the mart for generations.

It's July 2005 and the now unrecognisable mart does indeed resemble a bomb site. My brother Martyn – a mouth musician extraordinaire whose rapid-fire chanting of numerals makes, to uninitiated ears, a remarkable abstract poetry – has sold the mart for housing. All the pens and sheds have been swept away, and the site is a swirl of dust, JCBs, dumper trucks and cement mixers. The estate is to be called Drovers Point (no apostrophe), and the children at Tregŵyr Junior School have chosen names for the streets: Heol y Gwartheg, Yr Hen Gorlan, Llys y Farchnad, Tir y Farchnad, Clos y Porthmon, Clos Tregŵyr – agricultural names, on the whole, struggling to cast a Welsh spell over Taylor Woodrow's identi-homes with their blandly English generic names: the Ashbourne, the Fernlea, the Malbury, the Clifford.

Suburban anonymity descends on the last institution keeping Gowerton from settling into dormitory village mode. It's now a cleaner, quieter but less colourful place than it used to be in its industrial and agricultural heyday.

Gowerton has had several names. Its first, naming a junction of farmers' and drovers' tracks near today's Welcome to Gower pub, was Ffosfelin (ditch + mill) after a cornmill built near the river Llan in 1680 and demolished in 1939 (one of its millstones is on display outside the library in Mansel Street). That much of the surrounding land was no more than a boggy morass has suggested to some that the hamlet's original name was Ffosfelen (yellow ditch). When coal was discovered beneath the marshy ground in the 1800s, mines were sunk, the land was drained and houses were built. The growth of Ffosfelin was spurred on by the building of two railway lines – the Swansea to west Wales line (1852) and the Swansea to Pontarddulais line (1876) – which crossed each other at Ffosfelin and which enabled the easy transportation of coal. The burgeoning village then changed its name to Gower Road and in 1885 it became Gowerton, because too many letters intended for the village were ending up in Gower Road, Sketty.

Steel, ultimately, was the making of Gowerton – with one steelworks, the Elba (1872-1967), predominating. Gowerton, indeed, was the Elba. Named after the island off the west coast of Italy, a one-time source of ore, the works was situated on land at the north-western edge of the village. Its half dozen smokestacks, with 'Baldwins' in huge letters down the largest of them, dominated the skyline for miles around, until the works was demolished in 1973 and levelled off, eventually, for the 1980 Dyffryn Lliw National Eisteddfod.

The only physical traces of the works are in Mill Street: a curved fragment of wall marking the works entrance (immediately south of the notoriously low railway bridge) and the Elba's testing laboratory, now the Gowerton Medical Centre. The housing estate that occupies the works site commemorates its history with street names such as Llys Elba, Llys Baldwin and Clos Leighton Davies. Which brings me to another declaration of family interest, for Leighton Davies (1894-1980) – or Captain Leighton Davies as he was known – was my maternal grandfather.

He and his family, like his father before him, lived in 'the big house' (since demolished) overlooking the village – and, crucially, the works for which he, like his father before him, was responsible. Known as The Mount, it had been built in 1880 by the industrialist Colonel John Roper Wright (1843-1926) who established the Elba as a successful steelworks after its failed early days. By the time my mother Gloria was born there, in 1926, the family had long 'gone up in the world': public school, English in speech and name, Conservative in politics, chauffeurs, maids, gardeners, ponies, deluxe volumes of Shakespeare (pages uncut) – all the trappings befitting a captain of industry. Yet theirs were humble origins. My great grandfather John Davies (1864-1927) was born at the Lamb and Flag pub in Waunarlwydd, and started his working life at the Elba, aged 15, as a mill boy. A Hollywood scriptwriter could not have made a better job of John Davies's rags-to-riches tale. He ended his life as a knighted magnate of the steel industry, Sir John Cecil Davies (he added the Cecil himself; Gowerton's Cecil Road is named after him). On the day of his funeral, 20,000 steelworkers across Wales downed tools and stood respectfully in five minutes' cap-doffed silence.

Both Sir John and his son seem to have had a paternalist care for their workers and the people of Gowerton. My grandfather and his wife Molly are remembered still, by older residents, for the annual Christmas films and sweets they provided for local children at Gowerton's Tivoli cinema. Another benefaction was the pavilion my grandfather gave to the cricket club in 1922 – still doing service on the athletics ground just north of the railway embankment that bounds the old Elba site.

I decide, in the dusty whirlwind of the vanished mart, to pay the pavilion a visit. With me are my daughters Angharad and Branwen.

As pupils at Ysgol Gyfun Gŵyr, the Welsh-medium comprehensive school, they share with me their experiences of today's Gowerton – or Tre-gŵyr – as we walk through the village, in exchange for some memories of my own.

What fascinated me about Gowerton were the trains, not the mart – whose ineluctable routines bored me. Where Gorwydd Road swings left into Sterry Road there used to be a gated level crossing accompanied by a pedestrian bridge over the Swansea to Pontarddulais (or LMS) line. I'd spend hours on this bridge – which was painted a curious, glistening grey – licking an ice cream or sucking the flavour out of an ice lolly while waiting for steam trains to pass below, enveloping me in rewarding billows of steam and smoke. The line closed in 1965, and the associated station – Gowerton South – was demolished. Gowerton North, on the Swansea to west Wales line, then became simply Tre-gŵyr /Gowerton.

The girls and I carry on down the main street. It used to be called Station Road, but it was renamed Sterry Road after the coalowner Alfred Sterry (1823-1876) who founded the Elba works in 1872. The King Balti on our left used to be Hibbert's stores where, on our way home from the mart, we'd pick up our groceries in large boxes smelling of Daz or Omo. Opposite, in what is now the Ming Fai takeaway, was Garfield Morgan the barber's, where, as the sixties got hairier, I grew increasingly resistant to Mr Morgan's regulation Brylcreemed Mohawk.

The Contented Sole fish and chip shop, the girls tell me, is very popular with pupils from both their school and Gowerton Comprehensive, as is Thomas News opposite. The rivalry between the neighbouring schools is not always as friendly as might be wished, the police having been called in now and then to keep the warring factions apart.

The Ty Gwyn Mawr pub, with its topless 'y'[15], was built in 1884 as the London North Western Railway Hotel. Toplessness seems to be something of a tradition here. The pyramidal tower with which it was originally topped out was removed in 1974, and in 2005, at a sitting of the licensing authority, eyebrows – if not temperatures – were raised at complaints from neighbours about topless trampolining in the pub's beer garden.

Radical toplessness, if that isn't too contradictory a term, has also afflicted the Conservative Club, which flies *y Ddraig Goch* and seems bashful these days about its political affiliations, advertising itself simply as Gowerton Club. When it opened in 1886, with financial backing from Roper Wright, it was the first Conservative Club in Wales – and an audacious stab, I suppose, at what used to be called class collaboration. Constructed of furnace slag and Aberthaw limestone, it was topped by a 'crazy spirelet'[16] (the fanciful upper half of which was lopped off a couple of years ago). The weekly newspaper *Tarian y Gweithiwr*[17] was deliciously scathing of the new venture: "... the Tories have built a kind of Pandemonium as a scientific frontier for the Jingoes of Gower Road, a Temple in which are worshiped God and Bacchus and in which are united Bible and Beer. One day in the week they congregate together to learn a little from the Bible and old Mothers' Creeds, the other six days of the week they gather to the same Babel to drink, argue and gamble for similar purposes which are, it is said, absolutely necessary to fit men to be enlightened and conscientious Tories ..."

All sorts of people, and not just Tories, used the club, which soon established itself as an amenity for the whole village, with its banquets, concerts, whist drives, schoolroom facilities – and, today, its £6.95 Sunday lunches. Inevitably, my grandfather, as his father before him, was a generous patron of the Conservative Club which, well into the 1990s, was known as the Leighton Lounge.

Another boozer with family associations is the Welcome to Gower (1850s) at the western end of Sterry Road. My great-great-grandfather, Thomas Davies (Sir John's father), was landlord here from 1875 to 1880, when the pub – as the Gower Inn or the Gower Road Inn – was at the heart of village life. Poet (in Welsh, of course), wit, education campaigner and instigator of the famous Gower Road fairs (the last of which was held in 1965), he was a leading member of the Village Vestry, a sort of parish council which met regularly at the pub. I'd like to have met him.

As we turn right into Mill Street, I think of another relative I'd like to have met, a woman who kept a gin shop in a house – still extant – called Tŷ Gwyn, which my mother says was frequented mainly by women, the pubs in those days being men-only establishments.

Mill Street is notorious for traffic jams. In the days of Elba too there would be holds-ups here, caused by works trains coming and going on a level crossing, two of their shunting engines – to the delight of us kids – named after our mother, Gloria and Bunty (a nickname), and a third after our uncle, John.

Passing under the railway bridge, where Mill Street becomes Victoria Road, we turn left into the athletics ground and head across the sun-crisped pitch to the old pavilion with its dazzling white roof. There to meet us is Graham Young, chairman of the cricket club, who invites us in to have a look. It was used for both cricket and rugby changing rooms, one room per team, with a large central room for functions and a kitchen at the rear. Every inch of the redwood flooring is pitted with nearly a century's worth of being stomped over by studded boots. It's been superseded lately by more modern – and characterless – accommodation. "The question now," says Graham, "is whether to renovate it or demolish it. We'd love to keep it, but we're afraid of what troubles we might encounter if we start renovating. And it costs £1000 a year to insure."

Evidence of the Jenkins/Davies connection with Gowerton, in auctioneers' parlance, is going, going, (almost) gone.

notes

1 A Japanese literary form in origin, combining haiku and haiku-like prose.

2 Two others were Richard Savage (d. 1743) and Julia Ann Hatton (Ann of Swansea; 1764-1838).

3 It's fitting, perhaps, that as well as meaning a shaft of stone, an obelisk was also a mark used in ancient texts to point out a corrupt or doubtful passage.

4 From Ephesians, IV.25 and the First Book of Esdras, II.12 respectively.

5 John Beynon, 'An old lie out', in James A. Davies (ed.), A Swansea Anthology (Seren, 1996).

6 There were, in addition, twelve smaller collieries, slants or levels.

7 A few hundred metres to the west, however, towards the southern end of the popular fishing pool that is skirted by the bike path, there's the entrance to a mining tunnel which, unlike most such tunnels in the Swansea area, has not collapsed. It's grilled and padlocked against entry.

8   T.J. Morgan (1907–1986) was father of the National Assembly's First Minister Rhodri Morgan (1939) and of the writer and historian Prys Morgan (1937). The family lived for many years in Bishopston, where Prys Morgan still lives.

9   Swansea's premier late-drinking spot for those who prefer sociality to the conversation-zapping blitzpop of downtown venues.

10 Although a (somewhat aseptic) blues band, Dave Edmunds' Love Sculpture made their name – and the Top Ten – with a seven-minute headlong assault on Khachaturian's 'Sabre Dance', their compulsive *grand finale* whenever they played in Swansea.

11 Literally, 'Is there peace?', the question that is thrice asked at the chairing and crowning ceremonies of the National Eisteddfod, to which the audience thrice replies in the affirmative, 'Heddwch'.

12 Future.

13 As evidence that a government subsidy had been paid on the animal, so that the animal couldn't be 'recycled' and the subsidy claimed a second time.

14 Before 1927, the mart was held on alternate weeks in a field behind the Commercial pub and on the green at the King Arthur Hotel, Reynoldston.

15 The Ty should be Tŷ.

16 John Newman's adjudication.

17 Literally, 'The worker's shield'.

NORTH

THE LOWER SWANSEA VALLEY

Swansea wasted no time, when the opportunity arose in the 1960s, in obliterating all but a few traces of the industries which, over a 250-year period, had made it 'Copperopolis', a world leader in the production of not only copper, but also steel, tinplate and zinc.

In its metallurgical heyday, the landscape of the Lower Swansea Valley had been one of the awe-inspiring wonders of the industrialising world. George Borrow, touring 'Wild Wales' in 1854, had stood transfixed by the "accursed pandemonium" of smoke, filth and fire which he observed from the valley side. "So strange a scene I had never beheld in nature," he wrote. "Had it been on canvas, with the addition of a number of diabolical figures … it might have stood for Sabbath in Hell … and would have formed a picture worthy of the powerful but insane painter Hieronymous Bosch." By the mid twentieth century, when the abandonment of heavy industry in favour of service industries was well under way, this exhausted industrial landscape was spectacular still – for the extravagance of its devastation and the seeming impossibility of doing anything to make good one of the most polluted places on earth.

A post-war 'clean sweep' mentality combined with an urgent commitment, after the Aberfan disaster of 1966, to rid the post-industrial environment of its most degraded and dangerous features, and to reclaim derelict sites for new uses. Coal, copper, steel and tinplate may have been the making of old Swansea, but for many of those charged with the re-making of post-war Swansea, memories would have been all too raw of how their immediate forebears had lived lives of unremitting hardship. In their drive, to quote the poet Bryn Griffiths,

> to erase the stain of the past,
> to seed earth soured by a century
> of slag and sulphur fumes,
> to heal the cankered sore that
> is today Landore

the authorities gave hardly a second, sentimental thought to certain structures within the wreckage which industrial archaeologists informed them were of major international importance. They called in the Territorial Army, during the 1960s, to raze to the ground half a dozen such sites.

Between 1960 and 1990, the Lower Swansea Valley was indeed transformed, especially the devastated valley bottom between the A48 Llansamlet–Morriston road in the north and the Hafod to the south – an area on the map looking like a stubby, upended bottle pointing towards the sea. Particularly striking, east of the Tawe, are extensive plantations of larch, pine, birch and alder on land that it was once assumed would never again support life of any kind. The region became renowned as a laboratory for pollution and reclamation scientists. Where there were huge boulders of fused slag, mounds of multi-coloured toxic waste, crumbling smokestacks, decaying smelter sheds and abandoned sidings there's now an American-style enterprise 'park', with banal rows of retail sheds, offices and car parks, together with light industrial and manufacturing units. Dotted among them are a couple of ponds, teeming with coarse fish, and the lawn-fringed Fendrod Lake, dug out of the highly contaminated Fendrod marsh as a flood prevention measure, with its ducks and swans, picnic tables and fishing stages. If the dry ski slope and the Morfa athletics stadium have come and gone, there's no escaping the dazzling white, £30m Liberty Stadium at Landore, home of the Swans and the Ospreys since 2005. Looking like a multi-limbed, metal crab that could scuttle sideways at any moment, the stadium compels attention as the dominant structure in a landscape in which leisure and consumerism are now kings.

In spite in the insouciant haste with which the trappings of heavy industry were swept away, the Lower Swansea Valley nevertheless contains over twenty industrial sites of national and international importance – not that Swansea encourages any interest in them. It's

possible to follow an industrial trail of sorts, but you have to find your own way, there being no readily available published guide. It's a landscape of superlatives, with traces at every turn of 'the world's first this' and 'the world's largest that', but unless you've read up on the area, you have next to no idea what you're looking at.

There are those elsewhere for whom Swansea's renowned history is a magnet. It's a

sweltering July morning in 2006, and I'm walking the valley with Dr
Keir Reeves, a cultural historian from the University of Melbourne,
who's touring key post-industrial sites in Europe, chief among them
the china clay district of Cornwall, the world heritage site at
Blaenafon – and Swansea. He's been commissioned by the
Australian government to come up with plans for the development
of the former gold-mining region of Victoria as a world heritage
environment. He's hoping that Swansea might give him some ideas
– while I'm thinking, the longer we walk and talk, that Keir might
have some ideas for Swansea.

I've warned him that as far as industrial remains are concerned
there's not that much to see – although submerged, like an industrial
Pompeii, beneath the retail sheds, the newer suburbs and the redis-
tributed copper waste that was used to level off a chaotic landscape
there are undoubtedly important structural and mechanical remains.
Tramping along a tarmacked former railway line to the east of the
Tawe, we can delight in the stretch of new forest that borders the
path, but we also share a sense of regret at how the greening of parts
of the valley has obliterated so much of the industrial heritage.

The banks of the river that ferried the copper ore – from Cornwall,
Anglesey, Cuba, Chile and elsewhere – directly to the coal that was
used to smelt it, are walkable only here and there. From the Quay
Parade bridge near the docks, both banks look promising. But after
about 300 metres, the west bank path comes to an abrupt halt at the
fence that surrounds the massive black sheds of the engineering firm
Unit Superheating. A string of commercial and light industrial
concerns, and thereafter housing in the Hafod, keep the western
riverbank inaccessible for nearly a kilometre. The best bet is therefore
the eastern path. Its riverside stretch, before it veers right to skirt the
forestry, is dotted with Swansea Harbour Trust mooring bollards,
reminders of the almost continuous wharves that once lined the river
as far as Morriston.

While the presiding genius of the western side of the valley – up
ahead of us, on a crag overlooking Landore – is Morris 'castle', that
of the eastern side, immediately to our right, is Kilvey Hill, its black-
ened western flank still smarting from centuries of sulphurous
pollution. In this morning's bright sunlight, Kilvey's underlying
Pennant sandstone, exposed by the odd (disused) quarry, gleams a
rich dark gold.

The first major industrial site we come to is that of the White Rock
Copperworks (1737-1929). To the poet Bryn Griffiths, who was

raised nearby, "The ruins of White Rock was our secret playground, our Rome, our Thebes, our Lost City of Incas, Aztecs, whatever (we were literary kids). And there was the scrap works alongside, which we raided for weapons (real ones), left over from World War II." Cleared by the TA in the early 1960s, the site was designated the White Rock Industrial Archaeology Park in the 1980s when significant remains were excavated and consolidated. It was the first copper smelter to be built on the east bank of the river and the third of what would eventually total eleven riverside copperworks. Its most obvious feature is a spiral path inscribed playfully on a broad grassy mound. This is all that remains of a monstrous spoil tip, the bulk of which – 186,000 tonnes of it – was dumped on the site of the Upper Forest and Worcester tinplate works four kilometres away at Morriston, where it formed a platform above the flood-plain of the Tawe for the construction of the Morganite Carbon factory. Other notable features include part of the Pennant sandstone smelting hall known as 'The Great Workhouse', a cut-and-cover canal tunnel, sandstone quays, and a re-excavated and beautifully conserved seventeenth-century river dock – perhaps the most evocative remnant of all. Forget the overgrown greensward underfoot and the thick foliage on either side of the river, and imagine the Tawe confounded again with flame and industrial ferment, and a laden Cape Horner – thrusting bowsprit, towering masts – looming majestically through the noxious smokes billowing from all sides, her local crew thronging the deck, desperate to get ashore after six to nine months at sea. If Swansea had a more visionary attitude towards its industrial and maritime heritage, there might be ambitious plans for the reconstruction of one of its famous copper-ore barques, such as the *Zeta* (1865-82), after which the holy Catherine was named.

What goods were made from the ore the Cape Horners brought home? Copper sheathing for the hulls of timber ships (hence that term of assurance 'copper bottomed'), bolts, hinges, glazing bars, roofing material, coins, harness parts, buttons, buckles, toys, kitchen utensils, boilers, pipes, vats, rollers, wires, plates. Many of these things were manufactured in centres such as Birmingham, Bristol, Liverpool and London, after Swansea had produced the raw material in the form of fine copper ingots. Swansea copper also played a shameful role in the slave-dependent economies of the eighteenth and nineteenth centuries. Various Swansea smelters produced copper 'rods' and horse-shoe shaped bronze 'manillas' for bartering for slaves in Africa, White Rock being an early producer of manillas.

Directly opposite the White Rock site, and all but lost in a jungle of buddleia, birch and ivy, is the saw-toothed roof of the Vivian company's loco shed, built to house Britain's first ever standard-gauge articulated locomotive. Deciding on a closer examination, we cross the river via the A4217 road bridge, taking stock as we go of the wider human environment: Morriston to the north – dominated by the ornate steeple of Tabernacl – the first and largest of the settle-ments founded by the coppermasters; the terraces to the east built for their workers by the Grenfell family and known as Grenfelltown (now Pentrechwyth); the self-contained copperworkers' community of the Hafod to the immediate west; the terraces of Brynhyfryd, Landore and Plasmarl, and the huge chapels of quintessentially Welsh design – Siloh Newydd, Dinas Noddfa – scattered domineeringly among them.

"This is one hell of a landscape," says Keir. "I was expecting something, sure, but nothing as fascinating as this."

What he finds difficult to understand is why Swansea appears so reluctant to celebrate its unique industrial heritage and why the few internationally significant structures that remain are so shamefully neglected, as if being willed to destruction by the elements, vandalism and time.

The most prominent industrial relics on the valley bottom, which we pass en route to the loco shed, are proclaimed by their smoke-stacks[1]: two engine houses belonging to the Vivian's Hafod Works (1810-1924), which by 1842 was the largest copperworks in the world. Built in the early 1860s and 1910 respectively, these roofless, rotting structures are supposedly secured against vandals by a spiked fence, some of which has been cut away to provide relatively easy access for the graffiti artists who have evidently been at work on their walls. Fenced doubly securely within the fence is some rolling machinery, evidently so 'valuable' that, for years, it's been exposed on all sides to the weather. Uphill from the engine houses is the Landore Social Club, which used to be the works office. Opposite the club is a chunky sandstone structure, a rare survivor of the 54 limekilns once dotted along the Swansea Canal, for burning Mumbles limestone.

The loco shed is unfenced, other than by the almost impenetrable buddleia. You can just make out through the foliage large letters in white brickwork, along its eastern wall, spelling out 'V & S [i.e. Vivian and Son] Ltd No. 1 SHED'. The shed is built chiefly of the Vivian company's light grey, slag-based 'patent' brick, which tends, in time, to crumble. The somewhat spayed walls are mostly intact, but the shattered roof is dangerously unstable. Without urgent attention, the collapse of this important building will surely be complete in a year or two.

The graffitists have been up to their expert, if garish, labours along a riverside wall nearby, and they have managed to get inside some robustly fenced remains of the historic Morfa Works (1835-1980), just round the corner at the Landore park-and-ride. Distinguished by its skeletal clock turret and the exposed timbers of its roof, charred after a recent fire and close to caving in, this late nineteenth-century, Grade II listed building was the works' electrical powerhouse before becoming the canteen building of Yorkshire Imperial Metals, the last owners of the combined Hafod and Morfa works. Nearby is an old rolling mill shed, now used by Swansea Museum as a store, which at the time of its construction in the 1840s was the largest of its kind in the world.

We continue upriver on the west side of the Tawe. On the opposite bank, incorporated into the huge Addis plastics factory, are three re-roofed smelting halls (c.1838-42) of the old Upper Bank Works (1757), in which the first ever Mutz Yellow Metal was made for the sheathing of ships' hulls. With their characteristic ventilated gable ends and the foundations of furnaces under their floors, these Grade II listed structures are the last roofed smelting halls in Swansea. The whole site has been earmarked for residential development – Barratt Homes' £100m, 550-unit Copper Quarter scheme – and conservationists have been campaigning to save the sheds from demolition.

The council eventually decided to permit demolition of two of them, but to insist on the retention of the best preserved as a 'landmark' building in the new (and necessarily well-heeled) 'community', enisled by whizzing traffic and the out-of-town shopping sheds you find all over Britain: Sports World, TK Maxx, Morrisons, Pizza Hut, Next, George.

Another gently decaying Grade II structure nearby is the remarkable iron and timber bascule bridge (1919), over which slag was transported from the Morfa works to tips on the east side of the Tawe. By means of hydraulic power – the filling of a water tank at its western end – its deck would tilt upwards, to allow sailing ships to pass along the river.

The path continues alongside the Liberty Stadium and between the towering stone piers of Brunel's magnificent Landore Viaduct (1847-50), most of which was built originally of timber. This bridge too was designed to give clearance to sailing ships.

It was on a site just south of the viaduct that, in the 1860s, Wilhelm Siemens perfected the open-hearth process that revolutionised the production of steel. Nothing now remains of the Landore Siemens Steel Company works which, by 1873, was one of the world's four largest steelworks. Nor is there any trace, just north of the viaduct, of the earliest copper-smelting works in the valley, the Llangyfelach Copperworks (1717).

We carry on towards Morriston, switching – over a new footbridge at Plasmarl – to the east bank. Here, on a triangular plot in the lee of Makro, is the Pantyblawd Road site of the only statutory 'gipsy' encampment in the county. The gipsies, or travellers as they call themselves, have long been part of the valley scene, and have frequently suffered persecution. Any 'trouble' in valley communities is usually perceived to be the doing of 'rough' elements from elsewhere in the valley, with the 'gypsies' often – and unfairly – getting the blame.

On the outskirts of Morriston, we turn back towards town, taking a detour through the Hafod, currently undergoing a major programme of renovation. The re-rendering of many of the terraces of what is the best conserved copperworkers' township in Swansea is startlingly attractive.

By the end of our tour, Keir is astonished that, in spite of the late twentieth century 'obliterations', so much survives of the industrial whirlwind that made Swansea's name – from the remains of works and transportation systems, to the communities built for the workers and some of the mansions the magnates built for themselves in Swansea west. "If anywhere in Wales deserves world heritage status it's Swansea," he says. "Swansea should go for it. It ticks just about every world heritage box."

The conservation and promotion of Swansea's industrial heritage is obviously way beyond Swansea's financial capabilities (pressing immediate needs include a daunting £180m to refurbish the city's 113 schools). Without the international recognition (and funds) that would flow from achieving something like world heritage status, it seems inevitable that the neglect and deterioration will continue. Whether Swansea has the vision to pursue such an ambition – which might represent in the longer term a more creative opportunity for the city than the current obsession with building flashy waterside apartments for the rich – must, sadly, remain in doubt.

MORRIS CASTLE

Morris Castle, whose ruined twin towers stand sentinel high above Landore, was considered by the poet Edward Thomas (1878-1917) to be "the only thing in Swansea to satisfy a taste for the medieval pictur-esque". But Morris Castle – or Castell Graig or Trewyddfa Castle – is not a castle. It's what remains of a block of flats – Wales's earliest, and among Europe's first tenement-style accommodation since Roman times. It was built around 1773 by the coppermaster Sir John Morris I (1745-1819), the founder of Morriston, to house colliers employed at his Treboeth pit. It may have been the first construction in Swansea in which copper slag blocks were used.

Not, you might think, an entirely insignificant structure. But, like most industrial-era relics in Swansea, don't expect to find it signposted. On the contrary, if you manage to work out that one of several possible approaches to its crag at Cnap-Llwyd – the northern approach – is alongside number 191 Trewyddfa Road, you'll be greeted by an official

sign that warns 'UNSAFE STRUCTURE KEEP AWAY'. The main
southern approach, up an offshoot of Trewyddfa Road and past a
house with a magnificent pigeon loft out the back, is scarcely more
welcoming: in a worked-out quarry immediately below the towers,
there are three or four charred fir trees under which fires have been
lit with wooden pallets, to recover wire and scrap metal from cables
and car seats – a common illegal activity in secluded pockets of
wasteland.

We clamber up to the castle around the lip of another old quarry,
to be rewarded by an almost complete panorama – of the Tawe valley,
Kilvey Hill, Swansea Bay, Townhill and Treboeth, with the view to the
north obscured by the pines cresting the 16 rolling hectares of Parc
Llewelyn (1878) half a kilometre away. What's left of the apartment
block are its turret-like south-eastern and south-western corners, with
four fireplaces apiece (one at basement level, and one for each of the
three storeys), and a ragged topping of hart's tongue fern. Half of the
south-eastern tower, felled by a storm in 1987, lies in chunks among
the couch-grass and brambles.

The flats were built chiefly of Pennant sandstone dug from
quarries immediately to hand, with some brick here and there, and
string-courses of black, rectangular blocks cast from iron-oxide slag
produced at Morris's copper works. They're inviting surfaces for
graffitists. Marv, Monk and Betty – or their admirers – have scaled to
the top floor to leave their signatures there. Tash, Tom, Deenis and
Monky have been busily repetitive elsewhere. These blocks were a
common by-product of the copper industry. Although slag blocks
were more durable than brick or stone, few buildings were
constructed entirely of the material. But they were used in industrial
buildings where aesthetic considerations were less important, and –
sparingly – as quoins and decorative features in housing and chapels.
They're most evident today as coping stones for wall tops, cast either
as half-round blocks or as triangular blocks squared off at the base.
See, for instance, the garden walls of copperworkers' terraces in the
Hafod, or the wall the Vivians built in Brynmill Lane to seclude their
Singleton estate from plebeian attentions.

With an exterior covered in white lime plaster setting off the
regular striations of jet-black slag, and with its four castellated towers,
Morris castle must have been a dramatic landmark – as it was
intended to be, by both Morris and his English architect John
Johnson. It was part of the unified aesthetic vision Morris enjoyed,
from his Palladian-style mansion of Clasemont (also designed by

Johnson), of the entire Morris-controlled landscape. Walter Davies (1761 – 1849), in his *General View of the Agriculture and Domestic Economy of South Wales* (1810), describes the apartment block as a "lofty mansion, of a collegiate appearance, with an interior quadrangle, containing dwellings for 40^2 families, all colliers, excepting one tailor, one shoemaker, who are considered as useful appendages to the fraternity." The approach road from the north is still discernible on the ant-hilly, heather-clad plateau, as are the boundary banks of the garden plots Morris provided for his workers.

The views may have been spectacular, and the air – at least initially – may have been sweeter than down in the valley, but the long, uphill trudge from work did not appeal to the tenants of Morris castle. In 1811, by which time the Morrises themselves had been driven from Clasemont by the valley's noxious fumes, the apartment block was advertised for sale. It was still in residential use in 1850, but by the 1880s it was in ruins.

FFOREST-FACH

We're going to the dogs, my younger daughter Branwen and I. Our destination: the Swansea Greyhound Stadium in Fforest-fach[3].

Traffic jams, Tesco's superstore, Walkers crisps, countless factories, warehouses and retail sheds: such, for most non-residents, is the image of this amorphous suburb sprawling either side of a 2-km stretch of Carmarthen Road. Two hundred years ago, before extensive exploitation of the underlying Graigola seam, it was indeed a forested rural backwater. But all that changed during the nineteenth century, as the collieries sucked in mine workers and their families, the Swansea–Carmarthen railway line cut through to the north in the 1850s, and the small country village became a substantial community.

It was robustly Welsh in language and culture until well into the 1960s, as testified by the abundance of Welsh street and place names: Maes-y-Felin, Ty'n-y-Waun, Rhodfa'r Brain, Ffordd y Brain, Ystrad Uchaf, Heol Dynys, Heol Calfin, Penllwyn-eithen Uchaf.

Apart from one or two distinctive old chapels, Fforest-fach seems to be undergoing a relentless cleansing of historic memory. But as old buildings fall to the general 'improving' zeal, the occasional patriot keeps faith with the past. At Fforest-fach cross, diagonally opposite the Marquis pub (which sprang, seemingly overnight, from the ashes of an earlier, burned-out boozer), is the red-brick post office, which for decades boasted a home-made sign reading Tŷ Tywysog Llywelyn (Prince Llywelyn House). Tens of thousands of traffic-jammed motorists, over the years, must have pondered that sign's significance, and some, perhaps, will have felt like revving their engines in homage to Llywelyn ap Gruffudd (Y Llew Olaf; c.1225-82), the 'last prince'[4] of an independent Wales. About ten years ago, the 'Llywelyn' dropped off the rotting board. I notice now, as Branwen steers left into Carmarthen Road, that the 'Tŷ Tywysog' has also gone.

A traffic snarl-fest worse even than the cross at rush-hour is Parc Fforestfach, the vast shopping hell, dominated by Tesco, at the north-western edge of the built-up area. The car park may be big enough for you to lose your car in, but it is still hopelessly inadequate. 'Parking rage' fights have been known here, often coming to a frenzied, seasonal head at Christmas: in December, 2005 it took no less than two hours for motorists to leave the car park, which itself was gridlocked for four.

At the junction with Ffordd Cynore – where the Fforest Motel conveniently burned down one day, making yet more room for Parc Fforestfach – we turn left, and, after about a kilometre, reach a sharp bend in Ystrad Road, where we turn right into the Greyhound Stadium car park. Races are held every Tuesday and Saturday throughout the year, beginning at 7.30 p.m., and on bank holidays at 11.00 a.m. We're early – not only for the races but for Christmas: it's an Indian summer's evening in late September, but there's a neon sign on the red-brick clubhouse wall wishing us 'Merry Xmas', surmounted by a beaming plastic Santa. Or perhaps we're early for the races, and late for (last) Christmas. Plenty of time, either way, to soak up the pre-race atmosphere – the generation of which, at this stage, looks like being up to Branwen and me. We pay £4 each at the turnstile and pass through to the forecourt outside the Trappers Social and Sports Club, where a young couple at a picnic table are staring at their empty glasses. The only other sign of life is a clutch of kids kicking a football about in the middle of the oval field around which the freshly mown greensward of the race track invitingly runs. It's been a long hot summer. The contents of half a dozen hanging baskets outside the clubhouse long ago succumbed to thirst, and the commentator's box at the finishing line is similarly festooned with dead vegetation.

Time for a pint. In the Trappers Club – red plush chairs and benches, fading rustic scenes on the walls – we negotiate two pool tables at the entrance and a scrambler motorbike propped nearby. Four or five drinkers are half watching a rugby match on S4C. We take our drinks back to the forecourt and the livelier company of swifts reeling and swooping in the warm dusky light. The lovers have gone, but the punters are starting now to trickle through the turnstile. The smell of hot chip fat begins to fill the air, the lights come on around the track and the impromptu footballers leave for home.

That the place doesn't exactly exude professionalism is due partly to its status as a privately owned 'independent' track (like Wales's other two tracks, Bedwellte and Hengoed, Ystrad Mynach), rather than a track that's 'registered' and subject to National Greyhound Racing Club (NGRC) rules. Animal welfare organisations have long been concerned that the unregulated independent tracks lack the official safeguards that protect dogs in the registered sector from exploitation and eventual abandonment (or killing) at the end of their racing lives, aged three to five years. Exposés in the media of the ways in which dogs have been battered to death, poisoned, drowned, shot or left to starve to death have shocked the animal-loving public, turning many against the sport. But there has been a rapprochement in recent years between the welfare groups and the tracks, Fforest-fach in particular holding fundraising events to support the rescuing and re-housing of has-been hounds.

Eventually about a hundred spectators pitch up, often in family groups, aged from about eight to eighty. Many of them spend most of the evening in the clubhouse, eating sausages and chips and drinking, and taking little apparent interest in the actual races – which are short.

After gathering on the weighing platform, the six dogs (usually) per race are paraded up the greensward on their way to the starting traps in the far corner, and the last bets are placed with the tote and the three bookies. Business tonight is hardly booming. There is much squatting and cocking of legs at this point, the dogs having been trained, it seems, to excrete whatever they can at the very last minute. After they're settled in the traps, there's a metallic whirring, and the 'hare' or 'rabbit' (the sport developed from hare coursing) – a white nylon glove-like bag swollen with air – zips past us at 45 m.p.h and, as it rounds the bend in front of the traps, the dogs are released. They're an instantaneous blur of rippling muscle and pounding legs, covering about sixteen yards a second, a speed unmatched by any other breed of dog on earth. They come thumping up the home stretch, over the finishing line and on round the bend by the traps, where the rabbit is whipped out of their reach with only a split second to spare. It's all over in 17.50 seconds.

The first two races tonight are 'sprints', of 312 yards each. The remaining five are 525 yards – about one and a half times round the track – which the dogs cover in under 30 seconds. For most races there's a first prize only, of a modest £25, although international prizes elsewhere can run into thousands. When greyhound tracks first opened in Wales in the late 1920s, the sport became popular with miners and steelworkers, who could afford a dog and relished the possibility of making good money, but greyhound racing is too expensive these days to be enjoyed as a hobby.

We get chatting, between races, with Paul James from Aberdare and his girlfriend, who are racing two dogs tonight and who have brought a big 'puppy' along to get him used to the atmosphere. There's no mistaking their enthusiasm for the sport. Fforest-fach, says Paul, "is as good a track as any in Britain", and people come to race their dogs here from as far afield as Cornwall, Cumbria and Ireland.

'It's a shame that greyhound people have such a bad name,' he says. "Greyhounds are the only breed of dog to be mentioned in the Bible, and two thousand years of breeding has gone into these dogs. Greyhounds are the only pedigree dog. They are wonderfully intelligent animals with really distinctive personalities. They absolutely love racing, but they are also great dogs just to have around the place, they are so loving. I call them 40 m.p.h. couch potatoes."

Paul, who has had five world records with greyhounds, has another passion: politics. A Plaid Cymru candidate, he came within twelve votes of winning a seat on his local council at the last elections. With the tenacity of one of his greyhounds, he's confident of bagging that hare for Plaid the next time round.

The prospects for the dog track itself are less propitious. The lease on its council-owned site expires in 2010, and there are fears it could be redeveloped as a business park.

TOWNHILL

Townhill, on its 180-m high ridge, is – even by the standards of a city known for its distinct urban villages – a place apart. Its approaches are so steep that they could be conquered, when public transport was first attempted there, only by special buses brought in from

Switzerland. In wintry weather, it's often only Townhill that catches the snow; when skies are low, Townhill can be lost to sight beneath a bandage of mist for days on end. And at night, there's nowhere like Townhill for attracting the attentions of the police helicopter, ploughing round and round with its imperiously inquisitive, crime-hungry beam.

'Townhill has its problems, certainly,' says my creative writing student Zoë Murphy, who's showing me round her native patch one sunny June morning. "But it's not as bad as people say. I'm proud of the place. Everyone sticks together, and families are really supportive of each other."

People up here tend to be patriotic, and they are surrounded by Welsh street-names (Taliesyn, Granogwen, Tan y Marian, Cadrawd, Islwyn, Creidiol, Glyndŵr). But most know little about the preachers, poets, hymn-writers and freedom-fighters behind those names, and they have an eccentric way with some of the pronunciations: Pantycelyn Road, for instance, is routinely rendered and 'Panteeseelin'.

Until the 1920s, Townhill – known in medieval times, when it was forested, as Crowewode (Crow wood), later as 'the mountain' and eventually as 'the Town Hill' – was mostly farmland. Zoë lives in Mayhill, the eastern half of the ridge, on Mayhill Road, one of several notably straight thoroughfares established on old farm tracks dating from the enclosure of the hill in 1762, when the Duke of Beaufort helped himself to 60-ha of the best land, on the flat summit, and Swansea's burgesses divided up the rest. Some of these straightish stretches are no doubt much older: Powys Avenue and Graiglwyd Road coincide roughly with the Ancient Church Way, between Mountain Pleasant and Cockett, which Cockett people traversed to reach St Mary's in town, before Cockett had its own church (1856).

I leave my bike in the security of Zoë's living room, and we make our way up Mayhill Road, passing the dowdy Fairfield Social Club, which is the nearest Townhill gets these days to having a pub. At the roundabout at the top, where the dominant building is Our Lady of Lourdes RC church, and where Townhill proper begins, there used to be a pub, the Rum & Puncheon, but it was demolished in the 1990s. If the Rum was a bit of a 1960s box, Townhill was once famous internationally for its aspirational architecture. To our left, on Townhill Road, is Townhill Community School (1924), one of many distinguished buildings designed by Swansea's imaginative borough architect Ernest Morgan (1881-1954). He played a leading role in the

development of Townhill, which was driven by an idealistic determination to provide working-class people, many of them fugitives from town-centre slums, with the most salubrious and spacious housing that public resources could devise. No more cramped rows and 'courts', squalid back-to-backs, and narrow, lugubrious streets. Inspired by Garden City principles and in consultation with Raymond Unwin, the movement's guru, Swansea drew up plans in the early years of the last century for a Townhill garden city of mainly four-unit terraces and semi-detached houses, of a somewhat rustic, slate-hanging, half-timbered design, and focused on village-green-type circuses such as Mayhill's Llewelyn Circle and Cadwaladr Circle. The prototypes are still there, if much altered. But the First World War disrupted the scheme, and it was not until 1919 that work began on the houses in Pantycelyn Road, which must have the most spectacular views of any public housing in Britain.

It's to the grassy frontage of Pantycelyn Road, with its 'sleeping policemen' to deter boy racers (a persistent nuisance hereabouts), that I like to bring visitors to Swansea. With the exception of the less accessible Kilvey Hill, it's the best viewpoint from which to encompass the lie of Swansea's land: the river-mouth, port and working-class communities to the east; then, nearer at hand and west of the river, the city-centre shops, offices and club-land, the Vetch, the prison and, at the sea's edge, County Hall; immediately to our south, the middle-class and student enclaves of the Uplands, Brynmill and St Helen's, with the Guildhall and the rugby and cricket ground; then, beyond the university and Singleton Hospital, the extensive greenery of Swansea west and Gower. I brought a friend from India here once. Impressed, he gestured towards the thick forest around Clyne. "Are there," he asked intently, "tigers in your jungles?"

Townhill's most prominent structure, visible for miles around, is its 1929 water tower, which doubles as a support for communications aerials. The Pennant sandstone wall of the adjacent reservoir is topped with forbidding lengths of barbed wire which not even the resourceful youth of Townhill have been able to clamber over.

Zoë and I cut across the playing fields of Paradise Park, opposite the reservoir, having decided on a coffee in the new (and prize-winning) Phoenix Centre. Owned and managed by the Community and Development Trust Ltd., the Phoenix Centre – as its hopeful name implies – is making a determined contribution to the regeneration of the community. Built on the site of the old Blue Club, it has a library and information centre, a crèche and a wide range of sports facilities; it offers job training, health and legal advice, computer recycling and Hot Tap (tap dancing). Its busy and friendly café – where my (real) coffee is bracingly poky – serves the most sumptuous breakfasts in Swansea. The boss notices me taking down the prices – the Full Monty (£6.00), which would keep you going for a week, the slightly smaller Merlin Crescent (£3.95), the Dyfed Avenue (£2.95), the Powys Avenue (£2.00) – and hopes I'm not from the tax people.

The café is plastered with memorabilia of West End AFC, the Townhill soccer team. Like the culture of Townhill as a whole, it's very male focused. "There's not much for girls to do up here except have babies and work out things like income support," says Zoë who, with her degree and her artistic interests, can feel a little isolated. "Everyone adores gold up here – the women just love mwsh bling and swearing and smoking and shouting loud at each other. All ages, not just the young, they all love gold."

Pugilism and religion are dominant themes of the roundabout just south of the Phoenix: competing for attention with several churches are the Gwent Amateur Boxing and Sporting Club and the Samurai Olympic Judo Club.

We head down Powys Avenue to Graiglwyd Square, where there are a few shops. A weakness of Garden City planning is that it struggles to provide the population density that makes for a community large enough to sustain all the shops and amenities that a properly functioning community requires. Unlike the situation in, say, the Uplands, the ordinary needs of Townhill people – a newspaper, a dentist, a pint of bitter – are rarely to be met within walking distance of their homes. Busy streets police themselves. But airy, ambiguous spaces can lead to a vacillating sense of ownership, and a perception of insufficient privacy and security. Kids hanging about kicking balls can become kids hanging about throwing stones – as recently experienced by a friend of mine who was driven from her once pleasant home on the hill after repeated attacks on her house and car.

Consequently, some people south of the Townhill Fish Bar, particularly in Pentyla Road, like to give Cockett rather than Townhill as their address. "But Townhill is where they live," says Zoë, "so they'd better accept it."

Pentyla Road borders a large playing field popularly known as the Ganges (after a Mr Gangee who was once the field's caretaker). The field was retained by the Duke of Beaufort following enclosure in 1762 and it keeps its original triangular shape. With the hawthorn hedge that runs along Pentyla Road, it's the last significant remnant of the ancient common land of Townhill. It's therefore of historical, cultural and environmental importance. Rare birds have been spotted here, including, in 2006, the black-throated thrush from the Urals, and bats have been filmed in the hedge. It abounds in bugle flowers, daisies, dandelions, goldfinches and swifts. But local residents, including the poet and playwright Phil Stockton, have been fighting what looks like a losing battle to prevent the council from removing the hedge and building on the field. The council's 'experts' have decided, against a mass of historical evidence, that the hedge is no more than 20 years old and not worth preserving. Phil's poem 'The Field' concludes:

> Of course the planners (who, we know, know best)
> say this place is perfect for one use,
> then plan away (with lack of foresight blessed)
>
> and plot a course of natural abuse.
> Officially, they'll wreck this fallow space,
> and put some Barratt Boxes in its place.

Zoë remembers flirtatious kissing games in the Ganges, "with the boy picking a dandelion clock, getting the girl to open her mouth for a kiss – and then shoving the dandelion clock between her teeth."

Having reached the hill's western edge, we wander back towards Mayhill, via Pantycelyn Road and that spectacular view. At several

points below us, cut into the steep southern slopes, are disused
Pennant sandstone quarries, such as Rosehill, from which the building blocks of old Swansea were hewn. This glorious stone is blue-grey
in colour when freshly quarried, but its high iron content eventually
rusts, turning it that rich russet brown which is honeyed balm to the
eye, especially in late evening sunlight.

Mayhill suffered extensive damage during the 1941 bombing
raids. In the worst single incident of the war, 46 residents and fire-
fighters were killed when a stick of bombs hit a row of houses in Teilo
Crescent. Zoë points to an open space at the junction of Teilo
Crescent with Elfed Road, which is where two houses were bombed
and never rebuilt. But most bombed houses were rebuilt after the war
– by Swansea apprentices, each team with its own trademark plaque;
they emblazon the walls of many houses in Mayhill.

At the end of Nicander Parade, below a patch of grass known as
The Grubber, we come to a dell which hosts one of the sources of the
Washing Lake, a stream which ran down Mount Pleasant and fed
into the town moat, on the western side of the medieval defences,
eventually joining the Pill or Cadle stream. Known also as Nant y
Prys or Nant Prees, it was an important water supply for early
Swansea. Zoë remembers the stream as being "beautiful and clear" at
this point, but now it's a chaos of golden irises, polluted water, plastic
crates, paint cans and spilled paint, presided over by an abandoned
armchair. "Like this area as a whole," she says. "Beautiful things and
ugly things."

Nearby, on the south-eastern rim of Mayhill, is one of Swansea's
indisputably beautiful things, Ernest Morgan's circular-seeming
(from below) but actually D-shaped Mayhill School, known these
days as Seaview School, with its superb views not only over the city,
Gower and the Severn Sea, but also over the Black Mountains and
the Brecon Beacons. There's surely not a school in Wales that is more
imaginatively designed and sited. But its tower, says Zoë, can look
creepy, especially at dusk: it's the abode, for local kids, of a ghost
called Milly Molly Mandy.

On the gorse-bushed open grazing in front of the school is a scene
typical of Townhill and Mayhill: a gleaming black Welsh cob mare,
with her dun foal asleep at her feet, and, a few metres away, a piebald
pony nibbling at the coarse grass. People on the hill are fond of
horses, even sometimes keeping them in their rear gardens. There are
pigeon lofts too, and you're never very far from a dog. The mare, with
foal in tow, approaches us for a nuzzle and the pair follow us for a

while, as we drop down the slope to the old Jewish cemetery, a high-walled enclosure at one end of rubbish-strewn Berwick Terrace. It's the oldest structure on the hill, having been leased to Swansea's comparatively large Jewish community in 1768 – in what was then peaceful pasturage on the outskirts of town. When the cemetery reached capacity it was replaced by a special enclosure

at Oystermouth Cemetery. The wrought iron gates, with Star of David motifs, are chained shut, but loosely enough for us to squeeze between them for a wander among the intermittently vandalised graves, half sunk in a sea of waving grasses and wild flowers. There must be 300 or 400 of them, topped in most cases with the star of David, and inscribed in Hebrew and English.

Hip-hop is blasting from a set of speakers outside a front door in the somewhat run-down High View, which not so long ago was Shelley Crescent (as Long Ridge, which runs parallel, used to be Byron Crescent). "This is where they dump the druggies," Zoë murmurs. "They changed the names to try to change the image."

We look down on a couple of streets above Mount Pleasant that haven't dropped their associations with (less morally incendiary?) English poets, Wordsworth Street and Milton Terrace. Still visible on the kerbstones are the faded red-white-and-blue decorations of the Queen's jubilee celebrations in 1977. "None of that this last time," says Zoe. "We seem to have had enough of that lot, thank god."

Poem of the good settler

Came for a day:

setlo am oes ...[5]

notes

1 Two hundred years ago, there were 600 smokestacks in the valley.
2 It seems, in fact, to have been designed for twenty-four families.
3 Little forest.
4 Many will feel that that title belongs to Owain Glyndŵr (c.1354–1415/6).
5 'stayed a lifetime'. A later version – 'Came for a day / setlo ar fyw 'n fodlon' – appears on the walls of the housing association building in Christina Street.

PHOTOGRAPHS

WORKS CONSULTED

Adams, Sam, *Thomas Jeffery Llewelyn Prichard*, University of Wales Press, 2000

Alban, J.R., *The Guildhall, Swansea*, Swansea, 1984; *The 'Three Nights' Blitz'*, City of Swansea, 1994

Amis, Kingsley, *A Look around the Estate*, Jonathan Cape, 1967

Arthur, Nigel, *Swansea Since 1900: Ninety Years of Photographs*, South Wales Evening Post, 1988; *Swansea at War*, Archive Publications, 1988

Balchin, W.G.V. (ed.), *Swansea and its Region*, Swansea, 1971

Boatswain, Andrew and Oborne, Susan (eds.), *Cityscape – A View of Swansea and its Development*, Swansea City Council, 1996

Boorman, David, *The Brighton of Wales. Swansea as a Fashionable Resort, c.1780?c.1830*, Swansea, 1986

Bromley, Rosemary D.F. and Humphrys, Graham (eds.), *Dealing with Dereliction: The Redevelopment of the Lower Swansea Valley*, University College of Swansea, 1979

Campbell, Rhoda, *Water Under the Bridge*, D. Brown and Sons Ltd., 1997

Conran, Tony, *Castles*, Gomer Press, 1993

Cornish, Tony, *Francis Frith's Around Swansea*, Frith Book Company, 2000

Cuthill, Robert *'That Tin Shack': The Story of The Vivian Hall*, Blackpill, 1990 (publisher not known)

Bywgraffiadur Cymreig 1951–1970, Y, London 1997

Davies, James A. (ed.), *A Swansea Anthology*, Seren, 1996; *Dylan Thomas's Swansea, Gower and Laugharne*, University of Wales Press, 2000

Davies, John, *Cardiff*, University of Wales Press, 2002; *A History of Wales*, Penguin, 1994

Davies, John; Jenkins, Nigel; Baines, Menna; and Lynch, Peredur I., *The Welsh Academy Encyclopaedia of Wales*, University of Wales Press, 2008

Davies, Marie Stickler, *Swansea Jack*, R & S Brown, 1986

Dictionary of Welsh Biography Down to 1951, The, London, 1959

Elwin, Malcolm, *Landor, a Replevin*, Macdonald, 1958

Ferris, Paul, *Dylan Thomas*, Penguin, 1978

Gabb, Gerald, *The Story of the Village of Mumbles*, D. Brown and Sons Limited, Cowbridge, 1986; *The Life and Times of the Swansea and Mumbles Railway*, D. Brown and Sons Limited, Cowbridge, 1987; *Swansea and its History, Volume 1*, Swansea, 2007

Gamwell, S.C., *The Official Guide & Hand-book to Swansea and its District*, Swansea, 1880

Gillham, Mary E., *Swansea Bay's Green Mantle*, D. Brown and Sons Limited, Cowbridge, 1982

Goodall, Peter J.R., *For Whom the Bell Tolls*, Gomer Press, 2001

Gower (1948–), the journal of the Gower Society

Griffiths, R.A., (ed.) *The City of Swansea. Challenges and Change*, Sutton, 1990

Grove, Philippa and Keevil, Nance, *The Stairway to Cefn*, P.E.N. Publications, 2000

Hughes, David, *Tidy Boy*, Swansea Poetry Workshop, 1998

Hughes, Stephen, *Copperopolis, Landscapes of the Early Industrial Period in Swansea*, Royal Commission on the Ancient and Historical Monuments of Wales, 2000

Ingham, Karen (ed.) with Minhinnick, Robert, *Paradise Park*, Seren, 2000

Jenkins, Ruth (ed.), *Courage: Women's Essays on Life in Swansea*, Cartersford Publications Wales, 2004

Jones, W.H., *The History of Swansea and of the Lordship of Gower*, Volume I, Carmarthen, 1920; *The History of Swansea and of the Lordship of Gower*, Volume II, Royal Institution of South Wales, 1992; *History of the Port of Swansea*, Carmarthen, 1922

Lang, Jeff and Scoville, André, *Then & Now Morriston*, Tempus 2000

Loxton, William, *The Swansea I Remember*, Sou'wester Books, 1990

Marshall, Ray and Gabriel, Derek, *The Great Pub Crawl, A Story of Swansea Pubs*, Raydek Books, 1994

Miskell, Louise, *'Intelligent Town', An Urban History of Swansea, 1780–1855*, University of Wales Press, 2006

Mitchell, Adrian and Steadman, Ralph, *Who Killed Dylan Thomas?*, Tŷ Llên Publications, 1998

Morgan, John, *John Morgan's Wales*, Christopher Davies, 1993

Morgan, Prys (ed.), *Writers of the West / Llenorion y Gorllewin* (Vol. 4, West Glamorgan), West Wales Arts Association, 1974

Morgan, W. Ll., *The Castle of Swansea*, George Simpson & Co., Devizes, 1914

Mullard, Jonathan, *Gower*, Collins, 2006

Newman, John, *The Buildings of Wales: Glamorgan*, Penguin, 1995

Owen, J Alun, *Swansea's Earliest Open Spaces*, Swansea City Council, 1995

Porch, Richard, *Swansea: History You Can See*, Tempus, 2005; *Swansea City Centre Heritage Trail*, City and County of Swansea, 2007

Read, Peter, *God's Botherer*, Swansea Poetry Workshop, 2001

Rees, J. Hywel, *Talking about Gowerton*, Gowerton Community Council, 1992

Rees, Lloyd, *Swansea Poems*, Christopher Davies, 2000

Reeves, Ken, *A Stroll Through Old Swansea*, Sou'wester Books, 1991

Roberts, Alun, *Discovering Welsh Graves*, University of Wales Press, 2002

Robins, Nigel Alan, *The Enclosure of Townhill* (City of Swansea, 1990); *Homes for Heroes: Early Twentieth-Century Housing in the County Borough of Swansea*, City of Swansea, 1992

Rogers, W.C., *A Pictorial History of Swansea*, Gomer Press, 1981; *Historic Swansea* (ed. Bernard Morris), West Glamorgan Archive Service, 2005.

Scoville, André, *Morriston's Pictorial Past*, D Brown & Sons Ltd, 1988; *Images of Wales: Swansea, Landore, Clydach and Morriston*, Tempus, 2000; *Images of Wales: Morriston*, Tempus 2002.

Secombe, Harry, *Arias & Raspberries*, Robson Books, 1989

Stead, Peter, *Swansea City Guide*, Christopher Davies, 1992

Stony Stories, Swansea City Council, 1985

Strawbridge, Don, *Swansea Bay …the coastal route*, Gower Society, 2007

Super, R.H., *Walter Savage Landor*, John Calder, (?) 1954

Ross, J.E. (ed.), *Letters from Swansea*, Christopher Davies, 1983

Stephens, Meic (ed.), *The New Companion to the Literature of Wales*, University of Wales Press, 1998

Stock, Ray, *Swansea in the Golden Age of Postcards*, Christopher Davies, 1995.

Swansea 1960s – 1980s (Images of Wales series), City and County of Swansea, 2002

Swansea Before Industry, Swansea City Council and West Glamorgan County Council, n.d.

Thomas, N.L., *The Story of Swansea's Districts and Villages* (2 vols., Neath, 1964; Swansea, 1969); *Of Swansea West: The Mumbles: Past and Present* (Swansea, 1978); *The Story of Swansea's Markets* (Swansea, 1966)

Vaughan Thomas, Wynford, *Portrait of Gower*, Robert Hale, 1983

Williams, Glanmor, *Swansea, an Illustrated History,* Christopher Davies, 1990

ACKNOWLEDGEMENTS

Among the many people whose memories, suggestions, company on walks and all manner of practical assistance have been invaluable in the writing of this book, I am particularly grateful to (in alphabetical order) David Britton, Robin Campbell, Helen Clarke-Woods, David Cobb, Helen Davey, Spencer Davi(e)s, Stevie Davies, Gerald Gabb, Roger Gale, Gordon Gibson, John Goodby, Bryn Griffiths, Angharad and Branwen Jenkins (my daughters), Ruth Jenkins, Wally Jenkins, Peter Thabit Jones, John Lancaster, Andy Limnea, Gloria MacLeod (my mother), Louise Miskell, Sue Morgan, Bernard Morris, Zoë Murphy, Cath and Dennis Parker, Malcolm Parr, Richard Porch, Glyn Pursglove, Anna Ratcliffe, Jon Rees, Ioan Richard, Ron and Pam Rumble, Phil Stockton, Phil Taylor, the late Alan Thomas, Ceri Thomas (Bonymaen), Jen Wilson, Dave Woolley and ever-helpful staff at Mumbles Library and at the library of Swansea University. I am grateful to the series editor Peter Finch for commissioning book and to the team at Seren for their diligent and painstaking labours. My *compañera* Margot Morgan, with whom I enjoyed many a Swansea ramble, kindly read a draft of this book, and I thank her warmly for the suggestions she made for its improvement.

Versions of several of this book's sections or chapters appeared initially in *Planet: the Welsh Internationalist*. Most of the haiku (the short, generally three-line poems) are taken from my two haiku collections, *Blue* (2002) and *O For a Gun* (2007), both of them published by Planet Books of Aberystwyth. The longer poems come from my collections *Acts of Union: Selected Poems 1974-1989* (1990), *Ambush* (1998) and *Hotel Gwales* (2006), all published by Gomer Press of Llandysul. Both Planet Books and Gomer are gratefully acknowledged.

INDEX

THE AUTHOR

Nigel Jenkins (born 1949) is one of Wales's foremost writers. He is the author of collections of poetry, haiku, and essays, and co-editor of *The Welsh Academy Encyclopaedia of Wales*, published earlier this year. His travel book, *Gwalia in Khasia*, won the Arts Council of Wales Book of the Year prize in 1996. Brought up on a farm in Gower, he travelled and worked away from Swansea for several years before returning to work as a writer and broadcaster. He is currently a lecturer on Swansea University's Creative and Media Writing Programme.